CANONICAL TESTAMENT
Monsignor W. Onclin Chair 2004

KATHOLIEKE UNIVERSITEIT LEUVEN
Faculteit Kerkelijk Recht
Faculty of Canon Law

CANONICAL TESTAMENT

Monsignor W. Onclin Chair 2004

UITGEVERIJ PEETERS
LEUVEN
2004

ISBN 90-429-1463-7
D.2004/0602/69

© 2004, Uitgeverij Peeters, Bondgenotenlaan 153, B-3000 Leuven (Belgium)

INHOUDSTAFEL / TABLE OF CONTENTS

TIEN JAAR MONSIGNOR W. ONCLIN CHAIR
TUSSENBERICHT OF TESTAMENT?

RIK TORFS

In 1995, tijdens mijn eerste jaar als voorzitter van de faculteit kerke-lijk recht, die nu in de wandeling overigens zeer welluidend *BFKR* wordt geheten, vond de allereerste uitgave van de *Monsignor W. Onclin Chair for Comparative Church Law* plaats. Tenminste, in de vorm waarin hij nu algemeen bekend is, namelijk met twee vermaarde buitenlandse gast-hoogleraren die een week lang aan de studenten college geven, met een plechtige academische zitting ter afsluiting en met een publicatie voor het nageslacht. Die publicatie fungeerde tegelijk als visitekaartje voor de buitenwereld, als een relatiegeschenk dat niet gauw gauw in een *sky shop* moest worden opgepikt, maar uit de bloedeigen facultaire boekenkast stamde. De academische zitting van haar kant was elk jaar weer een verzamelpunt voor canonisten uit Vlaanderen en Nederland, alsook voor studenten en oud-studenten uit de hele wereld. En zo heeft de Mgr. W. Onclin Chair tien succesvolle edities gekend. Ik ben daar erg dankbaar voor. Tegelijk blijf ik hoopvol naar de toekomst kijken, ofschoon niet naïef, want wat komen gaat is hoogst onzeker, nu de aca-demische overheid van de KULeuven de vrije werking van onze facul-teit aan banden heeft gelegd en een voorzitter benoemde die haar ver-trouwen geniet, doch niet tot onze faculteit behoort, noch formeel, noch met zijn hart. Kortom, onderstaand relaas over tien jaar Monsignor W. Onclin Chair kan zowel een tussenbericht blijken te zijn als een tes-tament, dat zal de toekomst uitwijzen. In beide gevallen is het nuttig even terug te blikken. Natuurlijk niet om romantische verhalen uit het verle-den op te dissen. Ons adres is niet *Huize Avondrood*. Maar wel om te ver-duidelijken welke visie aan tien jaar Mgr. W. Onclin Chair ten grondslag lag. Deze visie heeft uiteraard te maken met ons vak, maar evenzeer met kerk, wetenschap en samenleving. Het is een visie die enerzijds heeft geleid tot succes en internationale uitstraling, maar die anderzijds in de ogen van sommigen hinderlijk en gevaarlijk was, en die dus de huidige problemen waarmee onze faculteit kampt, in de hand heeft gewerkt.

Zes accenten die tijdens de voorbije edities van de Monsignor W. Onclin Chair werden aangebracht, soms expliciet, vaak impliciet, breng ik hier kort in herinnering. En ik probeer ook aan te geven waarom het echt om *accenten* gaat, en niet om lapalissades. Een lapalissade zou zijn: wij pogen de liefde van Christus juridisch gestalte te geven. Of nog: de kerk als *communio* laten wij bij onze kerkrechtelijke benadering geen oogwenk los. Zo'n formules zijn verwerpelijk, juist omdat ze te mooi zijn om iets tegen in te brengen. Hun volmaaktheid maakt hen kwetsbaar, maar met de realiteit van het kerkelijk recht hebben ze weinig te maken, en dat is schuldig verzuim. Accenten moeten dus echt op iets heel bijzonders wijzen, op het verschil, op enige gevoeligheid voor middelpuntvliedende kracht. En nu volgt het lijstje.

I. DE THEORETISCHE FUNDERING VAN HET KERKELIJK RECHT

Misschien klinkt het vreemd, wanneer juist dit punt speciaal met rood wordt aangekruist. Is kerkelijk recht immers niet heel vaak *louter* theorie? Woorden, woorden, woorden. Vele normen van het kerkelijk wetboek zijn wensen, aansporingen of dogmatische stellingnamen. En zelfs normen die op het eerste gezicht erg praktisch ogen, zoals bepalingen uit het strafrecht en het procesrecht, worden vaak niet, of bijzonder moeizaam toegepast. Maar dat is het nu precies: verschillende sprekers tijdens de sessies van de W. Onclin Chair, ik denk hier heel in het bijzonder aan Cormac Burke, Helmuth Pree en Ruud Huysmans hebben gezocht naar de *werkelijke* theorie die aan het canonieke systeem ten grondslag ligt. Ze hadden het dus niet over hoe het canonieke recht er in theorie uitziet, maar wel over de echte (vaak ongeschreven) theoretische inspiratiebronnen van het recht zoals het praktisch werkt, of bewust beoogt om niet te werken. Nog anders gezegd: in hun analyses was de theorie geen *alternatief* voor de praktijk. Zij zochten eerder naar de alternatieve, soms impliciete theorie, die aan de praktijk, of de afwezigheid ervan, ten grondslag ligt. Kortom, diverse van onze auteurs spoorden de theorie op die een louter theoretische benadering van het canoniek recht poogt te schragen.

Ruud Huysmans vroeg zich af hoe het komt het dat er in de kerk recht is dat vaak niet echt werkt. Helmuth Pree schudde aan de boom van het *ius divinum*. Dat laatste komt en gaat. Het lijkt onwrikbaar, maar in de loop der eeuwen veranderde het vaak. Cormac Burke verantwoorddde zijn gestrengheid bij het behandelen huwelijksdossiers: personalisme betekent veel inzet, de wil om door te gaan. In die zin leidt de doorgedreven aanwezigheid van personalistische ideeën in het huwelijksrecht niet tot een automatische toename van het aantal nietigverklaringen.

Welke ideeën liggen *echt* aan het canoniek recht ten grondslag? Waar situeert zich zijn waarachtige theoretische fundering? Deze vragen werd tijdens de academische zittingen van de Monsignor W. Onclin Chair niet uit de weg gegaan.

II. EMPOWERMENT

Wat kunnen gewone stervelingen met het canoniek recht beginnen? Welke betekenis heeft het voor mensen die geen bisschop of kardinaal zijn, het nooit zullen worden, of het misschien niet eens *willen* worden? Het kerkelijk wetboek van 1917 was er vooral voor de clerici. Dat van 1983 bood ook leken een kans, of een kansje. Sommige auteurs gingen daar ook echt op in: Jim Coriden, Roch Pagé, wijlen Jim Provost. Zij behoorden tot een generatie van canonisten die uit het recht een maximale dosis vrijheid wilde puren, die begreep dat alles in het werk moest worden gesteld om creatieve mensen die niet van betutteling houden, toch een plaatsje binnen het kerkelijke systeem te gunnen. In de streek waar zijzelf vandaan komen, Noord-Amerika, lukte dat niet helemaal, en in West-Europa is het niet echt anders gelopen. Toch blijft hun vraag naar *empowerment* actueel. Zij verwoordt een hunkering naar verbeelding, een zoektocht naar creatieve mensen, en dat alles binnen de kerkstructuren. De vlucht naar de spiritualiteit, naar de veilige binnenkant, die vele jongere katholieken kenmerkt, was aan de generatie Coriden-Provost-Pagé niet besteed.

Thomas Green had het ook over *empowerment*, maar dan van de bisschoppenconferentie. In Amerika leeft die vraag sterk, het bisschopsambt zoals het in de praktijk wordt ervaren, leunt nauw aan bij de (hoge) theologische duiding ervan. Bij ons ligt dat moeilijker. Kardinaal Danneels kon erg populair worden omdat hij bisschop en kardinaal was, maar het is niet omdat iemand bisschop of kardinaal is, dat hij noodzakelijk populariteit verwerft. Het bisschopsambt is een aardig opstapje, doch biedt geen enkele garantie.

III. DE DONKERE ZIJDE VAN HET CANONIEK RECHT

Die donkere zijde zijn wij de voorbije jaren niet uit de weg gegaan. Het troosteloze optimisme van de beroepsglimlachers hebben wij daarentegen wel links laten liggen. De donkere zijde: John Beal behandelde zeer technisch en gedetailleerd, en dus een beetje gevaarlijk, het dossier van *sexual abuse*. Hij deed dat in 2000. Zijn tekst bleek voor de Verenigde Staten uitermate nuttig en praktisch te zijn, en leverde in Vlaanderen een volle bladzijde in *De Morgen* op. Opeens bleek immers hoe kerkelijk recht niet op echte confrontaties met het profane recht en op massieve druk van de samenleving was voorbereid. Kerkelijk recht betekende, officieel althans, klaroengeschal. Maar plotseling waren er *a lot of dirty things*. Niet simpel. Het is alsof een prachtig uitgedoste militaire muziekkapel plotseling naar de loopgraven wordt gestuurd. Een kogel ketst af op een trombone. De muziek klinkt ogenblikkelijk anders.

Boeiend is hoe de kwetsbaarheid van het kerkelijke systeem de maatschappelijke aandacht ervoor heeft vergroot. Tegenover de gevoelerigheid, de sentimentaliteit, de retoriek van het opgesmukte recht, staat de gevoeligheid, het respect voor de werkelijkheid van het canonieke recht uit de gore buitenwijken, *suburban canon law*. Gevoelerigheid versus gevoeligheid, valse sentimenten tegenover echte gevoelens: de publieke opinie heeft daar een veel scherper oog voor dan vele mensen vermoeden.

IV. VERGELIJKING

De *Monsignor W. Onclin Chair* was bedoeld om *comparative church law* aan bod te laten komen. Dat is ook gebeurd. De vergelijking vond godzijdank niet plaats op een al te kleine oppervlakte, werd dus nooit navelstaarderij. Zij beperkte zich niet tot een vergelijking tussen de CIC 1983 en de CCEO 1990. De vergelijking van details leidt immers al te gemakkelijk tot volslagen blindheid voor ideologische vooronderstellingen. Details kunnen prachtig zijn, vooral als zij erin slagen op een zeer beperkte ruimte heel veel te ontsluieren. Het detail openbaart dan het geheel. Maar het detail kan ook tot het tegengestelde resultaat leiden. Dan onthult het niet, maar versluiert het. Wie op die wijze details met elkaar vergelijkt, verliest er zich in. Door de studie van het detail neemt de kennis niet toe, maar af. Zo geschiedt wanneer het detail niets meer met het geheel te maken heeft. Het verwordt tot een afleidingsmanoeuvre. Dat gevaar dreigt heel reëel wanneer twee systemen worden vergeleken die *bijna* dezelfde zijn.

Charalambos Papastathis en Pieter Coertzen hebben, in het raam van de Monsignor W. Onclin Chair, bredere vergelijkingen gemaakt. Het orthodoxe en het hervormde perspectief verschillen wezenlijk van het katholieke. Die wezenlijke verschillen maken dat de verwondering over het eigen systeem groter wordt. Ze betreft niet slechts het detail, maar ook de basisopties. Een charme van de orthodoxie is dat de kerkpolitieke machtsstrijd – tussen allerlei patriarchaten bijvoorbeeld – er nauwelijks verhuld aanwezig is. Een charme van NG-kerk in Zuid-Afrika is dan weer hoe authentiek wordt gezocht naar een symbiose tussen adequate rechtsbescherming en Bijbelse wortels.

De rechtsvergelijking bedreven in het raam van de Monsignor W. Onclin Chair was nooit normatief. Er werd niet gezocht welk systeem zich het dichtst bij de wil van God bevond. Dat zou natuurlijk anders zijn gelopen in een vergelijking tussen de CIC 1983 en de CCEO 1990: de theologische fundering is wezenlijk dezelfde, dus houdt vergelijking onvermijdelijk ook competitie in.

Competitie met de professoren Coertzen en Papastathis hebben wij als katholieke kerkjuristen vanzelfsprekend nooit nagestreefd. Gastvrijheid vonden wij belangrijker. Niet alleen in de culinaire zin dan. Gastvrijheid betekent ook: mensen ontvangen in het eigen huis, uitgaan van het eigen systeem, zonder dat het eigen systeem *per se* het allerbeste hoeft te zijn. Het is immers mogelijk te wonen in een huis met gebreken en er toch heel veel van te houden.

Die attitude wijst allerminst op relativisme. Daarvan zou wel sprake zijn indien er geen eigen huis meer is, of wanneer dat samenvalt met de plaats waar iemand zich toevallig bevindt. Dat was duidelijk niet het uitgangspunt van tien jaar Monsignor W. Onclin Chair. Vergelijking beduidde verrijking, waardeoordelen bleven uit.

Soms vraag ik mij af of wij, volgens de regels van het spel, die waardeoordelen toch niet hadden moeten uitspreken. Inderdaad, als canoniek recht een theologische wetenschap is (de betwiste, maar toch ook veel toegejuichte stelling van Mörsdorf en Corecco), en als de exclusieve waarheid wordt gehuldigd door de rooms-katholieke kerk, bestaat er dan ook zoiets als *waarheid* en *onwaarheid* van rechtsregels en juridische concepten? Betekent zulks dan ook dat ons rechtssysteem, ontologisch gezien, alleen maar het beste kan zijn?

Goed toch dat wij ons deze vraag nooit openlijk hebben gesteld.

V. KERK EN STAAT

Uiteraard bleven de lezingen in het raam van de Onclin Chair niet beperkt tot intern kerkelijk recht. Uitsluitend binnen de lijntjes kleuren leidt immers tot een kleurloze tekening. Iemand hoeft geen *trendwatcher* te zijn om te beseffen dat een canonist die zich tot het interne kerkelijk recht beperkt, kiest voor de irrelevantie en voor een comfortabele marginaliteit, want zelfs al verkondigt hij domheden, *who cares*? Een onzichtbare rol in de marge: dat wilde onze faculteit natuurlijk vermijden. Canoniek recht kan, vandaag, niet los worden gezien van de plaats die religie bekleedt in de profane maatschappij. Dus nodigden wij diverse sprekers uit die vooral in de juridische verhoudingen tussen kerk en staat expertise hebben verworven.

En toch maakten wij ook hier (impliciet) een aantal keuzes, die bij dit tussenbericht (of testament?) enige verduidelijking behoeven. Wij zochten geen sprekers aan die, in onvervalste negentiende-eeuwse stijl, demarcatielijnen tussen de competentie van de kerk en die van de staat poogden te trekken. Evenmin brachten wij pleidooien, vanuit binnenkerkelijk perspectief, om het statuut van de kerk in de profane samenleving te beveiligen of te versterken. Integendeel, wij kozen voor een moderne benadering. Iván C. Ibán analyseerde de mogelijkheden van het concordaat, waarachter een ruimere aandacht voor een contractueel, niet louter publiekrechtelijk *Staatskirchenrecht* schuilgaat. Naast vernieuwde belangstelling voor het *contract*, kenmerkt ook de sleutelrol die voor mensenrechten is weggelegd het huidige kerk-staat-discours. James Wood maakte daar, vanuit een Amerikaans perspectief maar met een wereldwijde ervaring, levenslang werk van. En Jiří Rajmund Tretera beleefde de *Wende* in Tsjechië, of hoe kerk-staat-verhoudingen plots vanuit een ander paradigma vertrokken, een paradigma waarbij de mensenrechten een centrale rol vervulden.

Er was trouwens nog een derde insteek. Kerk-staat-verhoudingen hebben ook met precisiewerk te maken, met het aan elkaar smeden van canoniek recht en profaan recht, zoals een Amerikaanse en een Russische raket aan elkaar worden gekoppeld. Frank Morrisey bewandelde dat pad toen hij in 1996 de katholieke gezondheidszorg analyseerde.

Kortom, niet alleen breidden wij kerkelijk recht uit tot de verhoudingen tussen kerk en staat. Binnen deze verhoudingen opteerden wij bovendien voor de modernere trends: contractueel *Staatskirchenrecht*, de sleutelrol van mensenrechten, het ambachtelijk verenigen van profane en canonieke normen.

VI. MET HART EN ZIEL

Tijdens de W. Onclin Chair werden er altijd onderwerpen behandeld, invalshoeken gekozen, discoursen ontwikkeld, die wij belangrijk vonden.

Wij zochten naar beoefenaars die van het vak hielden, die het met hart en ziel beoefenden, die geen huurlingen waren, mensen voor wie kerkelijk recht een roeping was, een deel van henzelf. Dat laatste is niet evident. Vele clerici – die misschien wel als clericus geroepen zijn, want dat is een heel ander vraagstuk – studeren canoniek recht omwille van zeer utilitaristische redenen: zo'n studie is niet zelden een opstapje naar een mooie carrière in de kerkelijke hiërarchie. Wij kozen voor sprekers die voluit in het vak geloofden, en die de diepste fundamenten ervan verkenden. José Maria Serrano Ruiz bijvoorbeeld, de canonist die het huwelijksrecht na Vaticanum II het diepst beïnvloedde, die inzag dat het werkelijk *au sérieux* nemen van de mens als persoon en van elk huwelijk in al zijn relationele aspecten, ook tot de erkenning van de *incapacitas relativa* moet leiden. Of Ladislas Örsy, die aantoonde dat een theologie van het kerkelijk recht mogelijk was in *korte zinnen*. Korte zinnen en helderheid illustreren dat er geen onverenigbaarheid bestaat tussen *duidelijkheid* en *diepgang*.

In feite schuilt hier ook de kwetsbaarheid van het canonieke denken dat aan de Monsignor W. Onclin Chair ten grondslag lag: in een vaak speelse sfeer was de ondertoon bloedernstig. Wij vonden dat er *werkelijk* wat op het spel stond, dat canoniek recht mensen kan bevrijden en gelukkig maken. Voor ons was het geen vak, geen studierichting, die nu eenmaal geprogrammeerd staat in een universiteit die bij name katholiek is, maar eigenlijk gewoon een heel grote universiteit beoogt te zijn in het geseculariseerde Vlaanderen. Die universiteit wil, op het vlak van geloof, vooral geen gezeur. Zij verkiest een ornamenteel, ongevaarlijk, naar binnen gekeerd en op zichzelf gericht discours. In de religieuze sector – zo luidt impliciet de boodschap – moet veel worden gesproken, maar wordt best maar heel weinig gezegd. Vooral niet als het andere, veel belangrijker, economisch getinte, oriëntaties van het universitaire bedrijf in de weg zou kunnen staan. Geloof mag, zolang het niet al te serieus wordt. En de dingen worden pas echt bedreigd, wanneer achter een wolk van ironie en een schijnbaar badinerend discours, een zeer ernstige benadering van het kerkelijk recht verscholen gaat. Wanneer iets overblijft van de evangelische subversiviteit. Met daarin onder meer de wil om het zout der aarde te zijn, om het debat in zowel kerk als samenleving aan te zwengelen en herbergzaam te maken. Met hart en ziel. Kerkelijk recht als samenzwering.

Wij hebben tien mooie jaren gehad. En misschien zal ook de toekomst ons genadig zijn. En zelfs als de mechanismen van de macht te sterk blijken te zijn, de rancune te groot, de kloof te diep, zelfs dan is niet alles tevergeefs geweest. In zijn essaybundel *In die vroegte* citeert de Zuid-Afrikaanse auteur Hennie Aucamp een passage van collega-schrijfster Olive Schreiner (1855-1920), een passage die uitgroeide tot één van zijn levensmotto's, tot iets waarnaar hij teruggrijpt, zo schrijft hij, "wanneer dit my aan die moed ontbreek om 'n beginselsaak in die openbaar te verdedig, of 'n onpopulère standpunt te stel."

Het lijkt bijna of dit citaat heel speciaal is geschreven voor onze geliefde faculteit kerkelijk recht, zoals zij zich het voorbije decennium heeft ontwikkeld, zoals zij gedurende dit academiejaar werd vervolgd en heeft geleden: "It never pays the man who speaks the truth, but it pays humanity that it should be spoken."

TEN YEARS MONSIGNOR W. ONCLIN CHAIR.
AN INTERIM REPORT OR A TESTAMENT?

RIK TORFS

In 1995, during my first year as President of the Faculty of Canon Law, which is now known by the honourable name of *BFKR*, the first event hosted by the *Monsignor W. Onclin Chair for Comparative Church Law* took place. At least that was the first time it took place in the form in which it is now generally known, with two renowned foreign guest professors spending a week teaching students, rounded off with a ceremonial academic lecture and a publication for posterity. That publication also served as a calling-card for the outside world, as a complimentary gift that you could not just pick up in a *sky shop* but came from our very own faculty bookshelf. As for the academic lecture, each year it served as a meeting-point for canon lawyers from Flanders and the Netherlands and also for students and former students from all over the world. In this way the Monsignor W. Onclin Chair has passed through ten successful years. I am very grateful for that. At the same time I am still hopeful as I look to the future, although there can be no naïvety as it is very uncertain what will happen now that the academic authorities at the KU Leuven have restricted the freedom of action of our faculty and appointed a President who does not belong to our faculty, either formally or in his heart. In short, only the future will tell whether the update below on ten years of the Monsignor W. Onclin Chair is to be an interim report or a Last Will and Testament. Whatever the case, it is useful to take a look back at those years. Not to indulge in romantic stories of the past, of course. We are not living at *Sunset Cottage*. Nevertheless, we want to set out the vision that has supported ten years of the Monsignor W. Onclin Chair. This vision of course has a lot to do with our subject, but also with the Church, learning and society. It is a vision that has brought success and an international reputation, but which, in some people's eyes, has been difficult and dangerous and has therefore contributed to the problems now facing our faculty.

I would like to recall briefly six emphases that have been brought out in previous editions of the Monsignor W. Onclin Chair, sometimes explicitly and sometimes implicitly. I will also seek to point out why these really are *emphases* and not platitudes. A platitude would be: we try to give expression to the love of Christ in a legal context. Or: we never lose sight of the church as *communio* in our approach to canon law. Formulae like these are useless, precisely because they are so beautiful that nothing can be said against them. Their perfection makes them vulnerable, but they have little to do with the reality of canon law, and that is culpable negligence. So our emphases must point out something quite specific, to some kind of a difference, to an area where centrifugal force comes into play. And here is the list.

I. THE THEORETICAL FOUNDATIONS OF CANON LAW

It may seem strange that precisely this point should be underlined in red. After all, is not canon law very often *pure* theory? Words, words, words. Many norms in the Code of Canon Law are aspirations, incitements or dogmatic statements. Even those norms which seem at first sight to be very practical, such as the stipulations of penal law and procedural law, are often put into practice with great difficulty or not at all. But that is precisely the point: a number of speakers during the W. Onclin Chair sessions, and I am thinking in particular of Cormac Burke, Helmuth Pree and Ruud Huysmans, have sought for the *real* theory underlying the canonical system. Hence they have not spoken about what canon law looks like in theory, but about the real (and often unwritten) theoretical sources of inspiration for the law as it works in practice, or as it consciously intends not to work. In other words: in their analyses theory was not an *alternative* to practice. They have tended to look for the alternative and sometimes implicit theory underlying the practice or its absence. In short, a number of our authors have traced the theory that seeks to support a purely theoretical approach to canon law.

Ruud Huysmans asked himself how it is that there is law in the church that often does not really work. Helmuth Pree shook the tree of the *ius divinum*. This comes and goes. It seems to be unchanging, but over the centuries it has changed often. Cormac Burke accounted for his strictness in dealing with marriage cases: personalism means hard work, and the will to persevere. In that sense the consistent presence of personalistic ideas in marriage law does not automatically mean an increase in the number of annulments.

What ideas *really* underlie canon law? Where can its true theoretical foundations be found? These questions were not avoided during the Monsignor W. Onclin Chair academic lectures.

II. EMPOWERMENT

What can ordinary mortals do about canon law? What significance does it have for people who are not bishops or cardinals and never will be, or perhaps do not even *want* to be? The 1917 code of canon law was primarily for the clergy. The 1983 code also gave the laity a chance, or at least a small chance. Some authors have looked very carefully at this area: these include Jim Coriden, Roch Pagé and the late Jim Provost. They belonged to a generation of canon lawyers who wanted to distill as much freedom as possible from the law, a generation that understood that every effort had to be made to make room within the church system for creative people who do not like fault-finding. In the area where they come from, North America, they have not been entirely successful, and things have not been all that different in Western Europe. Nevertheless, their demand for *empowerment* is still just as pressing as ever. It expresses a hunger for imagination, a search for creative people within the structures of the Church. The flight into spiritually, into the safe inner sphere, that has been the solution found by many younger Catholics was not an option for the Coriden-Provost-Pagé generation.

Thomas Green also spoke about *empowerment*, but he was talking about the Bishops' Conference. This is very much a current question in America, where the office of bishop as it is experienced in practice is close to its (high) theological interpretation. In this country the situation is more difficult. Cardinal Danneels is highly popular because he is a bishop and a cardinal, but a person does not necessarily acquire popularity simply by being a bishop or a cardinal. The office of bishop is a nice promotion, but it offers no guarantees.

III. THE DARK SIDE OF CANON LAW

We have not avoided this dark side in recent years. The dismal optimism of the professional smilers is something that we have left behind us. The dark side: John Beal gave a very technical and detailed, and therefore slightly dangerous, treatment of the issue of *sexual abuse*. He did this in 2000. His text turned out to be extremely useful and practical for the United States, and in Flanders it resulted in a full page article in *De Morgen*. That is because it immediately showed how canon law is not prepared for real confrontations with secular law and massive pressure from society. Canon law, at least officially, was meant to be a clarion call. All of a sudden, however, there were *a lot of dirty things*. It was not a simple situation. It was as if a military musical band dressed up in full colours were suddenly sent off to the trenches. A bullet bounces off a trombone. Suddenly the music sounds different.

It is interesting to see how the vulnerability of the ecclesiastical system has increased society's interest in it. In contrast to the touchy-feely sentimentality and rhetoric of ostentatious law, we find a sensitivity and respect for reality in canon law from the less fashionable parts of town, or *suburban canon law*. Touchy-feeliness versus sensitivity, false sentimentality versus real feelings: public opinion has a much sharper eye for this than many people suspect.

IV. COMPARISON

The *Monsignor W. Onclin Chair* was intended to bring *comparative church law* up for discussion. It has done just that. Thank goodness the comparison did not take place in too small a space, so it never became an exercise in navel-gazing. It was not limited to a comparison between the CIC 1983 and the CCEO 1990. Comparisons of details all too easily result in a complete blindness to ideological preconceptions. Details can be wonderful, particularly if they can elucidate a great many things in a very limited space. In these cases, the detail reveals the whole. The detail, however, can also have the opposite effect. In these cases it does not reveal, but conceals. If anyone tries to compare details in this way, he will be lost in detail. The study of detail leads to less knowledge rather than more. This is what happens when the detail no longer has anything to do with the whole. It degenerates into a distraction manoeuvre. This danger is very real when two systems are being compared which are *almost* the same.

Charalambos Papastathis and Pieter Coertzen, in the context of the Monsignor W. Onclin Chair, have made wider comparisons. The Orthodox and Reformed perspectives have significant differences from the Catholic one. Those significant differences lead to more attention for our own system. This concerns not only the details, but also the most fundamental choices. One delightful thing about orthodoxy is that the power-struggle of church politics – between the various Patriarchates, for example – is barely concealed at all. And one wonderful thing about the NG Church in South Africa is the authentic search that takes place for a symbiosis between adequate legal protection and Biblical roots.

The legal comparison that has taken place in the context of the Monsignor W. Onclin Chair was never normative. No attempt has been made to discover which system was closest to the will of God. The situation would naturally have been different in a comparison between the CIC 1983 and the CCEO 1990: the theological foundation is essentially the same, so any comparison inevitably also implies competition.

As Catholic canon lawyers, we never, of course, sought to compete with Professors Coertzen and Papastathis. We considered hospitality to be more important. And not only in the culinary sense. Hospitality also means: receiving people in one's own house and working on the basis of one's own system, without one's own system having *per se* to be the best of all. After all, it is possible to live in a house with defects and nevertheless to love it very much.

That attitude certainly is not any indication of relativism. It would be if one no longer had a home of one's own, or if it coincided with the place where one simply happened to be. That was clearly not the starting-point for ten years of the Monsignor W. Onclin Chair. Comparison meant enrichment, and value-judgments were left outside the door.

Sometimes I wonder whether, in accordance with the rules of the game, we ought to have uttered those value-judgments after all. Indeed, if canon law is a theological science (the disputed but also much-welcomed assertion of Mörsdorf and Corecco) and if the exclusive truth is honoured by the Roman Catholic Church, then is there also such a thing as *truth* and *untruth* in legal rules and juridical concepts? Does this therefore mean that our legal system, from an ontological perspective, cannot fail to be the best?

It is a good thing that we never asked ourselves this question openly.

V. CHURCH AND STATE

Of course the lectures given within the context of the Onclin Chair have not been limited to internal church law. Always colouring carefully within the lines results in a colourless drawing. It is not necessary to be a *trend watcher* to see that a canon lawyer who limits his attention to internal church law is choosing irrelevance and comfortable marginalisation, because even if his statements are stupidity itself, *who cares*? An invisible role on the margins: this is, of course, what our faculty wanted to avoid. Today canon law cannot be seen in isolation from the place of religion in secular society. We have therefore invited a number of speakers who have acquired expertise above all in the juridical relationships between church and state.

Nevertheless, here too we have (implicitly) made a number of choices that require some clarification in this interim report (or Last Will and Testament?). We did not look for any speakers who would try to draw demarcation lines between the competencies of the Church and those of the State in the unadulterated nineteenth-century style. We also made no plea, from a perspective within the church, for any safeguards or strengthening of the status of the church within secular society. On the contrary, we chose to take a modern approach. Iván C. Ibán analysed the opportunities of the concordat, which conceals a much wider interest in a contractual and not purely public-law based *Staatskirchenrecht*. In addition to renewed interest in the *contract*, the key role of human rights is defining the church-state dialogue today. James Wood has devoted a lifetime of work to this issue, working from an American perspective but with worldwide experience. Jiří Rajmund Tretera experienced the *Wende* in the Czech Republic, or the way in which Church-state relations suddenly came to be based on a different paradigm in which human rights took the central place.

There was also a third perspective. Church-state relations also involve precision work, the forging of canon law and secular law into one, just as American and Russian rockets are linked together. Frank Morrisey walked that road in 1996 when he analysed Catholic health care.

In short, we have not only extended church law to include the relations between Church and State. Within these relations we have also opted for more modern trends: contractual *Staatskirchenrecht*, the key role played by human rights and the skillful merging of secular and canonical norms.

VI. WITH HEART AND SOUL

Through the activities of the Mgr. W. Onclin Chair we have always dealt with subjects, chosen perspectives and engaged in dialogues that we considered to be important. We have looked for those who love our subject and worked in it with all their hearts, not for hired hands, but for people for whom canon law was a vocation, part of themselves. Such people are not easy to find. Many clergy – who may perhaps have a vocation to be clergymen, for that is a compeltely different matter – study canon law for very utilitarian reasons: this kind of study is quite often a step up to a good career in the church hierarchy. We have chosen speakers who believe firmly in the subject and who have explored its deepest foundations. José Maria Serrano Ruiz, for example, the canon lawyer who influenced marriage law most deeply after Vatican II and perceived that really taking a person *au sérieux* as a person and taking each marriage seriously in all its relational aspects, must also lead to a recognition of *incapacitas relativa*. Or Ladislas Örsy, who demonstrated that a theology of canon law could be formulated in *short sentences*. Short sentences and understandable language illustrate that it is not impossible to reconcile *clarity* and *depth*.

In fact it is here that we find the vulnerability of canonical thought underlying the Monsignor W. Onclin Chair: in what is often a playful atmosphere, the undertone has been deadly serious. We have found that there *really is* a great deal at stake, that canon law can set people free and make them happy. For us, it was not a subject, not a department, which cannot fail to exist in a university which is Catholic by name, but which in fact only wants to be a very large university in secularised Flanders. Above all, when it comes to faith, that university does not want any complaining. It would prefer an ornamental, innocuous, introverted and inward-looking discourse. In the religious sector – thus runs the implicit message – you should use many words, but preferably say very little. Particularly not if it might stand in the way of the other, far more important and economically oriented aspects of university life. Faith is permissible, as long as it does not become too serious. And things are only really become threatening when a cloud of irony and what seems to be a jolly discourse conceals a very serious approach to canon law. When something of its evangelical subversiveness remains. This includes the desire to be the salt of the earth, to promote discussion both in the church and in society and to make it inhabitable. With heart and soul. This is canon law as a conspiracy.

We have had ten good years. And perhaps the future will also be good to us. Yet, even if the mechanisms of power do turn out to be too strong, the ill-will too great and the gulf too deep, even then it has all not been in vain. In his collection of essays *In die vroegte* South African author Hennie Aucamp cites a passage from another writer, Olive Schreiner (1855-1920), a passage that grew to become one of the mottos for his life, something for which he reaches, as he puts it, "wanneer dit my aan die moed ontbreek om 'n beginselsaak in die openbaar te verdedig, of 'n onpopulère standpunt te stel." (when I cannot find the courage to defend a question of principle in public, or to take an unpopular stand).

It almost seems that this quotation has been specially written for our beloved faculty of canon law, as it has developed during the past ten years, and as it has been persecuted and suffered during this academic year: "It never pays the man who speaks the truth, but it pays humanity that it should be spoken."

QUOD OMNES TANGIT...

BAS DE GAAY FORTMAN

I. PROLOGUE:
HUMAN RIGHTS BETWEEN STATE AND CHURCH

In a multi-facetted judgment the European Court of Human Rights unanimously condemns Italy for that state's failure to comply with the Rome Treaty's provisions guaranteeing defence rights to citizens in the so-called Pellegrini case[1]. The adversarial principle enshrined in what constitutes a fair hearing in the sense of art 6 § 1, holds under all circumstances, the Court rules, including procedures of *Ecclesiastical Courts* insofar as these would be granted civil effect (*exequatur*). The facts in the case of Pellegrini versus Italy are as follows:

Ms Pellegrini had married Mr Gigliozzi in April 1962. The marriage was a *matrimonio concordatorio*, meaning that their religious ceremony was valid in the eyes of the state, too. Some 28 years later the Rome District Court granted her petition for judicial separation while ordering Mr Gigliozzi to pay her a monthly maintenance allowance. Soon after she presented her case to the state court, however, her husband had submitted another petition to the Lazio Ecclesiastical Court, requesting to have the marriage annulled on the ground of consanguinity. The issue was that although her mother and his father were first cousins no evidence of any request for *dispensatio* appeared to be available. Notably, Mr Gigliozzi's interest in his annulment petition was more than purely religious: if a marriage is null and void, it can have no legal effects whatsoever, including an obligation to pay *mantenimento*. Yet, Mrs Pellegrini had not been given any serious opportunity to prepare for the ecclesiastical case – she had been summoned to appear without knowing why – and neither had she been assisted by a lawyer. In her appeal case before the Roman Rota she was still not shown all the evidence on the basis of which the lower court had annulled the marriage – one seemingly crucial document nor the information provided by some apparent witnesses –

---

[1] European Court of Human Rights, Case of Pellegrini v. Italy (*Application no. 30882/96*), 20 July 2001.

and she had not been informed of the possibility to be assisted by a lawyer.

The Rota's judgment – of which Mrs Pellegrini received merely the operative provisions, her request for a full copy having been refused once more- was referred to the Florence Court of Appeal for a declaration that it could be enforced under Italian law (*delibazione*). That civil court did, indeed, declare the Rota's decision enforceable, and a few months later Mr Gigliozzi stopped paying Mrs Pellegrini's maintenance. She then went to the Court of Cassation which three years later dismissed her appeal. So the Court in Strasbourg became her final resort.

The European Court of Human Rights totally shatters the grounds for the Cassation Court's judgment, arguing that Mrs Pellegrini's defence rights had been irremediably compromised by the Ecclesiastical Courts while the State Courts had not appropriately examined the matter. Indeed, qualifications such as "irrelevant", "apparently not", "not satisfied", and "the so-called witnesses" are clear indications of some judicial anger in Strasbourg.

Naturally, among both secular and canon lawyers the Pellegrini case has attracted a great deal of attention, particularly in respect of Church-State relations[2]. Indeed, the crux of the matter is that an exequatur cannot be granted after just some marginal examination, but only once the state court in question has fully satisfied itself that the requirements of the Rome Treaty have been met, too. Yet, there are certain other important aspects of the case that so far have gone largely unnoticed. I am referring here to:

1. the way in which the European Court of Human Rights disregards the ecclesiastical proceedings as such;
2. the substantive justice aspects; and
3. the issue of law-finding and human rights in semi-autonomous environments such as an ecclesiastical context.

Let us now look first at consideration 40 of the judgment:

> The Court notes at the outset that the applicant's marriage was annulled by a decision of the Vatican courts which was declared enforceable by the Italian courts. The Vatican has not ratified the convention and, furthermore,

---

[2] See, for example, K. MARTENS, "Het Hof voor de Rechten van de Mens in Straatsburg over de interne kerkelijke procedure, het exequatur van een kerkelijk vonnis en de kwaliteitsgaranties van artikel 6 § 1 EVRM" (noot onder EHRM 20 juli 2001 Pellegrini t. Italië), *Tijdschrift voor Bestuurswetenschappen & Publiekrecht* 2003, 43-48; and R. TORFS, "E.H.R.M. 20 juli 2001", *Rechtskundig Weekblad* 2003-2004, 435-437.

the application was lodged against Italy. The Court's task therefore consists not in examining whether the proceedings before the ecclesiastical courts complied with Article 6 of the Convention, but whether the Italian courts, before authorising enforcement of the decision annulling the marriage, duly satisfied themselves that the relevant proceedings fulfilled the guarantees of Article 6. A review of that kind is required where a decision in respect of which enforcement is requested emanates from the courts of a country which does not apply the Convention. Such a review is especially necessary where the implications of a declaration of enforceability are of capital importance for the parties.

"The Vatican has not ratified the convention." The significance of this short sentence is obvious: as a jurisdictional entity the Holy See is unholy, at least from the secular-religious perspective[3] of universal inalienable rights. Notably, apart from this formal reason for a simple dismissal of ecclesiastical justice, substantial arguments for this unholiness are sometimes used, too. Thus, Jurgens has argued that rather than *with* the Church, human rights always had to be conquered *on* the Church[4]. The resulting judgment is the same: the Church constitutes a major obstacle to the implementation of human rights. Indeed, Pope John Paul II's question to Soviet president Gorbachew might be formulated in a slight variation to that familiar anecdotic joke as to the meaning of glasnost: "Those human rights, I hope, are just for outside the Church?" The answer, of course, is that they are not. The whole idea of universal and inalienable rights means that there are no individuals, communities or institutions to which these rights would not pertain. Indeed, violations of these rights affect all human beings: "Quod omnes tangit". It is in that light that we have to look inside, too. Indeed, our empirical focus today is what in human rights discourse is usually called "the public-private divide", *casu quo* in an ecclesiastical setting. But before we pursue our analysis there, one preliminary observation has to be made: the State is not holy either. While in the international venture for the realisation of human rights it has been designated as the guardian institution, the state is also known to be at the roots of gross and systematic violations.

---

[3] As for Human Rights as a secular religion, see M. KORZEC, "Onzin op stelten. Mensenrechten als wereldreligie", *Intermediair* 10 December 1993, and B. DE GAAY FORTMAN, "Religion and Human Rights: mutually exclusive or supportive?", *Studies in Interreligious Dialogue* 1996, 101.
[4] See E. JURGENS, "Are Freedom of Religion and a Special Legal Position for Churches, Necessary or Even to be Desired in a Liberal Democracy under the Rule of Law?", in H. WARNINK (ed.), *Legal Position of Churches and Church Autonomy*, Leuven, Peeters, 2001, 240.

The point is simply that human rights violations always follow from mis-use of power. Hence the challenge, affecting state and church alike, is to tie the use of power effectively to norms aimed at the protection of basic human dignity.

II. LAW-FINDING AND HUMAN RIGHTS IN SEMI-AUTONOMOUS ENVIRONMENTS

Before taking an inside view, let us first study the formal question once more: Should secular courts refrain from an examination of human rights implementation by ecclesiastical courts except when the latter's decisions come up for an exequatur? If so, that would be a clear expres-sion of the public-private divide: a world full of private domains, enclosed by Chinese walls within which human dignity is legally unpro-tected. While that divide is usually observed in respect of the family, i.e. an institution whose privacy is protected by human rights law too, it also pertains to the inside of associations, corporations and churches. Yet, this has to do with formal complications impeding public investigation and the collection of evidence, rather than with fundamental objections to interfere in what was supposed to be private. Thus, no state judge would refrain from a judgment on wife-battery simply because in a particular family this was regarded as a practice protected by customary intra-fam-ily law. In a similar vein national judges today are not inclined to accept self-regulation and self-adjudication of institutions where fundamental rights are at stake. In the Bausch judgment of the Court of Appeal in 's Hertogenbosch, for example, it was unequivocally decided that ecclesi-astical procedures cannot be exempt from the duty to respect a person's good name and fame and to maintain secular norms with regard to med-ical deontology[5].

Indeed, within the framework of their national jurisdiction state judges tend to be less restrictive in these matters than the European Court of Human Rights. This is, however, not our main concern here. "What drives processes of law-finding in ecclesiastical courts?" we wonder. The background to that question is, again, the Pellegrini case but now

---

[5] Hof 's-Hertogenbosch, 2 December 1998, hearing no. C971117/Ro. See B. DE GAAY FORTMAN, "The Regulae Iuris and Human Rights as Bridges Between Church and State", in H. WARNINK (ed.), *Legal Position of Churches and Church Autonomy*, Leuven, Peeters, 2001, 229.

from the perspective of the Rota. Surprisingly, so far no commentator has pointed to the substantive issue, *viz.* abuse of law. For let us assume that the three procedural requirements stipulated by the ECHR under article 6 § 1 had all been fulfilled, and that, indeed, Mrs Pellegrini had to acknowledge the existence of a document proving irrefutably that the marriage ceremony had been performed without any *dispensatio* from the consanguinity proscriptions. Should, then, Mr Gigliozzi have succeeded in his attempt to nullify the marriage with the effect that no *mantenimento* were to be paid? Notably, Mrs Pellegrini had given the Rota details of the financial arrangements between herself and her ex-partner while stressing that the annulment of the marriage would result in substantial repercussions on the latter's obligation to pay maintenance, which was her only source of income[6]. Thus, the Rota knew that an unqualified annulment would contradict an equitable outcome so flagrantly that any judges committed to find justice in "the case behind the case"[7] would search until they found the legal arguments substantiating a continuation of the maintenance ruling by the Rome District Court. Actually, that should not have been too difficult, as the time of *ius abutendi*[8] is long past, and to discern *abuse of law* in this particular case should not have been too difficult.

Hence, the case confronts us rather painfully with apparent deficiencies in law-finding in ecclesiastical courts. In line with the Canon Law principle *In iudiciis non est acceptio personarum habenda*, I assume now that the Lazio and Rota judges were not just looking for any argument that could bear out an annulment of Mr Gigliozzi's maintenance obligations[9]. In order to understand what went wrong, then, let us look at Wiarda's three types of law-finding[10]. Sideways, I note that Gerard Wiarda was a great judge who presided over many courts, including the European Court of Human Rights. The Utrecht Law Faculty to which I belong has honoured his professorship there in the name of its research institute: the G.J. Wiarda Institute for Law Research.

---

[6] *Pellegrini case* (supra n. 1)., paragraph 21.

[7] Each of the parties tends to present a separate case. By the case behind the case I mean the genuine conflicts of interests that often remain hidden behind the facts as these are presented and the arguments used by their lawyers.

[8] A term used particularly with regard to property.

[9] *Corpus Iuris Canonicis*: Sexti decretal., lib. v, tit.xii., de regulis iuris, Bonifacius VII, Regula xii.

[10] G.J. WIARDA, *Drie typen van rechtsvinding*, Vierde druk bewerkt en van een nabeschouwing voorzien door Mr T. Koopmans, Deventer, Tjeenk Willink, 1999.

The analysis of three distinct ways of law-finding goes back to Montesquieu who in his "De l'esprit des lois" discerns:

1. the *Republic* in which the laws are so clear and unequivocal that the judges are no more than "les paroles de la loi";
2. the *Despotic State* in which pure arbitrariness rules; and
3. the *Monarchy*, a kind of intermediate state in which if the law is clear and unequivocal the judges follow it, but where that is not the case they look for its *esprit*.

Wiarda argues that today most laws are so clear that their application in practice does not present judges with extraordinary problems of law-finding. The point is, however, that where the outcome of a strict grammatical interpretation were evidently inequitable, one could no longer speak of a clear case of heteronymous law-finding. "To apply the law" is, indeed, not an unequivocal matter. Particularism often clashes with universalist prescriptions. According to a popular saying in Latin America, "You do justice to your friends; the law you apply to your enemies."

I would argue now that in the Rota's Pellegrini case we touch upon two distinct deficiencies in law-finding. The first is an apparent rigidity in respect of the law as such. *Dura est lex sed lex*. That is, indeed, an unequivocal *regula iuris* but it means no less nor more than the legality principle in the sense of a guarantee against judicial arbitrariness. Doing justice implies a duty to examine the real interests at stake and to judge the conflict between these in the light of not merely the legal texts but also the norms and values behind these, as well as general principles of law. The latter have found a prominent place in the *Corpus Iuris Canonici*. They include the adage *summum ius, summa iniuria*, as well as the duty to apply these *regulae iuris* in respect of the Church itself: *Patere legem quam ipse fecisti*, a point appropriately made by Martens[11].

The second deficiency in the Rota's law-finding appears to be its isolation from the world we live in. Procedurally, for example, its neglect of what are generally considered to be prerequisites of due process, is remarkable. This brings us to a major issue: the intricacies of law-finding in semi-autonomous environments.

The term "semi-autonomous social field" was introduced by Sally Falk-Moore to define non-state institutions that have "rule-making

---

[11] K. MARTENS, "De nietigverklaring van het kerkelijk huwelijk op basis van een psychiatrisch verslag: over deontologie en onrechtmatige daad", *Rechtskundig weekblad* 1998-1999, 1296.

capacities, and the means to induce or coerce compliance" but at the same time are "set in a larger social matrix which can, and does, affect and invade it, sometimes at the invitation of persons inside it, sometimes at its own instance"[12]. What strikes us now in processes of law-finding in ecclesiastical courts, as manifested in a substantial number of recent cases[13], is the lack of an apparent interface with the larger social environment. Thus, in such processes there emerges a noticeable contradiction between internal heteronomy and external autonomy. How to explain the latter? I see two reasons. The first one is a continuation of the time of the Guelphs and the Ghibelins: the rivalry between Church and State as if there were just two competing autonomous socio-juridical fields. The second reason for the appropriation of autonomy instead of accepting semi-autonomy may well lie in the concept of the *societas perfecta*.

The Church as *societas perfecta*, as explained in a recent doctoral dissertation defended before this University, is a strictly hierarchically ordered monarchy in which all good things descend on the people, grade by grade, level by level: "from God to the Pope, from the Pope to the bishops, from the bishops to the presbyters, and finally to the lay people"[14]. In the Second Vatican Council, however, as Örsy concludes in his *Quo Vadis Ecclesia: the Future of Canon Law*, "the Fathers agreed and stressed that the Church was a '*communio*', modelled on, and participating in the nature of the Trinity which is a communion of three persons in one Godhead"[15]. Yet, as Torfs has observed, "*societas perfecta* thinking is far from dead"[16]. Such thoughts lie at the roots of autonomy ideology. One way in which an attempt is made to preserve autonomy, Torfs notes, is by limiting jurisdiction *ratione materiae*, i.e. to a field of activity in which ecclesiastical autonomy would seem obvious. Might such an evidently autonomous realm be delimited? Definitely, judgments in respect of the sacraments would seem to qualify for a purely autonomous social field; yet, it is precisely with regard to the annulment

---

[12] S. FALK MOORE, *Law as Process. An Anthropological Approach*, London, Routledge and Kegan Paul, 1983, 55-56.

[13] See, for example, H. WARNINK, *o.c.*, *passim*.

[14] A. SWAMINATHAN, *Communio Fidelium et Communio Ecclesiarum. Effectiveness of Governance Structures in the Church*, Doctoral Dissertation, Leuven, Catholic University, Faculty of Canon Law, 2003, 2.

[15] Quoted by SWAMINATHAN, *o.c.*, 1.

[16] R. TORFS, "Church Tribunals *secundum* and *praeter legem*", in *Canon Law Between Interpretation and Imagination. Monsignor W. Onclin Chair 2001*, Leuven, Peeters, 2001, 63.

of that wonderful sacrament called marriage that we already encountered an interface with the public-political domain.

Torfs deplores a retreat into *societas perfecta* autonomy as a purely defensive strategy, but also on a more remarkable ground:

> In view of the rich tradition of canon law, and the influence that it has had on secular law, it is shameful to have to observe that it should now, for theological reasons, choose an approach to law which is no longer relevant to society in general[17].

Notably, international human rights mean that the state cannot be considered as being completely autonomous either. Furthermore, a strong state requires a strong civil society and hence there is another good reason to keep significant social fields within the realm of semi-autonomy, too: the need for a dynamic interface between such vital institutions as the churches and the state.

This, then, would seem to be the appropriate moment to turn to an especially important historical development: the mainstreaming of a particularly remarkable *regula iuris* as ground rule for democracy.

III. QUOD OMNES TANGIT DEBET AB OMNIBUS APPROBARI

The *Corpus Iuris Canonici* contains an impressive number of ancient *regulae iuris*: general principles of law-finding that may throw clear light upon complicated cases[18]. Among these is that ground rule of democratic thinking and practice: *Quod omnes tangit debet ab omnibus approbari* ("What touches all, by all must be approved")[19]. This maxim had become part of Roman law, particularly within the context of *tutela* (guardianship). According to a Justinian law of AD 531 individual guardians can take decisions with regard to a common guardianship only with the consent of all. The principle also applied to concessions such as an aqueduct[20].

It was particularly in the period between the twelfth and fifteenth century that canonists revived the dormant *Quod omnes tangit* principle while

---

[17] *Ibid.*, 69.

[18] See B. DE GAAY FORTMAN, "The Regulae Iuris and Human Rights as Bridges Between Church and State", in H. WARNINK (ed.), *Legal Position of Churches and Church Autonomy*, Leuven, Peeters, 2001, 226-228.

[19] *Corpus Iuris Canonicis*: Sexti decretal., lib. v, tit.xii.,de regulis iuris, Bonifacius VII, Regula xxix.

[20] See Y.M.-J. CONGAR, "Quod Omnes Tangit ab Omnibus Tractari et Approbari Debet", *Revue historique de droit francais et étranger* 1958, 210-259.

using it to define relations within the Church, e.g. between the bishop and his chapter of canons[21]. Thus, from its purely procedural part in private law it acquired an institutional role in ecclesiastical government. Even more striking is the way in which the *regula iuris* was transplanted to the public-political realm, to begin with taxation. Then, as Pennington notes:

> ... by the beginning of the fourteenth century, kings all over Europe were summoning representative assemblies of their noblemen, clergy, and townsmen. When they did, the reason that they often gave for calling such assemblies was, "what touches all must be approved by all". Thus, *Quod omnes tangit* became the theoretical base for parliament[22].

So from a principle of juridical consent it became a rule for democratic consultation and consensus. Indeed, the most remarkable use of the maxim was by Bartolomé de las Casas who, in his *De thesauris in Peru*, written in 1565 when he was 91 years old, argued that legitimate secular power docs exist outside the church and that since the dominium of infidels (the Indians) was legitimate, the Spaniards did not have the right to usurp their title[23]. He begins his reasoning with the ground rule *Quod omnes tangit* as developed to regulate the affairs of a bishopric. His argument then bases itself on the premise – developed during those three centuries in medieval Europe – that rules and practices that are valid in ecclesiastical institutions ought to be valid in the secular polity as well. Thus, he argues, as summarised by Pennington:

> ... if one applied this principle properly, it would also be dangerous and undesirable if a prince or a bishop were given to an unwilling people. Nor should a king be given to a foreign people. Consequently, the pope cannot grant the Spanish king *dominium* in the New World without the consent of the Indians[24].

Notably, as we saw, in Roman law the word "omnes" had an extremely limited meaning. It is more than remarkable that the extension of that term to really all people was based on ecclesiastical theory. Here, indeed, we find a beautiful illustration of Torfs' "rich tradition of canon law". *Omnes*, I should like to stress, is a crucial term in human rights, as embodied in article 1 of the Universal Declaration of Human Rights

---

[21] See K.J. PENNINGTON JR., "Bartolome de Las Casas and the Tradition of Medieval Law", *Church History* 1970, 157 ff.

[22] *Ibid.*, 157.

[23] *Ibid.*, 151.

[24] *Ibid.*, 157-158.

(UDHR) – "*All* human beings are born free and equal in dignity and rights"[25] – as well as in the famous expression "obligationes erga *omnes*" in the judgment of the International Court of Justice in the Barcelona Traction Case[26].

While apparently eight to five ages ago secular developments got such an important impetus from ecclesiastical sources, later developments were less positive. Strikingly, Yves Congar ends his scholarly review of the *Quod omnes tangit* principle with the disheartening conclusion that all these good things had been completely eradicated by a definitive victory of the Roman doctrine of the pontifical Monarchy[27]. That was written in 1958, just before *societas perfecta* thinking was supposedly overruled by Vatican II with its *communio* concept. Yet, we cannot say that the principle of democratic consent is alive and well within the Catholic Church today. There are, indeed, manifest hesitations with regard to the first part of the maxim: the "all" who are affected, even within the Church. But even more problematic seems to be the second part: the endorsement by all. The principal reason why involvement of all in actual decision-making is supposed to be impossible in the Church is conceptual: the Rule of God versus the rule of the people[28]. Illustrative is a recent presentation by Professor Heribert Heinemann to the Academy of the Rottenburg-Stuttgart diocese in Germany. After dismissing the *Quod omnes tangit* rule as a non-genuinely ecclesiastical principle that was transplanted from Roman law straight into Pope Boniface VIII's *Regulae Iuris*, he stresses the special nature of the Church. His conclusion is that the Church does not need any democratisation, as the word "democracy" cannot be theologically founded[29].

There is a misunderstanding here, arising from the secular democratic development of decision-making by representation following from elections based on the majority principle. Notably, there is a certain tension between majority rule and individual rights[30]. But despite such set-backs,

---

[25] My italics.

[26] Case of the International Court of Justice Concerning the *Barcelona Traction, Light and Power Company Limited (New Application: 1962) (Second Phase) Belgium v. Spain*, ICJ 1970, Rep. 3.

[27] Y. CONGAR, *o.c.*, 258.

[28] A. SWAMINATHAN, *o.c.*, 204ff.

[29] See his *lecture notes* (12/03/2003) at http://www.akademie-rs.de/highlight/heineman.htm

[30] See J. ELSTER, "Majority Rule and Individual Rights", in S. SHUTE and S. HURLEY, *On Human Rights. The Oxford Amnesty Lectures 1993*, New York, Basic Books, 1993, 181-185.

"free and fair elections" has become the secular key-word. It should be realised, however, that this development is closely connected to the formation of a nation state of a legally and politically universalist character. Definitively, churches as institutions are of a different nature, but that does not exclude structural ways and means of "approbare" by all who are affected. As this issue is a little beyond the main thrust of this address, I should like to limit my remarks here to a call for consideration of a different principle of deliberation and endorsement by all: *sociocracy*. As developed in practice by a Dutch businessman – now holder of a Special Chair at Maastricht University- it maintains the hierarchical formation of the organisation while adding to the management structure an organisational structure: the sociocratic circles. Within the circle connected to a higher level in principal decision-making the lower level is always represented while the principle applied is not majority rule but consent, meaning that no-one feels a need for dissent.[31] With these short comments I leave it there: general consultation and consent is the challenge, and discussions on the theological foundations of liberal democracy just divert from the essence of the *debet ab omnibus approbari* rule as developed in canon law proper.

As this inaugural lecture addresses particularly the first part of the principle, i.e. *"Quod omnes tangit"*, let us turn now to that which touches all: human rights.

IV. RELIGION AND HUMAN RIGHTS IN A DOWNSTREAM AND UP-STREAM PERSPECTIVE

The notion of individual subjective rights transcending legal protection of other interests is not uncontroversial. As an illustration of the difficulties of the Church with "the rights of man" Jurgens, for example, quotes the Encyclical *Quanta Cura* of 1864. In this document the pope condemns the principle that "every man is free to embrace and profess that religion which, guided by the light of reason, he shall consider true"[32].

However, beside objections to ideas that would seem to put the human being above God, there are also religious endorsements of human rights of a "supra-natural" character. Such positive statements are based upon

---

[31] See G. ENDENBURG, *Sociocratie*, Delft, Eburon, 2002, 252 p.
[32] E. JURGENS, *o.c.*, 240.

the view that human rights in essence are God-given. A striking example is the way in which the Latin American bishops endorsed the human rights concept in a statement made in 1992:

> The equality of all human beings, created as they are in the image of God, is guaranteed and completed in Christ. From the time of his incarnation, when the Word assumes our nature and especially through his redemption on the cross, He demonstrates the value of every single human being. Therefore Christ, God and man, constitutes also the deepest source and guarantee for the dignity of the human person. Each violation of human rights is contrary to God's plan and sinful[33].

Thus, the gospel is seen as the deepest foundation of all human rights. But this *ius divinum* is grossly and systematically violated from day to day "not only by terrorism, repression and attacks... but also through the existence of extreme poverty and unjust economic structures which result in extreme inequality. Political intolerance and indifference with regard to the situation of general impoverishment reveal a general contempt for concrete human life on which we cannot remain silent." Hence, as a "pastoral action line" the bishops request the promotion of human rights in an effective and courageous manner "based on both the gospel and the social doctrine of the Church, by word, action and cooperation, and in that way to commit ourselves to the defence of the individual and social rights of human beings, peoples, cultures and marginalised sectors of society, together with persons in a state of extreme vulnerability and prisoners."

In this way the dialectics of religion and human rights seem to have been overcome in a complete synthesis. This has taken the form here of a document. But the history of the Catholic Church in South and Central America offers many practical examples of a leading role in human rights struggles, too: Bishop Helder Camara of Recife, Cardinal Paulo Evaristo Arns of São Paulo, Cardinal Silva Henriquez of the Vicaría de la Solidaridad in Chile, Archbishop Oscar Romero in El Salvador, Bishop Juan Gerardi in Guatemala and so many unknown Christians whose conviction inspired them to sacrifice their lives for the cause of other people's human dignity. Unfortunately, there are also cases of complete collaboration in periods of tyranny. Notorious, for instance, is the role of the Church in

---

[33] CELAM, 1993, 164: "La igualdad entre los seres humanos en su dignidad, por ser creados a imagen y semejanza de Dios, se afianza y perfecciona en Cristo. Desde la Encarnación, al asumir el Verbo nuestra naturaleza y sobre todo su acción redentora en la cruz, muestra el valor de cada persona. Por lo mismo Cristo, Dios y hombre, es la fuente más profunda que garantiza la dignidad de la persona y de sus derechos. Toda la violación de los derechos humanos contradice el Plan de Dios y es pecado."

the Argentine at the time of the *guerra sucia*. Decisive in this connection seems to be primarily one factor: the quality and conviction of personal leadership. Yet, this is not our major concern here today. The issue that takes our attention right now is how to perceive the role of churches in the worldwide struggle for the implementation of human rights, as not only a possible obstacle, but also a potential asset. For this purpose it seems useful to present a model of the human rights venture in two versions: first a downstream and then an upstream endeavour.

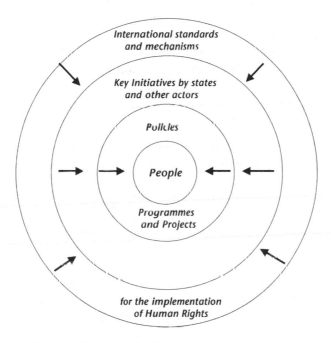

Figure 1: Human rights in a downstream perspective

The concentric circles presented above schematically exemplify human rights as a downstream effort: from standards set internationally downward towards people's daily lives. Human rights, I recall, constitutes an attempt to protect basic human dignity by law[34]. As an

---

[34] See B. DE GAAY FORTMAN, *Laborious Law, Inaugural Address on Accepting the Chair in Political Economy of Human Rights at Utrecht University, 21 May 2001*, The Hague, Institute of Social Studies, 2001, 3.

international endeavour this effort is of relatively recent origin. It is a venture of a highly juridical nature, grounded in three stages: standard setting, monitoring of observance of those norms, and enforcement. It is particularly the latter that has proved to be rather difficult. In that connection one touches upon semi-autonomous environments as problematic constraints to a full realization of human rights. The argument developed earlier on is that semi-autonomy can never imply an exemption of *obligationes erga omnes*. This is not just the effect of state responsibility, which was the route taken by the European Court of Human Rights in the Pellegrini case, but also a consequence of the character of semi-autonomous institutions as human rights duty bearers in their own right. Indeed, they must be seen as "actors", whose key initiatives are to be pervaded by the internationally accepted human rights standards.

However, this whole downstream venture is faced with three critical limitations[35]. Briefly, these may be summarised as follows:

1. Protection of human dignity by law assumes "law and order" in the sense that law functions as a way of guaranteeing security of people in their person, in their possessions and in their deals (implying enforcement of the rule that *pacta sunt servanda*), and settling disputes based upon conflicting interests in a peaceful manner. Yet, in many a politico-juridical setting the role of universalist state law is rather constrained.

2. The values behind human rights norms have to be "received" in the sense of a cultural reception of the law[36]. In reality there tend to be serious cultural constraints, although these may well differ from context to context, depending upon the concrete socio-cultural environment.

3. Human rights norms do not reflect all core aspects of justice in the same way. It is particularly in respect of the principle of equality as more than just formal equality of all before the law that their meaning is rather limited. The reason is that inalienable subjective rights

---

[35] For a more detailed discussion of these limitations see B. DE GAAY FORTMAN and M.A. MOHAMED SALIH, "The Life and Times of Religion and Human Rights", in W.E. A. VAN BEEK et al. (ed.), *Meeting Culture: Essays in Honour of Arie de Ruijter*, Maastricht, Shaker, 2003, 91-111.

[36] See B. DE GAAY FORTMAN, "Human Rights, Entitlement Systems and the Problem of Cultural Receptivity", in A. AN NA'IM et al. (ed), *Human Rights and Religious values: an Uneasy Relationship*, Grand Rapids, Eerdmans, 1995, 62-78.

tend to be formulated in a rather absolute manner: "everyone has the right to ...", whereas the struggle for social justice is directed against substantive inequality. As a result, human rights do not appear to function as an effective normative instrument in the fight against growing socio-economic inequality.

A short review of these limitations from an ecclesiastical perspective generates the following observations:

1. Churches tend to be law-oriented. Yet, as illustrated above, there still lies a problem in the practice of claiming autonomy in realms in which norms that touch all and obligations towards all prevail. Under growing public pressure, primarily from the churches' own constituencies, a development in a more obliging direction can now be observed, particularly with regard to sexual abuse.
2. In respect of women's rights and other issues related to intra-family relations, churches themselves often constitute a serious constraint.
3. Generally, faith-based views on justice take a deeper and more encompassing perspective than secular human rights discourse[37]. A clear example provides Christian social thinking as developed in both the Catholic Church and the Ecumenical Movement[38].

In respect of the churches and human rights, then, the effort is twofold: the mobilisation of churches as duty-bearers in the international venture to implement human rights, and religion as a spiritual source nourishing the conviction upon which respect for and protection of basic human dignity is to be based. A similar dual role applies to the old *Quod omnes tangit debet ab omnibus approbari* principle: it may serve as a driving force in efforts to overcome institutional obstacles through more participatory governance; and it may also function as an inspiration to embark upon the whole human rights venture *upstream*, i.e. from the perspective of *omnes* in the first part of our *regula iuris*. To understand what that means, let us now look at human rights as an upstream venture:

---

[37] See B. DE GAAY FORTMAN, "Religion and Human Rights: mutually exclusive or supportive?", *Studies in Interreligious Dialogue* 1996, 105-106.
[38] See B. DE GAAY FORTMAN and B. KLEIN GOLDEWIJK, *God and the Goods. Global Economy in a Civilizational Perspective*, Geneva, World Council of Churches Publications, 1998, chapter 3.

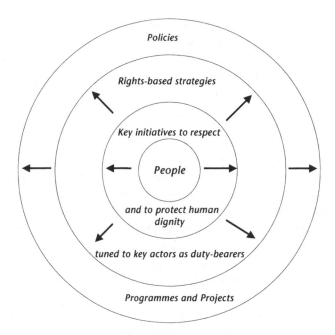

Figure 2: Human rights in an upstream perspective

Here the whole course of action begins with people in processes of self-identification as rights-holders. The challenge they are facing in their daily lives is to find protection against all abuse of power, and to acquire the fundamental freedoms and basic entitlements that follow from respect for everyone's basic human dignity. It is those at the grassroots themselves who know best what in their own context they are due. This, then, is to result in collective efforts to identify duty-bearers responsible for the constraints that the rights-holders face in their struggles for a decent life.

Yet, human dignity as the crucial idea on which the whole struggle is to be based, is a very difficult notion. It is particularly in a faith-based environment that the belief in the value of human life *per se* and the respectability of every human being as a unique creature may be inspired and transformed into a powerful conviction[39]. Of course, this is not to say that upstream involvement of the Christian churches were self-evident. Unfortunately, "us-them" divides, too, are sometimes generated

---

[39] See B. DE GAAY FORTMAN, "Religion and Human Rights: mutually exclusive or supportive?", *Studies in Interreligious Dialogue* 1996, 98-110.

by religious thought and action. Yet, it remains all the more important to acknowledge the potential of faith-based organisations in upstream ventures to respect and protect basic human dignity.

Downstream and upstream perspectives on human rights can be distinguished only theoretically; in reality they constitute two sides of what is basically one process: realization of the fundamental freedoms and basic entitlements that follow directly from the need to respect and protect the dignity of each and everyone. In this respect, too, the Pellegrini case is rather illustrative. Remarkably, while the European Court of Human Rights did compensate Mrs Pellegrini for some non-pecuniary damage, she was not awarded compensation for unpaid *mantenimento*. The point was that in the mean time she and Mr Gigliozzi had reached what the court calls "a friendly settlement". It is obviously unlikely that this upstream action would have been successful if Mrs Pellegrini had not linked her claims to international standards and mechanisms for the realisation of human rights.

Evidently, the case behind Mrs Pellegrini's trouble with Mr Gigliozzi had to with men-women relations in a context in which the Catholic Church plays a major part. In the final part of this lecture I shall go a little deeper into this important matter while examining a main impediment to do the full implementation of human rights: the exclusion of women in the term *omnes* through a public-private divide. The consequences of this deficit in the human rights mission tend to go much beyond the unfortunate effects of annulled marriages.

V. EPILOGUE: OVERCOMING THE PUBLIC-PRIVATE DIVIDE

A primary constraint to the implementation of human rights is, of course, *impunity*, which may be defined as all means by which persons responsible for major violations of human rights escape public exposure, trial and punishment. Commonly, the term is used especially with regard to crimes against humanity committed with official tacit or open approval in times of war or dictatorial rule[40]. It is generally considered to be a foremost failure in the functioning of states, to be addressed through institutional initiatives such as the recently established International Criminal Court.

---

[40] See Ch. HARPER (ed.), *Impunity. An Ethical Perspective. Six Case Studies from Latin America*, Geneva, WCC Publications, 1996, ix.

However, behind impunity is more than just deficient governance. We may, indeed, speak of a *culture of impunity* that begins at home. This constitutes a background to the slogan "women's rights are human rights". What seems to be theoretically self-evident, in practice meets two constraints in the international venture for the realisation of human rights. The first obstacle is the "privacy" of the family. As the Declaration of Beijing of 1995 has noted:

> Violence against women is a manifestation of the historically unequal power relations between men and women, which have led to domination over and discrimination against women by men and to the prevention of women's full advancement. Violence against women throughout the life cycle derives essentially from cultural patterns, in particular the harmful effects of certain traditional or customary practices and all acts of extremism linked to race, sex, language or religion that perpetuate the lower status accorded to women in the family, the workplace, the community and society[41].

Since governments tend to function in a political context that is not unrelated to culture as manifested in families and other private environmental settings, a call to states to combat domestic violence will tend to be insufficient. Notably, even such a simple appeal was too much for the General Assembly of the United Nations in 2003, adopting as it did, a lengthy resolution ending in merely one decision: "to continue its consideration of this question at its sixtieth session under the title 'advancement of women'"[42]. It is, indeed, the state itself that endorses and protects law that subordinates women. This is done indirectly, as Smart has noted: "the law does not 'give' power to men over women in the family... it legitimises the preconditions which create an unequal power structure"[43].

It is not just the dialectics of law and power that make it difficult for the state to intrude in the private sphere in order to enforce justice. The human right to privacy has resulted in legislation that makes it possible for those who beat their wives to slam the doors shut when others come to the rescue of these victims. Yet, the challenge of human rights implementation lies primarily in day-to-day observance and hence prevention of violations of women's rights, rather than merely in contentious action

---

[41] A/Conf.177/20, Platform of Action, par. 118.

[42] UNGA, 58th session, Third Committee, Agenda item 110, 03-61953.

[43] C. SMART, *The Ties that Bind: Law, Marriage and the Reproduction of Patriarchical Relations*, New York/London, Routledge and Kegan Paul, 1984, xii, quoted in S. ABEYESEKERA, *Women's Human Rights. Questions of Equality and Difference*, The Hague, ISS Working Paper, Feb. 1995, 47.

post factum. Hence, specific attention must be given to the role of civil society, which may be defined as "that segment of society that interacts with the state, influences the state, and yet is distinct from the state"[44]. Indeed, without participation of churches and mosques, schools, universities and social movements, it will be impossible to overcome the constraints of the public-private divide. This is, however, far from simple since some of these institutions, as we saw already, are precisely part of the problem.

The second obstacle to the full implementation of women's rights as human rights is, indeed, the cultural and religious setting in which traditional family law is often enshrined. Strikingly, while recognizing the universality of human rights as being "beyond question", the Vienna Declaration of 1993 notes that, "the significance of national and regional particularities and various historical, cultural and religious backgrounds must be borne in mind"[45]. The Beijing Declaration of 1995 adds that implementation is the sovereign responsibility of each state, in "full respect for various religious and ethical values"[46]. Religious institutions with their often-predominant positions in the realm of family law nourish these values, which are not always in conformity with international human rights standards. Take, for example, the "Riyadh Declaration on Human Rights in Peace and War", as accepted by the first international conference on human rights ever to be held in Saudi Arabia (October 2003). Article 14 declares: "Man and woman are partners in bearing the responsibilities of life on the base of the equitable integrations between them". Such formulations constitute unacceptable deviations from the principles of freedom and equality as enshrined in the Universal Declaration of Human Rights.

Pateman and Gross have argued that "to develop a theory in which women and femininity have an autonomous place means that the private and the public, the social and the political also have to be completely reconceptualised; in short it means an end to the long history of sexually particular theory that masquerades as universalism"[47]. What has to be examined carefully by religious authorities of all world religions is their own responsibility for a public-political conceptualisation of the family that still tends to exclude women from the approving *omnes* in questions

---

[44] N. CHAZAN, "Africa's Democratic Challenge", *World Policy Journal* 1990, 281.

[45] A/CONF.157/23, p. 5.

[46] A/CONF.177/20, Platform for Action, par. 9.

[47] C. PATEMAN and E. GROSS (ed.), *Feminist Challenges*, Sydney, Allen and Unwin, 1986, 9, quoted in S. ABEYESEKERA, *o.c.*, 52.

that touch them all. Sunila Abeyesekera, a scholar who impressed me already during her participation in the Institute of Social Studies' human rights programme, concludes her study of the international human rights venture with its underlying discourse as to the position of women as follows:

> I argue in favour of on-going moves to reconceptualise principles of equality, justice and rights within a framework that is inclusive of difference and plurality. This re-conceptualisation must base itself upon the "neutrality" of terms and concepts such as equality, justice and rights; it must also challenge existing assumptions about the "un-natural" division of the world into the separate spheres of public and private, and focus on the family as the critical site of contestation in the discussion of women's human rights[48].

Reconceptualisation, indeed, precedes operationalisation; and operationalisation of women's rights as human rights is a project of much wider significance than mere use of the structures of the *Convention for the Elimination of All forms of Discrimination Against Women* (CEDAW) and the Charter-based *Commission on the Status of Women* (CSW) could entail. It requires a restructuring and reculturing of relations within the family as well as in institutions at the *meso* level, including the churches. In efforts to overcome public-private divides it is, indeed, self-empowerment of women and a civil society oriented towards gender equality that may be regarded as factors of a considerably more influential nature than state policies. Thus, the involvement of non-state actors is to be seen as essential. A principal challenge is to transform these into communities in which what touches all is approved by all. The Church to which this old and prestigious university is aligned could make a major contribution here through a revitalisation of the organisational principle of true communion that pervades the whole New Testament as well as the history of the first Christian congregations: κοινωνια[49].

In the methodology presented in this lecture decision-making in *societas perfecta* structures evidently requires downstream corrections through the international project for the implementation of human rights. In contrast, the principle of κοινωνια (*communio*), may be seen as an upstream driving force to overcome obstacles to the implementation of norms that affect all.

---

[48] S. ABEYESEKERA, *o.c.*, 53.
[49] See Swaminathan's dissertation (*o.c.*, note 14), a doctoral project in which it has been a privilege to participate as a member of the Academic Jury.

VI. CLOSING WORDS

Rector, Ladies and Gentlemen,

Allow me to express my sincere thanks to the Catholic University of Louvain for the trust put into a non-canonist protestant as one of the holders of its prestigious Monsignor Willy Onclin Chair in Comparative Canon Law. With the faculty responsible for the respectable nomination to this rotating Chair I cherish a long-lasting collegiality, based on a striking commonness in academic orientation and commitment. I pay gratitude to the old and out-standing Faculty of Canon Law in general, and I thank my colleagues Rik Torfs, Hildegard Warnink and Kurt Martens in particular, for their collegiality and academic support.

Finally: one more detail in the lives of Mrs Pellegrini and Mr Gigliozzi. It was in April 1962, as I mentioned already at the outset of this lecture, that the two of them married. In that same month there were of course many other couples that entered into such a liaison. In one of these I was personally involved, together with my wife Ina. It is to her that I wish to dedicate this address.

Dixi.

CONTRIBUTIONS OF THE HOLY SEE TO THE REFINEMENT OF THE ROME STATUTE OF THE INTERNATIONAL CRIMINAL COURT

JOHAN D. VAN DER VYVER

On June 15 through July 17, 1998, the United Nations Diplomatic Conference of Plenipotentiaries was held in Rome, Italy, with a view to "finalizing and adopting a convention on the establishment of an international criminal court"[1]. The Rome Conference was preceded by deliberations in New York of an *Ad Hoc* Committee (1995) and a Preparatory Committee (1996-1998), operating under a mandate of the General Assembly of the United Nations to refine a *Draft Statute for an International Criminal Court* that had been prepared by the International Law Commission (ILC)[2].

The Preparatory Committee forwarded to Rome a 173-page *Draft Statute*, containing 116 articles and with approximately 1700 "brackets" indicating areas of disagreement[3]. At the Rome Conference, about 200 additional proposals were submitted in writing and numerous others derived from corridor discussions and informal negotiations[4]. In the final

---

[1] G.A. Res. 52/160 of 15 Dec. 1997 (annex), U.N. GAOR Supp. (No. 49), U.N. Doc. A/52/49, at 384, § 3.

[2] U.N. Doc. A/CONF.183/2/Add. 1 (14 April 1994).

[3] *Draft Statute for the International Criminal Court*, in REPORT OF THE PREPARATORY COMMITTEE ON THE ESTABLISHMENT OF AN INTERNATIONAL CRIMINAL COURT, U.N. Doc. A/CONF.183/2/Add.1 (14 April 1998) (hereafter "Draft Statute"). For an overview of the Draft Statute, *see* Lyn L. Stevens, *Toward a Permanent International Criminal Court*, in 6 EUR. J. CRIME, CR. L. & CR. JUSTICE 236, at 238-47 (1998).

[4] Hans-Peter Kaul, *Durchbruch in Rom: Der Vertrag über den Internationalen Strafgerichtshof*, in 46 VEREINTE NATIONEN 125, at 125 (1998); Roy S. Lee, *Introduction*, in THE INTERNATIONAL CRIMINAL COURT: THE MAKING OF THE ROME STATUTE: ISSUES, NEGOTIATIONS, RESULTS 1, at 13, 15 (ed.) Roy S. Lee. The Hague/London/Boston: Kluwer Law Int'l (1999); and *see also* Philippe Kirsch, *The Development of the Rome Statute*, in THE INTERNATIONAL CRIMINAL COURT: THE MAKING OF THE ROME STATUTE: ISSUES, NEGOTIATIONS, RESULTS 451, at 452 (ed.) Roy S. Lee. The Hague/London/Boston: Kluwer Law Int'l (1999); Philippe Kirsch & Darryl Robinson, *Reaching Agreement at the Rome Conference*, in (eds.) ANTONIO CASSESE, PAOLA GAETA & JOHN R.W.D.JONES, 1 THE ROME STATUTE OF THE INTERNATIONAL CRIMINAL COURT: A COMMENTARY 67, at 68. Oxford: Oxford Univ. Press (2002) (speaking of "over 1400 square brackets"); LEILA NADYA SADAT, THE INTERNATIONAL CRIMINAL COURT AND THE TRANSFORMATION OF INTERNATIONAL LAW: JUSTICE FOR THE NEW MILLENNIUM xii, at xv. Ardsley, N.Y.: Transnat'l Publ. Inc.

week of the Rome Conference, almost the entire Part 2 of the Statute dealing with "Jurisdiction, Admissibility and Applicable Law" remained in contention[5]. It became clear that no progress had been made in the endeavors of like-minded folk to achieve general agreement on the provisions of that Part which would constitute the back-bone of an effective, independent and impartial court.

The Rome Conference nevertheless culminated in the approval, by majority vote[6], of the text of the Statute of the International Criminal Court[7]. The Statute entered into force on July 1, 2002 following its ratification by 60 States. At the closing date (December 31, 2000), 139 countries had signed the ICC Statute[8], and as of date 92 States have deposited their instruments of ratification with the Secretary-General of the United Nations[9].

Among the celebrated participants in the Rome Conference was the delegation of the Holy See, comprising 11 members under the leadership of Monseignor Renato R. Martino, permanent observer of the Holy See at the United Nations. The delegation was noted for its positive contributions to the crafting of the Rome Statute. I propose to highlight some of those contributions in several particular areas:

A. the concept of gender;
B. the distinction between enforced and forced pregnancies;
C. the proscription of weapons of mass destruction;
D. the interests of defense counsel; and
E. general principles of justice pertaining to the qualification of judges and privileged communications.

It would be wrong, of course, to assume that those areas were the only ones in which the delegation of the Holy See contributed toward the drafting of the ICC Statute. The delegation threw its weight behind many of the intricate problems that had to be negotiated, it assisted in the forging

---

(2002), at 2-3 and M. Cherif Bassiouni, *Foreword*, in SADAT, *supra*, xii, at xv (mentioning "some 1300 parenthetical brackets").

[5] *See* Kirsch, *supra* note 4, at 455-56 and 458; and for an overview of the main matters of dispute, *see* Kaul, *supra* note 4, at 127-29; Hans-Peter Kaul, *Special Note: The Struggle for the International Criminal Court's Jurisdiction*, in 6 EUR. J. CRIME, CR. L. & CR. JUSTICE 364 (1998).

[6] The ICC Statute was adopted by 120 votes in favor, 7 against (including China, Israel the USA and four Arab States), and 21 abstentions.

[7] *Statute of the International Criminal Court*, U.N. Doc. A/CONF.183/9 (17 July 1998), *reprinted in* 37 I.L.M. 1002 (1998) (hereafter "ICC Statute").

[8] Belgium signed the ICC Statute on 10 September 1998.

[9] Belgium ratified the ICC Statute on 28 June 2000.

of compromises, and it spoke out strongly against positions taken that defied the principle of equal justice for all and the equal protection of the laws or were in any other way not conducive to basic principles of criminal justice.

A. THE GENDER ISSUE

The concept of "gender" features in the ICC Statute in several of its provisions. It is provided in general that the interpretation and application of law to be applied by the ICC must be "consistent with internationally recognized human rights, and be without any adverse distinction founded on grounds such as *gender*..., age, race, colour, language, religion or belief, political or other opinion, national, ethnic or social origin, wealth, birth or other status"[10]. The definition of crimes against humanity includes the condemnation of "[p]ersecution against any identifiable group or collectivity on political, racial, national, ethnic, cultural, religious, *gender*... or other grounds that are universally recognized as impermissible under international law, in connection with any act referred to in this paragraph or any crime within the jurisdiction of the Court"[11].

The reference to "gender" as a component of the non-discrimination clause in the section on "Applicable Law" was hotly debated in the Working Group and was initially opposed by delegations as far apart as the United Kingdom, Egypt, and the Holy See. A delegate from the UK expressed the opinion that the non-discrimination part of the interpretation clause was already included in the directive founded on "internationally recognized human rights" and was therefore tautological[12]; Egypt (and other Arab States) maintained that the word "gender" cannot be

---

[10] ICC Statute, *supra* note 7, art. 21(3). (Emphasis added.)

[11] *Id.*, art. 7(1)(h). (Emphasis added.)

[12] The objection raised by the UK stemmed from the wording of the provision in the Draft Statute forwarded to Rome by the Preparatory Committee, which provided: "The application and interpretation of law... must be consistent with internationally recognized human rights, *which include* the prohibition on any adverse distinction founded on gender..." Draft Statute, *supra* note 3, art. 20(3). (Emphasis added.) That objection was resolved by substituting "which include" with "and" so that the non-discrimination component would not be seen as a (tautological) exemplification of "internationally recognized human rights" but would acquire a standing in its own right alongside the human rights command.

translated into Arabic[13]; and concerns of the Holy See were centered upon the possibility that "gender" might be taken to include sexual orientation[14], and that could in turn implicate, as instances of persecution, disabilities attached to homosexuality by Roman Catholicism and perhaps most of the other mainstream religions, and indeed in many national legal systems. The concerns of the Holy See were shared by several countries where Roman Catholicism predominates and by a number of Arab States. China, perhaps for other reasons, also preferred a shortened version of the interpretation clause that would exclude the entire non-discrimination component[15].

Persecution as defined in the ICC Statute involves the commission of any of the crimes within the jurisdiction of the ICC inspired by a certain discriminatory intent based on a sectional prejudice[16]. Any crime committed that falls within the subject-matter jurisdiction of the ICC becomes the crime of persecution if the perpetrator was intent on severely depriving the victims of fundamental rights contrary to international law on grounds of, among other things, their gender. The definition of persecution also contains an open-ended clause in its prejudicial intent provisions denoting "other grounds that are universally recognized as impermissible under international law"[17].

A definition of "gender" was carefully crafted in negotiations behind the scenes with the Holy See (and some other delegations) in order to ensure that Gays and Lesbians will not come within the enumerated groups protected against acts of persecution[18]. Requiring in the open ended clause of the definition of persecution that the other instances of a discriminatory intent that would bring the rules of persecution to bear on the *actus reus* must be impermissible under international law was added to make doubly sure that condemnations of homosexuality are to be precluded from the reach of ICC jurisdiction[19].

---

[13] The Arab States finally resolved their problem by simply giving an Arabic form to the English word "gender".

[14] *See* Per Salant, *International Criminal Law Principles*, in THE INTERNATIONAL CRIMINAL COURT: THE MAKING OF THE ROME STATUTE: ISSUES, NEGOTIATIONS, RESULTS 189, at 216 (ed.) Roy S. Lee. The Hague/London/Boston: Kluwer Law Int'l (1999); SADAT, *supra* note 4, at 180.

[15] *See* Per Salant, *supra* note 14, at 215-216.

[16] Machteld Boot & Christopher H. Hall, *Crimes against Humanity, Persecution*, in COMMENTARIES ON THE ROME STATUTE OF THE INTERNATIONAL CRIMINAL COURT 146, at 150 (ed.) Otto Triffterer. Baden-Baden: Nomos Verlagsgesellschaft (1999).

[17] ICC Statute, *supra* note 7, art. 7(1)(h).

[18] *See* SADAT, *supra* note 4, at 160.

[19] *Id.*, at 159.

The definition of gender decided upon provides:

> For the purpose of this Statute, it is understood that the term "gender" refers to the two sexes, male and female, within the context of society. The term "gender" does not indicate any meaning different from the above[20].

The definition of "gender" leaves much to be desired. Why not clearly state the obvious, namely that gender denotes the role attributed to persons in society by virtue of their sex-related attributes? In his report on the Beijing Conference, the Secretary-General of the United Nations more precisely defined the concept of "gender" for U.N. purposes:

> ... in United Nations usage, gender refers to the socially constructed roles played by women and men that are ascribed to them on the basis of their sex. Gender analysis is done in order to examine similarities and differences in roles and responsibilities between women and men without direct reference to biology, but rather to the behaviour patterns expected from women and men and their cultural reinforcement. These roles are usually specific to a given area and time, that is, since gender roles are contingent on the social and economic context, they can vary according to the specific context and can change over time. In terms of the use of language, the word "sex" is used to refer to physical and biological characteristics of women and men, while gender is used to refer to the explanations for observed differences between women and men based on socially assigned roles[21].

The phrase "in the context of society" in the ICC definition of "gender" was intended to denote the sociological dimension of gender, while the second sentence was intended to exclude sexual orientation from the definition's enclave[22]. That, according to Cate Steains (the coordinator on gender issues at the Rome Conference), was the only definition Arab States and some other delegations were willing to accept[23]. As such, the definition represents "a delicate, hard-fought compromise among delegations"[24]; or, again, "the culmination of hard-fought negotiations that managed to produce language acceptable to delegations on both sides of the debate"[25].

---

[20] ICC Statute, *supra* note 7, art 7(3):

[21] IMPLEMENTATION OF THE FOURTH WORLD CONFERENCE ON WOMEN, *Report of the Secretary General*, para. 9, U.N. Doc. A/51/322 (3 Sept. 1996).

[22] *See* Cate Steains, *Gender Issues*, in THE INTERNATIONAL CRIMINAL COURT: THE MAKING OF THE ROME STATUTE: ISSUES, NEGOTIATIONS, RESULTS 357, at 374 (ed.) Roy S. Lee. The Hague/London/Boston: Kluwer Law Int'l (1999).

[23] *Id.*, at 374-75.

[24] *Id.*, at 371.

[25] *Id.*, at 374.

Basing the gender issue on the biologically-based male/female divide is in itself problematic. One has to be sensitive, namely, to the station in life of not only male and female but also of persons with, biologically, sexually ambiguous qualities, such as congenital adrenal hyperplasia (CAH)[26], the androgen insensitivity syndrome (AIS)[27], or those of the hermaphrodite[28]. It has been established that approximately 1.75% of newborn babies present some ambiguity as to sex. Their disposition in life is a gender issue but cannot be regulated on the based of the male-female divide. Coupling the definition of "gender" to that divide would therefore leave such persons out in the cold.

The concerns that prompted the definition of gender were perhaps unfounded. The ICC Statute made the prosecution of the crimes within its jurisdiction subject to strenuous threshold requirements that would preclude mere discrimination against any group of persons because of their sexual orientation. To qualify as a crime against humanity, the action taken must be part of a widespread or systematic attack against the group[29], and the *actus reus* constituting the crime of persecution must amount to a crime in its own right, such as killing members of the group, enslaving or deporting them, severely depriving them of their physical liberty, causing them to disappear and the like[30].

There are compelling reasons for holding that discrimination against persons on basis of their sexual orientation by and through the laws of *the State* is unacceptable. In evaluating group alliances of persons, a distinction should be made between institutional and collective communities. Differing in this regard from a collective community of people, an institutional community is one of which membership is not entirely voluntary[31]. In *Prosecutor v. Akayesu*, the International Criminal Tribunal for

---

[26] Persons with classical CAH are born with masculine appearing external genitals but with female internal organs, and they usually also have high levels of the male sex hormone, testosterone, in their blood.

[27] The child with classical AIS is born with male (XY) sex chromosomes, but the male genital development of the external genitals continue along female lines, and at the same time, the development of the female internal organs are suppressed. The person with AIS therefore has genitals that are completely female, but internally there are testes instead of a uterus and ovaries.

[28] The hermaphrodite is a person born with ovary and testicle tissue. The genitalia can vary from completely male or female to a combination of both.

[29] ICC Statute, *supra* note 7, art. 7(1).

[30] *Id.*, art. 7(1)(h) (requiring that persecution is to involve "any act referred to in this paragraph or any crime within the jurisdiction of the Court").

[31] The Dutch (Calvistic) legal philosopher, Herman Dooyeweerd (1894-1977), defined institutional communities as those "which by their inner nature are destined to encompass

Rwanda in the same context spoke of "'stable' groups, constituted in a permanent fashion and membership... which is determined by birth, with the exclusion of the more 'mobile' groups which one joins through individual voluntary commitment, such as political and economic groups"[32]. Persons belonging to the "stable" group do so on an involuntary basis, or – in the words of the Akayesu judgment – "automatically, by birth, in a continuous and often irremediable manner"[33].

The State is in this sense made up of an institutional community or "stable group" and for that reason alone ought not to enact laws or uphold practices that would marginalize any person or group of persons under its domain because of personal attributes over which that person or those persons have no control.

The Church may be in a different situation. As an institution separate from the State, it enjoys internal sphere sovereignty to regulate its domestic ecclesiastical affairs without state interference; and as a religious community, it has a right to self-determination, which – as defined in the 1992 Declaration on the Rights of Persons Belonging to National Ethnic, Religious and Linguistic Minorities – entails "the right... to profess and practice their own religion... in private and in public, freely and without interference or any form of discrimination"[34].

The right to self-determination of peoples is not absolute. The Declaration on the Rights of Persons Belonging to National or Ethnic, Religious and Linguistic Minorities excluded from the right to self-determination specific practices of a religious community that violate the national laws of a country and are contrary to international standards[35]. It is submitted that the national-law limitation is to be conditioned by the international-standards criterion: it presupposes municipal regulation that remains

---

their members to an intensive degree, continuously or at least for a considerable part of their life, and such in a way independent of their will." HERMAN DOOYEWEERD, A NEW CRITIQUE OF THEORETICAL THOUGHT, vol. 3, 187. Jordan Station, Ontario: Padeia Press (1984).

[32] PROSECUTOR v. JEAN-PAUL AKAYESU, para 510, Case No. ICTR-96-4-T (Sept. 2, 1998); and see also PROSECUTOR v. ALFRED MUSEMA, para. 163, Case No. ICTR-96-13-T (27 Jan. 2000); Paul J. Magnarella, Some Milestones and Achievements at the International Criminal Tribunal for Rwanda: The 1998 Kambanda and Akayesu Cases, in 11 FLA. J. INT'L L. 517, at 529-31 (1997); Antonio Cassese, Genocide, in 1 THE ROME STATUTE OF THE INTERNATIONAL CRIMINAL COURT: A COMMENTARY (eds.) Antonio Cassese, Paola Gaeta & John R.W.D. Jones 335, at 345. Oxford: Oxford Univ. Press (2002).

[33] PROSECUTOR v. AKAYESU, supra note 32, at para. 529-31.

[34] Declaration on the Rights of Persons Belonging to National or Ethnic, Religious and Linguistic Minorities, art. 2.1, G.A. Res.47/136 of 18 Dec. 1992, 47 U.N. GAOR Supp. (No. 49), at 210, U.N. Doc. A/RES/47/135 (1992).

[35] Id., art. 4.2.

within the confines of international standards and does not place undue restrictions upon the group interests of minorities.

Current state practice does not uphold the limitations inherent in the right to self-determination of religious communities dictated by the international standards criterion to the letter. For example, gender discrimination is condemned in almost all of the international human rights conventions and covenants, yet religious institutions that discriminate against women on gender grounds have thus far, successfully, claimed a sovereign right to conduct their affairs within the sphere of their internal household according to the dictates of their faith. And perhaps rightly so! Does one really want the State to compel the Roman Catholic Church (and others) to ordain women as priest (or as part of their clergy)?

This raises the question as to an appropriate criterion for separating those violations of "international standards" that do, and those that do not, exceed the limits of the right to self-determination of religious communities. There are no clear answers to this question. It would seem, though, that those customs and traditions that threaten the life or violate the physical integrity of members of the religious group clearly exceed the permissible confines of the right to self-determination of the group. Disabilities attached to individual members of a religious community based on gender or sexual orientation fall short of that impermissible threshold.

B. ENFORCED AND FORCED PREGNANCIES

One of the outstanding features of the Rome Conference was the positive role of the NGO community; and within that community, the Women's Caucus can perhaps be singled out as the one whose untiring efforts culminated in the achievement of almost all of their objectives.

Since earliest times, women have been particularly prone to sexual crimes; and for as long a time, international law has practically turned a blind eye to those atrocities. Rape, for example, is committed quite blatantly and with almost complete impunity as an instrument of, or a kind of free-for-all accessory attending, armed conflict[36]. "Around the world," said Kathleen Barry, "prostitution is considered a necessary and even patriotic service to 'our boys in uniform'"[37]. Until recently, international

---

[36] See Sarnata Reynolds, *Deterring and Preventing Rape and Sexual Slavery During Periods of Armed Conflict*, in 16 L. & INEQ. J. 601, at 605-06 (1998).

[37] KATHLEEN BARRY, FEMALE SEXUAL SLAVERY, 59 (1979).

humanitarian law addressed such offences in fairly general terms and, perhaps for that reason, quite ineffectively. Fionnuala Ni Aolain speaks of "the low status for sexual violations within the hierarchy of humanitarian law offences"[38].

The Rome Conference has laid a solid foundation to change all of that. A special achievement of the Conference was its positive response to the Women's Caucus in the NGO Coalition for an International Criminal Court (CICC) to afford concrete substance to international crimes against women. The Women's Caucus introduced, and most competently lobbied for, the inclusion in the ICC Statute of several matters[39], and was successful in almost all of their endeavors[40]. That did not come easy. In a *Discussion Paper* of July 7, presented to the Rome Conference by the Conference Bureau with a view to expediting the proceedings[41], the enumeration of gender-specific crimes in the definition of crimes against humanity and of war crimes remained unresolved; and although substantial support prevailed throughout the proceedings for such enumeration, the follow-up *Bureau Proposal* of July 10 recorded that the inclusion (or circumscription) of the gender-specific crimes remained subject to "further discussion"[42].

The successes of the Women's Caucus included in the end the inscrtion in the definition of crimes against humanity of "[r]ape, sexual slavery, enforced prostitution, forced pregnancy, enforced sterilization, or any other form of sexual violence of comparable gravity"[43], and similar proscriptions in the definition of war crimes in the case of international armed conflict[44] as well as armed conflict not of an international character[45]. At least as far as crimes against humanity were concerned, these offences could have been covered under the general rubric of outrages against personal dignity or humiliating treatment. Mentioning, on

---

[38] Fionnuala Ni Aolain, *Radical Rules: The Effects of Evidential and Procedural Rules on the Regulation of Sexual Violence in War*, in 60 ALB. L. REV. 883, at 888 (1997).

[39] See Patricia Viseur Sellers & Kaoru Okuizumi, *International Prosecution of Sexual Assaults*, in 7 TRANSNAT'L L. & CONTMP. PROBS. 45, at 73-80 (1997); Nicole Eva Erb, *Gender-Based Crimes under the Draft Statute for the Permanent International Criminal Court*, in 29 COLUM. HUM. RTS. REV. 401, at 424-34 (1998).

[40] See Brook Sari Moshan, *Women, War and Words: The Gender Component of the Permanent International Criminal Court's Definition of Crimes Against Humanity*, in 22 FORDHAM INT'L L.J. 154, at 176-78 (1998) (listing the "victories" of the Women's Caucus).

[41] *Discussion Paper*, U.N. Doc. A/CONF.183/C.1/L.53 (July 6, 1998).

[42] *Bureau Proposal*, U.N. Doc. A/CONF.183/C.1/L.59 (July 10, 1998).

[43] ICC Statute, *supra* note 7, art. 7(1)(g).

[44] *Id.*, art. 8(2)(b)(xxii).

[45] *Id.*, art. 8(2)(c)(vi).

the contrary, gender-specific crimes as a distinct category of crimes against humanity, and according to them a separate place in the list of such crimes, and of war crimes, was important to avoid speculations as to the criminal nature of those atrocities under the rubric of some general proscriptions and to ensure that law enforcement agencies would identify those specific acts as international crimes. Specifying the gender-based crimes has therefore been hailed as a major achievement of the Women's Caucus[46].

Already in the Preparatory Committee, there was wide support for including "rape, sexual slavery, enforced prostitution, enforced pregnancy, enforced sterilization, and any other form of sexual violence" that also constitute a grave breach of the Geneva Conventions[47]. However, in Rome the delegation of the Holy See raised the red flag in regard to the notion of "enforced pregnancy." This could implicate the prohibition of abortions.

Untiring efforts of the Holy See to secure that doctrines of the Church in support of the sanctity of life, marriage and the family are not contradicted in international instruments for the promotion and protection of human rights were evident at recent international conferences where those matters became an issue, such as the United Nations Conference on Environment and Development held in Rio de Janeiro on 3 to 14 June 1992, the International Conference on Population and Development held in Cairo on 5 to 11 September 1994, and the Fourth World Conference on Women held in Beijing on 4 to 15 September 1995[48]. And now also the Rome Conference for the establishment of an international criminal court.

Concerns of the Roman Catholic Church in regard to the increasing liberalization of abortion laws in many countries of the world prompted interventions by the Holy See delegation in Rome to secure precision in ICC usage so as to make it abundantly clear that the crimes within the jurisdiction of the Court would in no way contradict those concerns.

The question when life begins and becomes demanding of protection is one that cannot be resolved by scientific insights or rational argument.

---

[46] *See* Moshan, *supra* note 40, at 176-77 and 180-81.

[47] *See* Draft Statute, *supra* note 3, *ad* War Crimes, B.(p.*bis*); Christopher Keith Hall, *The Fifth Session of the UN Preparatory Committee on the Establishment of an International Criminal Court*, in 92 AM. J. INT'L L. 331, at 333-34 (1998).

[48] C. Migliore, *Ways and Means of the International Activity of the Holy See*, in CHURCH AND STATE; CHANGING PARADIGMS. MONSIGNOR W. ONCLIN CHAIR 1999, 31, at 38. Leuven: Uitgeverij Peeters (1999).

The very concept of life belongs to the realm of empirical mystery and wonder, and the view taken as to its origin in the process of procreation, one way or the other, is ultimately founded on religious faith, which in itself requires metaphysical intervention as a matter of grace. Faith in this sense comprises the acceptance of a premise for one's reasoning – a point of departure – without the backing of sensorial observation, scientific demonstration or rational proof.

The Church by its very nature and function has a vital role to play in the detection and cultivation of a particular belief structure that constitutes the basis of one's acceptance for the truth of a state of affairs without the backing of sensorial or scientific verification. The Church has a mission to carry out and spread the religious foundation of a belief beyond the confines of its inner ecclesiastical circle. In matters of faith, its voice must be heard loud and clearly!

The mission of the Holy See to uphold and to secure respect for basic tenets of the Roman Catholic Church in defense of life, matrimony and the family is well-known and at times caused delegations to regard proposals made by the Holy See with undue suspicion. For example, when the Preamble of the ICC Statute was under consideration, the Holy See delegation in informal negotiations proposed that a clause be inserted to emphasize that human beings are at the center of concerns for justice. This, according to the coordinator of negotiations on the preamble and final clauses (Tuiloma Slade of Samoa), "was widely regarded as an unacceptable effort to raise the abortion issue" and the clause was therefore rejected[49]. However, as far as "enforced pregnancy" was concerned, the Holy See made out a compelling case pertinent to the substance of crimes within the jurisdiction of the ICC.

Prior to the Rome Conference, the terms "forced" and "enforced" in the context of gender-specific crimes were used interchangeably and without precise conceptual differentiation. But there is a difference. Whereas "forcing" someone to do or to forbear something includes the element of overpowering that person – which, as pointed out by the International Criminal Tribunal for Rwanda in *Prosecutor v. Akayesu*, is not confined to physical force but also includes non-physical coercion, such as threats, intimidation, extortion and other forms of duress[50] –

---

[49] Tyuiloma Neroni Slade & Roger S. Clark, *Preamble and Final Clauses*, in THE INTERNATIONAL CRIMINAL COURT: THE MAKING OF THE ROME STATUTE: ISSUES, NEGOTIATIONS, RESULTS 421, at 426 (ed.) Roy S. Lee. The Hague/London/Boston: Kluwer Law Int'l (1999).

[50] PROSECUTOR V. AKAYESU, *supra* note 32, at para. 686.

"enforced" action denotes some form of legal or social sanction or superior order that compels or permits the observance or endurance of certain practices.

Limitations of access to abortions prescribed by law or dictated by religious doctrine could therefore indeed amount to "enforced pregnancy". Forced pregnancy, on the other hand, is thrust upon a women by the person who actually made her pregnant. The delegation of the Holy See was successful in persuading others that this was the case and "forced pregnancy" was consequently substituted for "enforced pregnancy".

The Pro Life lobby in Rome, particularly the Holy See, nevertheless wanted further guarantees. For that reason, a clause was inserted into the Article dealing with crimes against humanity proclaiming that the definition of "forced pregnancy" must not be interpreted "as affecting laws relating to pregnancy"[51]. A cross-reference to this provision in the Article dealing with war crimes[52] was intended to reinforce assurances that the Rome Statute was not concerned with the question of abortion. Perhaps that was superfluous: it ought to be obvious to anyone that "forced pregnancy" as a war crime, committed "in particular... as part of a plan or policy or as part of a large-scale commission of such acts"[53] and as a "serious violation[] of the laws and customs applicable in... armed conflict"[54] cannot possibly be interpreted to implicate the question as to the (il)legality of abortions.

Forced pregnancy is always a consequence of rape. It is mentioned in the ICC Statute alongside rape to indicate that this is a crime in its own right. The crime of forced pregnancy will not be committed if pregnancy was not the desired consequence of the rape – that is, desired by the rapist (*dolus directus*) – or has been foreseen by the rapist as an inevitable consequence of his act (*dolus indirectus*). If the rapist foresaw the pregnancy of his victim as a mere possibility (*dolus eventualis*), he will for purposes of ICC jurisdiction not be answerable for forced pregnancy, since the element of fault as defined in the ICC Statute excludes this form of intent[55]. The accused will nevertheless be guilty of the crime of rape.

This might raise the question why forced pregnancy should be given a place alongside rape in a criminal statute. The trauma which the victims

[51] ICC Statute, *supra* note 7, art. 7(2)(f).
[52] *Id.*, art. 8(2)(b)(xxii).
[53] *Id.*, art. 8(1).
[54] *Id.*, art. 8(2)(b).
[55] *Id.*, art. 30(2)(b).

of rape must inevitably suffer[56], is clearly aggravated when the rape results in pregnancy[57]. The rape of Muslim women as part of a strategy of ethnic cleansing is particularly obnoxious, because Muslim women who have been raped are likely to face rejection by their families and their communities[58]. Given these traumatic consequences of the rape, forced pregnancy will in the normal course of events warrant aggravating punishment.

The ICC did not seek to criminalize or to exercise jurisdiction for the prosecution of persons advocating and implementing the free choice option. The Holy See assumed the task of making doubly sure that the language used in the ICC Statute would not perhaps lend itself to abuse at some future date to contradict that intent. In the process, the Holy See initiated a refinement of terminology – distinguishing between forced and enforced action – which in itself constituted a significant contribution to the development of international-law usage. One might rest assured that national criminal justice systems throughout the world will imitate that usage for the better administration of justice.

C. WEAPONS OF MASS DESTRUCTION

The use, or threat to use, certain weapons, projectiles or material and methods of warfare in an international armed conflict constitutes a war crime. At the Rome Conference, the question whether or not nuclear weapons should be included in the list of prohibited weapons was particularly controversial[59].

The Vatican's opposition to weapons of mass destruction attested to by the Holy See delegation at the Rome Conference has been consistently acted upon since World War II. It was initially demonstrated through the symbolic ratification by the Holy See of the Statute of the International

---

[56] Catherine A. McKinnon, *Crimes of War, Crimes of Peace*, in 4 U.C.L.A. WOMEN'S L.J. 59, at 68 (1993); Laurel Fletcher et al., *Human Rights Violations Against Women*, in 15 WHITTIER L. REV. 319, at 320-21 (1994); Sharon A. Healey, *Prosecuting Rape Under the Statute of the War Crimes Tribunal for the Former Yugoslavia*, in 21 BROOK. J. INT'L L. 327, at 337-40 (1995); Amy E. Ray, *The Shame of It: Gender-Based Terrorism in the Former Yugoslavia and the Failure of International Human Rights Law to Comprehend the Injuries*, in 46 AM. U. L. REV. 793, at 804-06 (1997).

[57] McKinnon, *supra* note 56, at 65; Healey, *supra* note 56, at 337-40; Ray, *supra* note 56, at 809-10.

[58] *See* Healey, *supra* note 56, at 338-40; Ray, *supra* note 56, at 804-06.

[59] SADAT, *supra* note 4, at 267; Michael Bothe, *War Crimes*, in THE ROME STATUTE OF THE INTERNATIONAL CRIMINAL COURT: A COMMENTARY 379, at 396-97 (eds.) Antonio Cassese, Paola Gaeta & John R.W.D. Jones. Oxford: Oxford Univ. Press (2002).

Atomic Energy Agency of 1956[60] and the signing of the *Treaty on the Non-Proliferation of Nuclear Weapons* of 1968[61].

The Holy See more recently signed the *Comprehensive Nuclear-Test-Ban Treaty* of 1996 (on 24 September 1996) and ratified the *Convention on Prohibition or Restriction on the Use of Certain Conventional Weapons which may be Deemed to be Excessively Injurious or to Have Indiscriminate Effects* of 1980 (on 22 July 1997), the *Convention on the Prohibition of the Use, Stockpiling, Production and Transfer of Anti-Personal Mines and on Their Destruction* of 1997 (on 17 February 1998), and the *Convention on the Prohibition of the Development, Production, Stockpiling and Use of Chemical Weapons and on Their Destruction* of 1992 (on 12 May 1999). It also ratified and consented to be bound by *Protocol II to the Convention on Prohibition or Restriction on the Use of Land Mines, Booby-Traps and Other Devices* of 1996 on 22 July 1997, and *Protocol IV to the Convention (Entitled Protocol on Blinding Laser Weapons)* of 1995 on the same date.

The debate in the ICC was centered upon three options: a generic provision, initially proposed by New Zealand[62], that would confine the jurisdiction of the ICC to the use of "weapons, projectiles and materials and methods of warfare which are of a nature to cause superfluous injury or unnecessary suffering or which are inherently indiscriminate in violation of international humanitarian law"[63]; a short list of prohibited weapons mentioned by name; or a longer list of such weapons, mainly supported by non-aligned States, that added to the short list, nuclear weapons, anti-personal mines, and blinding laser weapons. The Holy See threw its weight behind the long list of expressly mentioned weapons, projectiles and materials and methods of warfare.

The dispute as to the in- or exclusion of nuclear weapons was mainly centered on the question as to whether or not their use is currently prohibited as a matter of customary international law[64]. In 1996, the

---

[60] Statute of the International Atomic Energy Agency, 276 U.N.T.S. 3.

[61] Treaty on the Non-Proliferation of Nuclear Weapons, 729 U.N.T.S. 161.

[62] *Proposal Submitted by New Zealand*, U.N. Doc. A/CONF.183/C.1/L.40 (2 July 1998).

[63] The proposal was based on a provision of Protocol I to the Geneva Conventions of 12 August 1949, which provides: "It is prohibited to employ weapons, projectiles and material or methods of warfare of a nature to cause superfluous injury or unnecessary suffering." *Protocol Additional to the Geneva Conventions of 12 August 1949, and relating to the Protection of Victims of International Armed Conflicts (Protocol I), 1977*, art. 35(2), U.N. Doc. A/32/144, 1255 U.N.T.S. 3, *reprinted in* 16 I.L.M. 1391 (1977).

[64] Philippe Kirsch & John T. Holmes, *The Rome Conference on an International Criminal Court: The Negotiations Process*, in 93 AM J. INT'L L. 2, at 7 (1999).

International Court of Justice (ICJ) received instructions from the General Assembly of the United Nations for an advisory opinion on the legality under international law of the use of nuclear weapons in armed conflict. The Court was equally divided (seven votes to seven) on the question whether the use of nuclear weapons would in all circumstances violate the norms of international law relevant to armed conflict. With the casting vote of the President, it finally endorsed the following general proposition:

> [T]he threat or use of nuclear weapons would generally be contrary to the rules of international law applicable in armed conflict, and in particular the principles and rules of humanitarian law.
>
> However,... the Court cannot conclude definitively whether the threat or use of nuclear weapons would be lawful or unlawful in an extreme circumstance of self-defense, in which the survival of a State would be at stake[65].

This opinion afforded to the super powers, who were dead against proclaiming the threat or use of nuclear weapons a crime under international customary law, a peg to hang their hats on.

The ICC Statute in the end proceeded on the assumption that not a single Convention dealing with *ius ad bellum* and which has been adopted since World War II reflects rules of customary international law. The Drafters settled for the "short list" of prohibited weapons, derived from the laws and customs of war dating back to no later than 1925[66]. It prohibits the threat or use of poison or poisoned weapons[67], asphyxiating, poisonous or other gases, and all analogous liquids, materials or devices[68],

---

[65] LEGALITY OF THE THREAT OR USE OF NUCLEAR WEAPONS, para 105E, 1996 ICJ 226.

[66] It must be emphasized that the 1980 *Convention on Prohibitions or Restrictions on the Use of certain Conventional Weapons Which May be Deemed to be Excessively Injurious or to Have Indiscriminate Effects* (U.N. Doc. A/CONF.95/15, *reprinted* in 19 I.L.M. 1523 (1980) was not the one that informed the inclusion in the ICC Statute of weapons, projectiles and material and methods of warfare which are of a nature to cause superfluous injury or unnecessary suffering, or which are inherently indiscriminate. The particular weapons prohibited by the Convention are not listed in the Convention itself but in protocols to the Convention, and those mentioned in the protocols are not (yet) included in the ICC list.

[67] ICC Statute, *supra* note 7, art. 8(2)(b)(xvii). This crime was taken *verbatim* from *Convention (No. IV) Respecting the Laws and Customs of War on Land, with Annex of Regulations, 1907*, art. 23(a), 36 Stat. 2277, U.S.T. 539, *reprinted in* 1 BEVANS 631 and 2 AM. J. INT'L L. (Supp.) 90 (1908).

[68] ICC Statute, *supra* note 7, art. 8(2)(b)(xviii). The essence of this crime dates back to the proscriptions of the *Geneva Protocol for the Prohibition of the Use in War of Poisonous or Other Gases and Bacteriological Methods of Warfare, 1925*, 26 U.S.T. 571, T.I.A.S No. 8061, 94 L.N.T.S. 65 (prohibiting "the use in war of asphyxiating, poisonous or other gases, and of all analogous liquid materials or devices"); and *see also* the *Declaration to Prohibit the Use of Projectiles, the Only Object of Which is the Diffusion of Asphyxiating or Deleterious Gases, 1899*, *reprinted in* 1 AM. J. INT'L L. (Supp.) 157 (1907).

bullets which expand or flatten easily in the human body, such as bullets
with a hard envelope which does not entirely cover the core or is pierced
with incisions (dumdum bullets)[69], and weapons, projectiles and material and methods of warfare which are of a nature to cause superfluous
injury or unnecessary suffering, or which are inherently indiscriminate
in violation of the international law of armed conflict, provided such
weapons, projectiles and material and methods of warfare are the subject
of a comprehensive prohibition[70].

The latter provision was probably intended to denote a wide-ranging
acceptance by a cross-section of the international community of States of
their illegality[71]. However, it was made subject to a further proviso: at
some future date, the weapons, projectiles and material and methods of
warfare considered to be "of a nature to cause superfluous injury or
unnecessary suffering or which are inherently indiscriminate" must be
identified by name; those weapons, projectiles and material and methods
of warfare must then be listed in an annex to the ICC Statute; and that
annex must be adopted in accordance with the procedures prescribed for
the amendment of the ICC Statute. These constraints render it unlikely
that new weapons of mass destruction will in the foreseeable future be
added to the list currently included in the ICC Statute[72].

As to the exclusion of nuclear weapons, the cynical observation of one
delegate is worth noting: if one person is killed (one could add, instantly
and therefore mercifully) by a dumdum bullet, the soldier who fired the
shot could be brought before the ICC (provided of course the threshold
requirements for the prosecution of war crimes have been satisfied), but

---

[69] ICC Statute, *supra* note 7, art. 8(2)(b)(xix). This crime finds its original source in
the *Declaration to Prohibit the Use of Bullets which Expand or Flatten Easily in the
Human Body, 1899, reprinted in* 1 AM. J. INT'L L. (Supp.) 155 (1907). Expansion of the
dumdum bullet upon impact causes significantly more damage to its target than would an
ordinary bullet of the same cartridge, and therefore, being a weapon that inflicts "unnecessary cruel wounds," it has for that reason been banned. *See* Bothe, *supra* note 59, at 408.

[70] ICC Statute, *supra* note 7, art. 8(2)(b)(xx). The original source takes one back to the earliest expositions of the rules of propriety that governs armed conflict: in this instance the *Declaration of St. Petersburg* of 1868, which stated that the use of arms which "uselessly aggravate the suffering of disabled men, or render their death inevitable" would be contrary to "the
laws of humanity." *Declaration Renouncing the Use, in Time of War, of Explosive Projects
Less than 400 Grammes Weight, 1868, reprinted in* 1 AM. J. INT'L L. (Supp.) 95 (1907).

[71] *See* Michael Cottier, *Preliminary Remarks on Subparagraphs (xvii-xx): Prohibited
Weapons: Drafting History*, in COMMENTARY ON THE ROME STATUTE OF THE INTERNA-
TIONAL CRIMINAL COURT 239, at 243-44 (ed.) Otto Triffterer. Baden-Baden: Nomos Ver-
lagsgesellschaft (1999).

[72] Antonio Cassese, *The Statute of the International Criminal Court: Some Preliminary
Reflections*, in 10 EUR. J. INT'L L. 144, at 153 (1999).

innocent civilians who have been mutilated by land mines will be left without redress in the ICC; or worse still, if millions of people are indiscriminately killed or mutilated by the explosion of a nuclear bomb, the incident will be of no concern to the ICC.

The dispute over nuclear weapons had a specific bearing on support for including biological and chemical weapons in the war crimes provisions of the ICC Statute. Many of the non-aligned delegations argued that if nuclear weapons were to be excluded, then the use of biological and chemical weapons as defined in the 1972 *Convention on the Prohibition of the Development, Production and Stockpiling of Bacteriological (Biological) and Toxin Weapons and on Their Destruction*[73], and the 1993 *Convention on the Prohibition of the Development, Production and Stockpiling and Use of Chemical Weapons and Their Destruction*[74] – seen by many as the "poor person's weapons of mass destruction" – ought also to escape the subject-matter jurisdiction of the ICC[75]. The Bureau's final compromise package that became the ICC Statute therefore did not contain either nuclear weapons or biological and chemical weapons in the list of prohibited weapons. However, there is a strong body of opinion that the use of biological and chemical weapons is included in the proscriptive provisions of the 1925 *Geneva Protocol for the Prohibition of the Use in War of Poisonous or Other Gases and Bacteriological Methods of Warfare*[76]. In 1969, the General Assembly of the United Nations in a Resolution on the *Question of Chemical and Bacteriological (Biological) Weapons*, recognized that the 1925 Geneva Protocol embodies generally recognized rules of international law prohibiting the use in international armed conflicts of all biological and chemical methods of warfare. It declared as contrary to the generally recognized rules of international law as embodied in that Protocol,

the use in international armed conflicts of:

(a) Any chemical agents of warfare – chemical substances, whether gaseous, liquid or solid – which might be employed because of their direct toxic effects on man, animals or plants;

---

[73] *Convention on the Prohibition of the Development, Production and Stockpiling of Bacteriological and Toxin Weapons and on Their Destruction, 1972*, art. I, 1015 U.N.T.S. 26, U.S.T. 583, T.I.A.S. No. 8062, 11 I.L.M. 309 (1972).

[74] *Convention on the Prohibition of the Development, Production and Stockpiling and Use of Chemical Weapons and on Their Destruction, 1993*, art. II(1), 31 I.L.M. 800 (1993).

[75] *See* Cottier, *supra* note 71, at 240-41.

[76] *Protocol for the Prohibition of the Use in War Poisonous or Other Gases and Bacteriological Methods of Warfare, 1925*, 26 U.S.T. 571, T.I.A.S No. 8061, 94 L.N.T.S. 65.

(b) Any biological agents of warfare – living organisms, whatever their nature, or infective material derived from them – which are intended to cause disease or death in man, animals or plants, and which depend for their effects on their ability to multiply in the person, animal or plant attacked[77].

The fact that new chemical, bacteriological and biological agents may have been developed subsequent to the date of the Protocol does not detract from its application to such new agents: the Protocol applies "regardless of any technical development"[78]. The 1972 *Convention on the Prohibition of the Development, Production and Stockpiling of Bacteriological (Biological) and Toxin Weapons and on Their Destruction* and the 1993 *Convention on the Prohibition of the Development, Production and Stockpiling and Use of Chemical Weapons and Their Destruction* must also not be seen as having replaced the 1925 Geneva Protocol. The former Convention reaffirms in its Preamble adherence by its States Parties to the principles and objectives of the 1925 Geneva Protocol, and the latter "reaffirms principles and objectives of and obligations assumed under the Geneva Protocol of 1925."

In the final plenary session of the Rome Conference, several countries who voted against the ICC Statute or who abstained in the final vote based their concerns on exclusion of chemical weapons and/or of nuclear weapons from the list of prohibited weapons, projectiles or material and methods of warfare. Those countries included India, Singapore, and Sudan (speaking on behalf of the Arab States)[79]. Mexico supported the adoption of the ICC Statute but nevertheless expressed its misgivings because of the exclusion of nuclear weapons. A representative of India, explaining his delegation's abstention, stated that by not including nuclear

---

[77] G.A. Res. 2603 (XXIV) of 16 Dec. 1969, in 24 U.N. GAOR Supp. (No. 30) at 16, U.N. Doc. A/7630 (1969); and *see also Report of the Secretary General on Respect for Human Rights in Armed Conflicts*, para. 192, U.N. Doc. A/7720 (20 Nov. 1969) (urging Member States of the United Nations, "in the interests of enhancing the security of peoples around the world," to make a clear affirmation that the prohibitions contained in the 1925 Geneva Protocol applies to the use in war of all chemical, bacteriological and biological agents).

[78] G.A. Res. 2603 (XXIV) of 16 Dec. 1969, *supra* note 77. The Report of the Secretary General refers to the application of the 1925 Protocol to chemical, bacteriological and biological agents "which now exist or which may be developed in future." *See also* LEGALITY OF THE THREAT OR USE OF NUCLEAR WEAPONS, *supra* note 65, at para. 85-86 (holding that the fact that nuclear weapons did not exist at the time when the rules of international humanitarian law were developed does not mean that their destructive use cannot be brought within the reach of those proscriptions).

[79] It was not clear which Arab States were included in the Sudanese intervention. Egypt and Jordan, for example, voted in favor of adoption of the ICC Statute.

weapons among those the threat or use of which was banned for purposes of the ICC Statute, the Conference was sending a wrong message that "the international community has decided that the use of nuclear weapons is not a crime"[80].

Earlier, in the final session of the Committee of the Whole, Mr. Rama Rao of India in an attempt to filibuster the proceedings[81], proposed two sets of amendments: the one to add to the list of prohibited weapons in the definition of war crimes, "weapons of mass destruction, i.e. nuclear, chemical and biological weapons"[82]. A motion proposed by Denmark that "no action be taken" was thereupon accepted by an overwhelming majority of the delegations. A brief interlude followed in which a few delegations explained their vote, including the one of the Holy See: The Holy See voted against India, but this must not be seen as any deviation from the Vatican's strong opposition to weapons of mass destruction!

The Rome Conference has not put the question of nuclear weapons to rest. There is an ongoing dispute between New Zealand and France over the issue that finds its roots in earlier litigation between the two countries on nuclear weapon tests conducted by France in the South Pacific region. In 1974, Australia[83] and New Zealand[84], in separate applications, invited the ICJ to condemn France for the carrying out of those tests. The Court declined to give a judgment in the matter, holding that the dispute was rendered moot by an undertaking of France to refrain from such tests in the future, but noting that "if the basis of this Judgment were to be affected, the Applicant could request an examination of the situation in accordance with the provisions of the [ICJ] Statute"[85].

In 1995, France announced that it would carry out a final series of eight nuclear weapon tests in the South Pacific, commencing in September of that year. New Zealand thereupon brought a further application for an examination of the situation, maintaining that the basis of the 1974 judgments was affected, within the meaning of the ICJ's above directive,

---

[80] It must be emphasized, lest the Indian intervention might be misconstrued, that criminal conduct not subject to the jurisdiction of the ICC does not for that reason become decriminalized.

[81] Since the Rome Conference had to conclude its business by midnight of that same day, entertaining at that stage any amendments to the "package proposal" prepared by the conference Bureau would have been fatal to the outcome of the Conference.

[82] *Amendments to A/CONF.183/C.1/L.76/Add.2, Proposed by India*, U.N. Doc. A/CONF.183/C.1/L.94 (17 July 1998).

[83] NUCLEAR TEST (AUSTRALIA V. FRANCE) CASE, 1974 ICJ 252.

[84] NUCLEAR TEST (NEW ZEALAND V. FRANCE) CASE, 1974 ICJ 456.

[85] 1974 ICJ 252, at para. 60; 1974 ICJ 456, at para. 63.

by France's announcement[86]. The Court again ruled against the applicant, holding that the 1974 judgment could not serve as the basis for condemning France's nuclear test program in the South Pacific, since France this time around intended to execute underground nuclear weapon tests while the 1974 judgment related to atmospheric tests only. New Zealand's submission that the rationale of the 1974 judgments, though confined to atmospheric tests (because those were the kind of tests in issue in those cases), also applied to underground nuclear weapon tests because of the risk to the marine environment inherent in both atmospheric and underground nuclear tests, was rejected by the Court. The Court did note, though, that "the present Order is without prejudice to the obligations of States to respect and protect the natural environment"[87].

The ICC Statute does not permit its ratification subject to reservations[88]. However, several States have added declarations to their instruments of ratification[89]. When France ratified the ICC Statute on 9 June 2000, it submitted a declaration stating that the ICC Statute "can neither regulate nor prohibit the possible use of nuclear weapons in the exercise of... [France's] inherent right to self-defense." New Zealand responded in a declaration attached to its instrument of ratification of September 7, 2000: if civilians or civilian targets are intentionally targeted in an armed conflict, or extensive collateral damages to property results from an attack while not justified by military necessity and carried out unlawfully and wantonly, the fact that nuclear weapons had been used in such attacks will not defeat the competence of the ICC to prosecute the war crime concerned.

D. THE INTERESTS OF DEFENSE COUNSEL

The ICC Statute does not regulate the interests of defense counsel. This shortcoming attracted the attention of Ms. Elise Groulx, President of a Montreal-based NGO, *Association Internationale des Avocats de la Défense*. At the Rome Conference, Ms. Groulx raised the question of

---

[86] REQUEST FOR AN EXAMINATION OF THE SITUATION IN ACCORDANCE WITH PARAGRAPH 63 OF THE COURT'S JUDGMENT OF 20 DECEMBER 1974 IN THE NUCLEAR TEST (NEW ZEALAND V. FRANCE) CASE, 1995 ICJ 288.

[87] *Id.*, at para. 64.

[88] ICC Statute, *supra* note 7, art. 120.

[89] Declarations are not binding on the Court but may be taken into account to establish the meaning of provisions in the ICC Statute.

defense rights in the NGO Coalition for an International Court, but could not persuade the group that this was a cause that could be addressed at that stage. There were too many important issues that remained in dispute, she was told, and bringing onto the agenda yet another matter that was bound to provoke controversy would further complicate conclusion of the overall task of the Rome Conference to agree on a Statute for the ICC within the allotted time.

Following the Rome Conference, Ms. Groulx persisted in her efforts to accommodate the interests of defense counsel within the structures of the ICC; and she soon found support for her efforts from the ranks of the Holy See delegation in the (post-Rome) Preparatory Commission. The delegation included a person who had been a defense counsel and who was therefore acutely aware of the problems encountered by that branch of the legal profession. As a matter of justice, it was seen to be important to recognize the role of defense counsel in a balanced and fair criminal justice system.

The support received from the Holy See and other key actors in the Polish, Italian and a number of Latin American delegations paid off. The Rules of Procedure and Evidence adopted in 2000 now instructs the Registrar of the ICC to organize the staff of the Registry in a manner that promotes the rights of the defense in accordance with principles of a fair trial[90]. He is required, to this end:

(a) to facilitate the protection of confidentiality of communications between the accused and his or her legal representative[91];

(b) to provide support, assistance, and information to defense counsel and, as appropriate, afford support to the professional investigators for the efficient and effective conduct of the defense;

(c) to assist arrested persons, persons suspected of a crime and who are about to be questioned by the Prosecutor or national authorities assisting in an investigation, and the accused in obtaining legal advice and the assistance of legal counsel;

(d) to advise the Prosecutor and the Chambers of the Court, as necessary, of relevant defense-related issues;

(e) to provide the defense with such facilities as may be necessary for the direct performance of the duties to be complied with by the defense;

---

[90] Report of the Preparatory Commission for the International Criminal Court, *Finalized Draft Text of the Rules of Procedure and Evidence*, Rule 20(1), U.N. Doc. PCNICC/2000/INF/3/Add.1 (12 July 2000).

[91] As to the protection of lawyer-client confidentiality, *see* ICC Statute, *supra* note 7, art. 67(1)(b).

(f) to facilitate the dissemination of information and case law of the ICC
     to defense counsel and, as appropriate, to cooperate with national
     defense and bar associations or any independent representative body
     or counsel and legal associations, including one that may be estab-
     lished with the assistance of the Assembly of States Parties, to pro-
     mote the specialization and training of lawyers in the law enunciated
     in the ICC Statute and the Rules of Procedure and Evidence;
(g) to ensure that the above functions are executed, and the financial
     administration of the Registry is carried out, in such a manner as to
     ensure the professional independence of defense counsel[92]; and
(h) to create and maintain a list of counsel who meet the criteria pre-
     scribed for lawyers in order to qualify for conducting cases in the
     ICC[93].

The Registrar makes recommendation on a variety of matters, for
example, putting regulations in place, to be approved by the Presidency,
that will govern the operation of the Registry[94] and which must include,
among other things, a provision that will afford to defense counsel appropriate and reasonable assistance from his or her office[95]. Criteria and procedures for the assignment of legal assistance to be included in the regulations will be based on a proposal by the Registrar, who in turn is
required to consult, as appropriate, any independent representative body
of counsel or legal association, including any such body whose establishment may be facilitated by the Assembly of States Parties[96].

At the Rome Conference, the idea emerged of having defense counsel
included in the structures of the ICC as a public defenders office of
some sorts[97]. The idea was soon abandoned – and for good reason: the
office of defense counsel that constitutes an organ of the Court could be
seen to implicate the independence of its office bearers[98]. Instead, the
Association Internationale des Avocats de la Défense, took the initiative,
under the leadership of Ms. Elise Groulx, in establishing an International

---

[92] Rules of Procedure and Evidence, *supra* note 90, Rule 20(2).

[93] *Id.*, Rule 21(2); and as to the criteria applying to defense counsel, *see* Rule 22.

[94] *Id.*, Rule 14(1).

[95] *Id.*, Rule 14(2).

[96] *Id.*, Rule 21(1).

[97] John R.W.D. Jones, *Composition of the Court*, in 1 THE ROME STATUTE OF THE
INTERNATIONAL CRIMINAL COURT: A COMMENTARY 235, at 240 (eds.) Antonio Cassese,
Paola Gaeta & John R.W.D. Jones. Oxford: Oxford Univ. Press (2000).

[98] *See contra*, Karim A.A. Kahn, *Organs of the Court*, in COMMENTARY ON THE ROME
STATUTE OF THE INTERNATIONAL CRIMINAL COURT 589, at 593 (ed.) Otto Triffterer. Baden-
Baden: Nomos Verlagsgesellschaft (1999).

Bar Association for purposes of defense counsel in the ICC. The French Government took an interest in the matter and sponsored a meeting of representatives of national bar associations from all over the globe, that was held in Paris on 5-6 December 2001, to make the International Bar Association (IBA) a reality. A follow-up conference was held in Montreal on 1-12 July 2002 that included more than 350 participants from 80 States. The IBA was established at that meeting.

In terms of the Rules of Procedure and Evidence, a Code of Professional Conduct for defense counsel is to be drawn up by the Presidency on the basis of a proposal made by the Registrar[99], who in turn is required to consult, as appropriate, any independent representative body of counsel or legal association, including any such body whose establishment may be facilitated by the Assembly of States Parties[100]. A primary task of the IBA was to draft a code of professional conduct for practitioners in the ICC to be presented to the Registrar of the Court. The code was circulated to interested parties in February 2003.

E. PRINCIPLES OF CRIMINAL JUSTICE

The Holy See has been said to be "the moral conscience" of the world today[101]. Its uncompromising commitment to the dictates of justice remained evident throughout the proceedings that attended the drafting of the ICC Statute and other instruments centered upon the creation of the International Criminal Court.

When the qualifications of judges of the ICC were debated[102], some delegations wanted to insert an age restriction that would disqualify persons who would otherwise be eminently qualified from serving in that capacity. The Holy See strongly, and successfully, opposed the age restriction since it would amount to discrimination pure and simple. The Holy See pointed out in informal negotiations that various forms of discrimination formed the basis of many crimes within the subject-matter jurisdiction of the ICC and that it would therefore be unwise to institutionalize a form of discrimination in a Statute designed to provide legal redress against other instances of discrimination.

---

[99] Rules of Procedure and Evidence, *supra* note 90, Rule 8.
[100] *Id.*, Rule 20(3).
[101] Migliore, *supra* note 48, at 38.
[102] *See* ICC Statute, *supra* note 7, art. 36(3).

The Rules of Procedure and Evidence of the ICC makes provision for upholding the confidentiality of privileged communications and information[103]. It protects the privileged status of communications made in the context of the professional relationship between a person and his or her legal representative[104], and of those made in the course of a professional relationship between, for example, a person and his or her medical doctor, psychiatrist, psychologist or counselor[105].

Privileged communications within the religious context was of extreme importance to the Holy See, and its delegation worked at great lengths to ensure that the confidentiality of priest-penitent confessions be respected and upheld by the ICC. In consequence of those labors, the Rules of Procedure and Evidence now provides:

> [T]he Court shall give particular regard to recognizing as privileged those communications made in the context of the professional relationship... between a person and a member of a religious clergy: and in the latter case, the Court shall recognize as privileged those communications made in the context of a sacred confession where it is an integral part of the practice of that religion[106].

CONCLUSION

The Holy See – diplomatic arm of the Vatican – has come to be a powerful agent in international relations. A count taken a few years ago showed that the Vatican entertained diplomatic relations with 169 countries. In 1948, the Food and Agricultural Organization became the first international institution to receive a permanent observer from the Holy See, and since then the Holy See has acquired standing in all the major specialized agencies and regional organizations. It became part of the United Nations system in 1951 by gaining membership of the executive council of the High Commissioner for Refugees, and has in due course acceded to Permanent Observer status at the United Nations in New York, Geneva and Vienna[107].

The Roman Catholic Church has been characterized, with a view to its role in international relations, as belonging to a category of transnational institutions referred to by some analysts as transovereigns; that is, "power-

---

[103] Rules of Procedure and Evidence, *supra* note 90, Rule 73.
[104] *Id.*, Rule 73 (1).
[105] *Id.*, Rule 73 (2) and (3).
[106] *Id.*, Rule 73 (3).
[107] Migliore, *supra* note 48, at 36-37.

ful political entities that are less than fully sovereign states, but more that just individuals who presently comprise them"[108]. There might be those who would question the standing within the international norm-creating arena afforded to the Holy See, given its parochial base. Other ecclesiastical institutions have not been granted the same status – though the voice of Islam is often conveyed through the representatives of Muslim States. Sovereignty of the Vatican within a defined territory constitutes adequate justification for affording *locus standi* to the Holy See as a transovereign.

And the Holy See has exercised its standing in international relations with distinction. It has assumed moral leadership in the world that by far exceeds the confines of its own ecclesiastical household[109], and which seeks to engage in activity "for the good of the international community"[110]. It may rightly be said that, today, the diplomacy of the Holy See "is not only recognized in international law and within the order of international affairs, but its presence is sought after and its activity is appreciated"[111].

The role of the Holy See in brokering peace and reconciliation in strife-torn communities, in substituting democratic political structures for totalitarian systems of government, and in promoting the fundamental rights and freedoms of peoples subject to repression, poverty and famine, has been well documented. The Second Vatican Council in Rome, while endorsing the principle that the Church should not be active in the secular realm of politics, nevertheless proclaimed a religious mission as the source of "commitments, direction, and vigor to establish and consolidate the community of men according to the law of God"[112]. It went on to assert that

> the Church is able, indeed it is obliged, if times and circumstances require it, to initiate action for the benefit of all men, especially of those in need, like works of mercy and similar undertakings[113].

The focus of this paper was on the contributions of the Holy See in norm-creating endeavors of the international community of States, with special reference to the drafting of the Statute for a permanent international criminal court. There is one decisive aspect that attended those contributions which, in conclusion, requires emphasis: participation of

---

[108] Timothy P. Terrell & Bernard L. McNamee, *Transovereignty: Separating Human Rights from Traditional Sovereignty and the Implications for the Ethics of International Practice*, in FORDHAM INT'L L.J. 459, at 460 (1994).

[109] *Id.*, at 472.

[110] Migliore, *supra* note 48, at 38.

[111] *Id.*, at 36.

[112] *The Conciliar and Post Conciliar Documents*, in VATICAN COUNCIL II, 942 (ed.) Austin Flannery) Liturgal Press (1984).

[113] *Ibid.*

the Holy See in international diplomacy does not rest upon the incentives of military power or economic strength[114]. It furthermore supercedes the moral constraints dictated by national self-interest.

In that respect, contributions of the Holy See at the Rome Conference stood in sharp contrast to those of many government delegations. Israel, for example, voted against adoption of the ICC Statute because of the inclusion in the subject-matter jurisdiction of the Court of a war crime comprising the transfer, directly or indirectly, by an Occupying Power of parts of its own population into the territory it occupies[115]; France had a bee in its bonnet about the prosecution of French soldiers in an international criminal tribunal and brokered a compromise in terms of which a State, upon ratification of the ICC Statute, can submit a declaration that would exclude the exercise of jurisdiction by the ICC over any war crime committed by a national or on the territory of the declaring State for a period of (no more than) seven years[116]; Australia added a declaration to its instrument of ratification of 1 July 2002 proclaiming that no person shall be surrendered to stand trial in the ICC unless the Attorney-General of Australia has issued a certificate authorizing his or her surrender, and so on. Clearly the most blatant defiance of the rule of law and the principle of equal justice for all came from no other than the United States of America[117].

The United States proceeded on the assumption that the ICC was to be a court "for others, not for us". It consequently insisted on strategies that would afford to the United States government the power to veto the prosecution of American nationals in the ICC. As stated by Ambassador at large for War Crime Issues and leader of the American delegation in Rome, David Scheffer:

> Any arrangement by which a UN-sponsored tribunal could assert jurisdiction to prosecute Americans would be political poison in Congress[118].

While the Rome Conference was in session, Senator Jessie Helms (R-NC), at the time chair of the Senate Foreign Relations Committee, in a letter dated 26 March 1998 informed Secretary of State Madeleine

---

[114] Migliore, *supra* note 48, at 31.

[115] *See* ICC Statute, *supra* note 7, art. 8(2)(viii).

[116] *Id.*, art. 124. France, as well as Colombia, attached an Article 124 declaration to their respective instruments of ratification.

[117] *See* Johan D. Van der Vyver, *The International Criminal Court: American Responses to the Rome Conference and the Role of the European Union*, Rechtspolitisches Forum 19, Institut für Rechtspolitik an der Universität Trier (2003).

[118] T.W. Lippman, *Ambassador to the Darkest Areas of Human Conflict*, in Washington Post, at A.19 (18 Nov. 1997).

Albright that "a treaty establishing... a [U.N. criminal] court without a clear U.S. veto,... will be dead on arrival at the Senate Foreign Relations Committee." However, the Rome Conference insisted on upholding the principle of equal justice for all and consequently rejected, what came to be known as, "American exceptionalism." The Clinton administration nevertheless on 31 December 2001 signed the ICC Statute.

However, when President George W. Bush took office, his administration embarked on a malicious campaign to discredit the ICC. It cancelled the American signing of the ICC Statute. It in 2002 enacted the American Servicemembers Protection Act which, among other things, authorizes the President to "use all means necessary and appropriate" (including military force) to bring about the release of US citizens (and the nationals of certain other countries) who are detained or imprisoned by or on behalf of the ICC[119], and instructs the President to use his veto in the Security Council to block each resolution authorizing any peace-keeping mission or enforcement operation designed to terminate a threat to the peace, a breach of the peace, or an act of aggression unless members of the armed forces of the United States are rendered "permanently exempt" from prosecutions in the ICC[120]. It embarked on a world-wide campaign to enter into agreements with as many States as possible that would preclude those States from ever surrendering an American national to stand trial in the ICC[121], threatening to discontinue military aid to those that refuse to enter into such agreements[122].

In June 2002, the United States actually vetoed a Security Council resolution for renewal of the mandate of the NATO peacekeeping mission in Bosnia-Herzegovina because the Council declined to adopt a proposal of the United States that would afford immunity from arrest, detention and prosecution in all Member States of the United Nations, save the one of their own nationality, to persons participating in United Nations peace-keeping operations. A compromise resolution was thereupon adopted, requesting the ICC not to proceed with any investigation or prosecution for a period of 12 months as from 1 July 2002 of any cases that might involve a contributing State not a Party to the ICC Statute in connection

[119] American Servicemembers Protection Act. P.L. 107-206, 116 Stat. 899, 22 USC 7401, § 2008(a) and (b), read with § 2013(3) and (4).

[120] *Id.*, § 2005(a).

[121] To date, approximately 70 States have given in to American pressures and have signed such impunity agreements.

[122] The United States has thus far cancelled military aid programs in approximately 40 States.

with acts or omissions relating to any operation established or authorized by the United Nations[123]; and following that, renewal of the peacekeeping mission in Bosnia-Herzegovina was approved[124].

The former Security Council resolution recorded that the suspension of investigations and prosecutions for a period of twelve months is to be renewed "for further 12-months periods for as long as may be necessary." The suspension of investigations and prosecutions was indeed renewed on 12 June 2003, but this time around three Member States of the Security Council (France, Germany and Jordan) abstained. Subsequently, the United States made it known that it would veto a resolution, sponsored by Mexico, aimed at increasing the protection of humanitarian aid workers in the conflict zones of the world, because the draft resolution referred to attacks against peacekeeping personnel as a "war crime as defined in the ICC Statute." Following removal of all reference to the ICC in the text, the resolution was adopted without an American veto[125].

The Holy See might also be said to promote its parochial self-interests. Interventions such as those relating to the concept of gender, forced pregnancies and confidentiality of privileged communications were clearly informed by doctrines upheld by the Roman Catholic Church. But there is a difference. The doctrines concerned are founded on religious conviction and a moral consciousness and not on assumed interests that do not even have the semblance of the dictates of justice and fair play.

---

[123] SC Res 1422 of 12 July 2002.
[124] SC Res 1423 of 12 July 2002.
[125] SC Res 1502 of 26 August 2002.

PERSONALIA

BAS DE GAAY FORTMAN was born in The Hague (the Netherlands) in 1937. He obtained master degrees in law as well as economics at the Free University, Amsterdam. In 1966, he received his doctoral degree. From 1967 until 1971 Bas de Gaay Fortman served as Acting Head of Economics at the University of Zambia in Lusaka. In 1971 he became Member of the Dutch Parliament (Second Chamber of the States-General) for the Radical Party (*Politieke Partij Radikalen*, PPR). In 1972 he was elected leader of this party, which subsequently took part in the government coalition (Cabinet Den Uyl, 1973-1977). During this period, he also served as Professor Extraordinary of Economic Development at the Institute of Social Studies (ISS) in 's-Gravenhage. In 1977 he left the Second Chamber of the States-General while being elected as Floor Leader for the *PPR* in the First Chamber (Senate). At the Institute of Social Studies he was appointed Professor Ordinary of Political Economy in which capacity he served until 2002 (Valedictory Address *Power and Protection, Productivism and the Poor*). In 1991 Bas de Gaay Fortman represented the Reformed Churches in the Netherlands (*GKN*) at the General Assembly of the World Council of Churches (WCC) in Canberra (Australia). That year he left the Dutch Parliament and became WCC Commissioner for the Unit on Justice, Peace and Creation. From 1995 until 1996 he represented the *GKN* in the Steering Committee for the merger with the Netherlands Reformed Church and the Evangelical Lutheran Church in the Kingdom of the Netherlands. In September 2000 Bas de Gaay Fortman was appointed Professor of Political Economy of Human Rights at Utrecht University. His research is situated in two fields: Political Economy of Intra-State Collective Violence, and Political Economy of Jurisprudence (with Emphasis on Human Rights). He published among others 'The *Regulae Iuris* and Human Rights as Bridges Between Church and State' (in H. Warnink (ed.), *Legal Position of Churches and Church Autonomy*, Leuven, Peeters, 2001).

RIK TORFS was born in Turnhout (Belgium) in 1956. He studied law (lic. iur., 1979; lic. not., 1980) and canon law (J.C.D., 1987) at the Katholieke Universiteit Leuven. After one year of teaching at Utrecht University (The Netherlands), he became professor at the Faculty of Canon Law (K.U. Leuven) in 1988. He was dean of the Faculty of Canon

Law between 1994 and 2003. Since 2000, he is visiting professor at the University of Stellenbosch (South Africa). In 2003, he was president of the *European Consortium for State-Church Research* of which he is still a member. He is also member of the editorial committee of the *Revue de droit canonique* (Strasbourg), member of the board of the *International Academy for Freedom of Religion and Belief* (Washington) and editor of the *European Journal for Church and State Research* (Leuven).

JOHAN VAN DER VYVER was born in Pietermaritzburg (South Africa) in 1934. He obtained the degrees B.Com. (1954), LL.B. (1956), and Honns. B.A. (in philosophy) (1965) of the Potchefstroom University for Christian Higher Education, and the LL.D. degree of the University of Pretoria (1973). He was also awarded the Diploma of the International and Comparative Law of Human Rights of the International Institute of Human Rights in Strasbourg, France (1986), and received the Doctor of Laws degree (*honoris causa*) of the University of Zululand (1993) and of the Potchefstroom University for Christian Higher Education (2003). He was formerly a professor of law in Potchefstroom and at the University of the Witwatersrand, Johannesburg in South Africa and is currently the I.T. Cohen Professor of International Law and Human Rights at Emory University in Atlanta, Georgia in the U.S.A.

PUBLICATIES / PUBLICATIONS
MSGR. W. ONCLIN CHAIR

Editor RIK TORFS
Editoral assistant KURT MARTENS

Canon Law and Marriage. Monsignor W. Onclin Chair 1995, Leuven, Peeters, 1995, 36 p.

R. TORFS, *The Faculty of Canon Law of K.U. Leuven in 1995*, 5-9.
C. BURKE, *Renewal, Personalism and Law*, 11-21.
R.G.W. HUYSMANS, *Enforcement and Deregulation in Canon Law*, 23-36.

A Swing of the Pendulum. Canon Law in Modern Society. Monsignor W. Onclin Chair 1996, Leuven, Peeters, 1996, 64 p.

R. TORFS, *Une messe est possible. Over de nabijheid van Kerk en geloof*, 7-11.
R. TORFS, *'Une messe est possible'. A Challenge for Canon Law*, 13 17.
J.M. SERRANO RUIZ, *Acerca del carácter personal del matrimonio: digresiones y retornos*, 19-31.
J.M. SERRANO RUIZ, *The Personal Character of Marriage. A Swing of the Pendulum*, 33-45.
F.G. MORRISEY, *Catholic Identity of Healthcare Institutions in a Time of Change*, 47-64.

In Diversitate Unitas. Monsignor W. Onclin Chair 1997, Leuven, Peeters, 1997, 72 p.

R. TORFS, *Pro Pontifice et Rege*, 7-13.
R. TORFS, *Pro Pontifice et Rege*, 15-22.
H. PREE, *The Divine and the Human of the Ius Divinum*, 23-41.
J.H. PROVOST, *Temporary Replacements or New Forms of Ministry: Lay Persons with Pastoral Care of Parishes*, 43-70.

Bridging Past and Future. Monsignor W. Onclin Revisited. Monsignor W. Onclin Chair 1998, Leuven, Peeters, 1998, 87 p.

P. CARD. LAGHI, *Message*, 7-9.
R. TORFS, *Kerkelijk recht in de branding. Terug naar monseigneur W. Onclin*, 11-20.
R. TORFS, *Canon Law in the Balance. Monsignor W. Onclin Revisited*, 21-31.

L. ÖRSY, *In the Service of the Holy Spirit: the Ecclesial Vocation of the Canon Lawyers*, 33-53.
P. COERTZEN, *Protection of Rights in the Church. A Reformed Perspective*, 55-87.

Church and State. Changing Paradigms. Monsignor W. Onclin Chair 1999, Leuven, Peeters, 1999, 72 p.

R. TORFS, *Crisis in het kerkelijk recht*, 7-17.
R. TORFS, *Crisis in Canon Law*, 19-29.
C. MIGLIORE, *Ways and Means of the International Activity of the Holy See*, 31-42.
J.E. WOOD, JR., *The Role of Religion in the Advancement of Religious Human Rights*, 43-69.

Canon Law and Realism. Monsignor W. Onclin Chair 2000, Leuven, Peeters, 2000, 92 p.

R. TORFS, *De advocaat in de kerk, of de avonturen van een vreemdeling in het paradijs*, 7-28.
R. TORFS, *The Advocate in the Church. Source of Conflict or Conflict Solver*, 29-49.
J.P. BEAL, *At the Crossroads of Two Laws. Some Reflections on the Influence of Secular Law on the Church's Response to Clergy Sexual Abuse in the United States*, 51-74.
CH.K. PAPASTATHIS, *Unity Among the Orthodox Churches. From the Theological Approach to the Historical Realities*, 75-88.

Canon Law Between Interpretation and Imagination. Monsignor W. Onclin Chair 2001, Leuven, Peeters, 2001, 88 p.

J. CORIDEN, *Necessary Canonical Reform: Urgent Issues for the Future*, 7-25.
R. PAGÉ, *Full Time Lay Pastoral Ministers and Diocesan Governance*, 27-40.
R. TORFS, *Kerkelijke rechtbanken* secundum *en* praeter legem, 41-61.
R. TORFS, *Church Tribunals* secundum *and* praeter legem, 63-84.

Many Cultures, Many Faces. Monsignor W. Onclin Chair 2002, Leuven, Peeters, 2002, 112 p.

R. TORFS, *Dwarsverbindingen*, 7-17.
R. TORFS, *Cross-connections*, 19-29.

J.R. TRETERA, *Systems of Relations Between the State and Churches in General (Systems of State Ecclesiastical Law) and Their Occurence in the Czech Lands in Particular*, 31-56.
A. MENDONÇA, Bonum Coniugum *from a Socio-Cultural Perspective*, 57-108.

***Canon Law, Consultation and Consolation. Monsignor W. Onclin Chair 2003*, Leuven, Peeters, 2003, 163 p.**

R. TORFS, *De opleiding kerkelijk recht na de Romeinse hervorming*. Per aspera ad astra?, 7-24.
R. TORFS, *The Roman Reform of the Canon Law Programme*. Per aspera ad astra?, 25-41.
T.J. GREEN, *The Legislative Competency of the Episcopal Conference: Present Situation and Future Possibilities*, 43-98.
I.C. IBAN, *Concordates in the European Union: a Relic from the Past or a Valid Instrument for the XXI Century?*, 99-157.

PREFACE

Southeast Asian Images is the concluding volume of my investigations of the culture of the public world in Thailand, the Philippines, and Indonesia. These four books parallel four others that appeared as Inside interpretations of Thai, Philippine, Indonesian, and Southeast Asian societies. The latter publications gave prominence to the life world of the urban middle-class population in the three countries concerned, and view the public world through the prism of the private sphere. In the present monograph, the contrary occurs. It highlights the public world as such, although it has to conclude that its culture cannot be understood without an adequate understanding of the private sphere of existence.

The idea to work on the culture of the public world came to me for various reasons. The first was the barely suppressed irritation of my Filipino colleagues at my early interpretations of everyday life in their country. No matter how carping Filipinos are at their own society, they are very sensitive to any foreign opinion on their social life. As a result, I decided to investigate their most often published ideas about themselves. By examining school texts, interpretations of history, newspaper reportage and opinion making, and fiction, I probed into the public discourse. In doing so, I was confronted with ways of thinking about the public world that challenged my way of seeing things public. I had hit on a very interesting topic.

My motivation was heightened when, after the fall of the Berlin Wall in 198, then President Bush began talking about a ùnew world orderû in which all and sundry would be democratic and respectful of human rights. Earlier in the decade, when still a vice president, he had had the temerity to praise Marcos as a democrat, so now, what did he really mean? However democratic regimes dress up and whatever universal declarations they sign, the local understanding and practice will vary from place to place, even if Washington or Westminster provide the aspired-to models.

At the same time the idea of globalization began to enter the public imagination. Among the thousand things the word may mean, one aspect is the spreading of worldwide habits, fashions, entertainments, and even ways of thinking. As an anthropologist, I dismiss this idea but at the same time am challenged to prove the groundedness of diversity. We may see the same things, but the ways in which they are understood vary greatly. This, in its turn, may have interesting consequences for the shape and motivation of emerging civil societies.

What made it worthwhile to pursue this investigation is the eminent comparability of the cultures concerned. From the point of view of private life, I could argue this for the Thais, Tagalogs, and Javanese in the beginning and concluding chapters of *Inside Southeast Asia*. In this volume it will appear that the thinking about the public realm in the three countries is also rather similar. The three are much more closely related to each other than to erstwhile colonial masters, and the adaptation and localization of foreign products, such as democracy and human rights, meet with similar obstacles.

I thank Cynthia Bautista, Rachel Harrison, Asker Mulder, Nina Tjomsland, and especially Silkworm Books' anonymous reader for commenting on parts of the manuscript. The chapter on Indonesian civics has been adapted from chapter 7 of *Mysticism in Java; Ideology in Indonesia* (The Pepin Press 1998). The reflections on the Philippine image of the nation are also part of *Filipino Images* (New Day 2000). The revised chapters on the current religious revival and the malaise of citizenship and nationalism originally provided a comparative dimension to Inside *Philippine Society* (New Day 1997). I am grateful to the publishers for their kindness in consenting to reproduce the substance of these chapters in the present volume. All other chapters, some of them initially conference papers, find their original book publication here.

The present collection is probably my last field research-based contribution to the study of Southeast Asia. The thirty-five years that I have been engaged in a direct encounter with its people have left me with innumerable debts of gratitude. These do not constitute a burden. On the contrary, they remind me of the goodness I received over the years of my active professional life. I have been very fortunate to hit upon Southeast Asia as the arena of my academic and more pedestrian pursuits. I therefore hope that this book will be received as a token of my gratitude, and that it may stimulate the interest of Southeast Asians in each other.

Chiang Mai, 2001

INTRODUCTION

This book contains a serious yet accessible investigation of the social imagination of modern Southeast Asians that aims at informing a broad public, inclusive of the academic audience. It is a pioneering study because there is very little interpretative work on the public world of modern urbanites. Somehow, anthropologists have excluded these new people and their equally recent urban environment—where culture is literally in the-making—from their purview. It is other researchers who write on middle classes and urban subjects, which they approach in a more structural, political, or spatial manner. Apart from their—recent—descriptions of lifestyles and consumer behavior, we still know very little about how people think and what they aspire to.

Similar to the other *Images* books, we shall approach the mental images people hold of their public world through written sources they produce for each other's perusal which serve as important elements of the public discourse and the formation of opinion. The sources made accessible here concern secondary school texts, the discussion among public intellectuals in essays and the press, interviews with members of that intelligentsia, and the images novelists evoke of life in present-day society. These source chapters deriving from vernacular texts have been complemented by two chapters that focus on observable behavior, which aim at explaining the current religious resurgence and disenchantment with the nation-state in Southeast Asia.

As a complement to *Inside Southeast Asia*, this inquiry into the culture of the public world also aspires to discover commonalities in the world of ideas of contemporary middle classes in the three countries concerned, and to compare their situation on the ground by reviewing issues, problems, and proposed solutions. This is specifically the subject matter of the first concluding chapter. The second conclusion summarizes the actual condition of society people experience—which also results in opinion and immediate imagery—that will be contrasted with the hoped-for. One of the events public intellectuals aspire to is the arising of a vigorous, influential civil society in order to civilize the state and public life in general. It is, therefore, the chances of such an arising occurring that will be evaluated in the last chapter. Before embarking in all this, let us first clarify the basic ideas that guide the analysis.

THE PUBLIC WORLD

A modern public world that consists of the institutions of the state, economy, and civil society is an arena in which citizens actively participate in public affairs. In Southeast Asia, this is a relatively recent phenomenon. If we imagine ourselves back into history to an era when we lived in peasant society or in small communities, public and private affairs were hard to distinguish, and powerful institutions, such as government, church, or monetary exchange, had not established themselves.

Following Habermas's ideas about the evolution of social complexity, such as those set forth in his *Theory of Communicative Action*, the first institution to specialize and to separate itself from the integrity of the communal, private life-world, is government, or politics. The near headman became a distant king, and a ruling class set itself apart from the commoners whom they henceforward commanded. Their affairs were public affairs in the sense that they very much demonstrated their power through ritual display and the pomp of state, but these affairs were not of the public: the latter merely served as spectators and mutes. In his *Negara*, Geertz labeled this condition a theatre state, which I also found a useful notion to think about certain one-party regimes, such as North Korea, or Suharto's Indonesia.

In the latter case, the state displayed itself on billboards, through endless sloganeering, media control, and periodic national celebrations, most importantly Independence Day, and the five-yearly election campaigns, rightfully dubbed the Festival of Democracy. In spite of this festive democracy, everybody knew that challenging the state was a very hazardous activity, and that politics and decision making were confined to and hidden by the walls of the presidential palace.

The second institution to free itself from the life-world of ordinary existence is the economy, or the market. What is meant is the increasing importance of money in social life. Relationships and goods become commodified, get assigned a value that stands apart from the persons or the needs involved. The economy appears to go its own way, irrespective of individual wishes, and gives rise to a market-driven society, an archetypical *Gesellschaft* in which people pursue their personal gain.

Both state and economy deeply influence ordinary existence through, for instance, bureaucratic impositions and the monetization of relationships. Habermas calls this the colonization of the life-world by the two independent subsystems of state and economy. I think this terminology is felicitous, because it reveals that their working imposes itself on private existence, and that the functioning of politics and economy is not subject to the logic and morality of the life-world. The two subsystems go their own way, guided by their own logic: the concern of politics and state is the accumulation of power, and that of economy and market is the accumulation of wealth. They do this irrespective of the needs of people whose life-world they penetrate. Obviously, these people are in need to defend themselves.

In order to defend oneself, one needs power, which may mean having guns, and/or ideas and knowledge, and/or money. When people start opposing the state or economic manipulation, they are expressing the fact that there is civil society. This civil society aspires to regulate the exercise of state and market power; it wants to civilize these or, at the very least, to influence the decisions made in the political and corporate spheres. In order to do so, civil society needs power; civil society is, therefore, political, and thrives best in an open, democratic environment that guarantees the freedoms of expression and association—in other words, the free exchange of ideas.

The force emanating from civil society is closely related to two important elements: an advanced level of education and sophistication of the middle classes, and their resources, or relative economic independence. These considerations are important to estimate the potency of civil society. While a critical mindset may appear as a basic condition, we should also be aware that when most educated persons are state-dependent, as civil servants or regimented subjects, it will be hard to imagine how they can successfully challenge the state. Independent professionals and a free press would seem to be better suited to influence public opinion and to eventually mobilize people to join a cause. More potential still can possibly be expected from those who enjoy economic resources.

The last point can be well illustrated by the early stirrings of civil society in Europe. Around the year 1100, merchants, bankers, and entrepreneurs had become potent enough to wrest privilege from the feudal lords. Through lending them money, the latter had to allow for market and urban freedoms, which soon resulted in walled cities within which free commoners—citizens—took care of their own affairs. In other words, their economic potency was their most powerful weapon against the impositions of the feudal state. They became the precursors of civil society.

In the case of Southeast Asia, we should be wary of comparing with Europe-inspired historical and theoretical models. In the countries under discussion, the conditions for the arising of civil society developed recently. Urban settings, middle classes, modern education, accelerated economic growth, and exposure to nationwide and global media are relatively new phenomena. Besides, while there is much that is cosmopolitan about contemporary civil societies in Southeast Asia, their culture is also pervaded by older ideas that spell the setting in which modernity has to be accommodated.

Because of this, Appadurai and Breckenridge argue, in their introduction to *Consuming Modernity*, that modernity is nobody's monopoly any longer, and that the development of what the authors call public culture will be nationally specific. Civil society in Southeast Asia should, therefore, be understood on the basis of its own origin and growth in a specific cultural-historical context.

Consuming Modernity highlights the consumptive side of public culture, such as sports, television, cinema, travel, radio, and museums. To this they could have added other manifestations of money- and market-driven life, such as the advertising, fashion, lifestyle, and recreation industries that exert a pervasive influence on the mental world of the middle classes. In this, they apparently agree with Horkheimer and Adorno's idea that the public at large is victim of the culture industry, and that it merely consumes 'culture' instead of creatively participating in it. In their *Dialectic of Enlightenment*, the latter even went so far as to predict Enlightenment's undoing because of the market-driven, asinine production of standardized 'culture' that prevents a critical public from arising. Whereas this pessimism can be argued theoretically, it is, thank goodness, not supported by the practice we can also witness in Southeast Asia.

Practice, and especially the new practice of attempting to influence public and corporate policy, not only needs ideas, or policy goals, but also needs to find support in public opinion. Both such ideas and public opinion in its diversity are reflections of the social imagination that is the subject matter of this investigation. This imagination is complex, showing conservative and progressive, dominant and innovative, traditional cultural and modern alternatives that arise as a response to massive societal change. Before turning to these, let us first trace the emergence of civil society in Thailand, the Philippines, and Indonesia.

EVOLUTION OF THE PUBLIC WORLD IN SOUTHEAST ASIA

In Thailand and many parts of Indonesia, state formation, and thus the setting apart of government and politics from the everyday concerns of ordinary people, took place long before the first Europeans arrived on the scene. In fact, they would probably not have been attracted to go there if trade and local economies had not been flourishing. Yet, inland states and maritime trade-oriented port cities had not spread everywhere, Manila and certain southern Muslim principalities being the minor exceptions in the Philippines. It is, therefore, of interest to trace the evolution towards complex social organization in those islands in order to illustrate the processes outlined in the previous section.

In the Philippines, a state as a political system imposing itself on a far-flung population only came into existence when the King of Spain established his dominion in the islands that are still known by his name. When that happened, the often mutually antagonistic tribes and communities of peasants, fishermen, warriors, and traders were brought into a subservient relation to a higher level of government that encompassed them all.

Because of the Spanish policy of justifying their conquest through Christianization, its early impositions had formidable cultural consequences. Economically, however, things remained very much the same. Like in earlier days, the population was subject to taxation by local power holders and continued to live under subsistence conditions.

In the Spanish colony, the appearance of the second component of the public world occurred rather late. Basically, the separation of the economy only evolved in the late eighteenth and nineteenth centuries when the country was gradually integrated into the world economy. The independence of the economy resulted in the emergence of a class of native entrepreneurs who sought higher education for their offspring. This became a salient possibility when the Jesuits returned to the archipelago in 1859. Not long after their introduction of modern, Western schooling, proto-nationalist ideas began to circulate, soon to be followed by demands for justice, abolition of privilege, self-determination, political representation, and national independence. In the 1870s and 1880s, we thus witness the arising of the intelligentsia as the vanguard of an emancipating citizenry, or civil society, in the Philippines. As their thinking matured, it led to the successful revolution against Spanish rule.

The relation between Western education and the arising of civil society is also clear in Thailand where the expansion and modernization of army and civil service required Western training which inevitably resulted in demands for democratic government versus royal rule and the privileges of the nobility. In the Netherlands East Indies, the territory that would become Indonesia, the Dutch were rather late in introducing modern schooling, but as soon as they did, cultural, commercial, and political demands against the colonial state were formulated, and, by the 1920s, a lively civil society flourished.

Regarding the development of early civil society, we should be aware of significant differences in the three countries under discussion. In the Philippines, the intelligentsia—known as *ilustrados*, enlightened ones—generally consisted of the sons of an affluent class of native landlords and entrepreneurs who thus had a firm basis in the country's economy. The new people who came up in Thailand and Indonesia had no economic independence. They arose because of the modernization of the state and its demand for well-trained personnel. In Thailand this resulted in a situation in which almost all modernly trained ethnic Thais could be absorbed by the burgeoning bureaucracy until well into the 1960s. Whatever existed as a civil society of free professionals was really marginal to the system, at the same time that the Chinese, highly educated or not, continued minding their business. In Indonesia, apart from the aristocracy-affiliated government administrators, the so-called *priyayi*, a rather diverse class of professionals came to the fore who protested the colonial arrangement. Their lively movement culminated in 1928 in the declaration of a future independent, unitary Indonesia.

It is clear that all intellectual awakening resulted in demands on the political status quo. Because of this challenging of the state, the Philippines temporarily liberated itself (1898–1901), the Thais, also temporarily, side-tracked the monarchy (1932–58), and the Indonesians nurtured the nationalism that would, in due course, bring the republic to life. The intensity of the challenges, or rather of the public discourse about the changes to be effected, was typically at its peak from shortly before to some years after these signal events. In the Philippines, the reform and Propaganda movements started in the 1880s, and it was only in the 1910s that nationalist discourse died down. In the Thai case, the community of students had discussions mainly in Paris in the 1920s, while the exchanges of utopian and democratic ideas vanished from the public mind when Marshal Phibun Songkhram established a dictatorship in 1938. In Indonesia, the open debate flourished from the 1910s until Sukarno put the lid on it by closing the Constitutional Assembly *(Konstituante)* in 1959.

These dates are important to understanding the kind of ideas that animated the debates. In the Philippines these took place much earlier than in Thailand and Indonesia. As a result, the Filipino exchanges were about emancipation vis-à-vis the Spaniards, nationalism and liberation, with no clear goals set to bring about social change. Despite the atrocities of their conquest, the Americans soon attracted a measure of attachment. They were hailed as enlightened modernizers after a long period of clerical obscurantism. Thus, while learning a new style of life and enjoying many civil liberties, the debates turned routine rather than challenging, and what society was hoped to become remained vague, only to be discussed by the marginal Left in the 1920s and 1930s (and fought for ever after!).

The Thai and Indonesian discourses matured much later than the early Filipino debates and were, therefore, more visionary. In the 1920s and 1930s, the influence of utopian socialism and humanism, with their visions of social and individual moral progress, was clearly reflected in the programmatic thought of the modern nation's founding fathers: society and persons were constructable. This was evident from economist Pridi Banomyong's grandiose plans for a socialist-style land reform in Thailand, and from Indonesia's declared ideals to found the country on the rule of law, to strive for social justice, and a humane, democratic society.

Whatever the high hopes of early civil society may have been, they soon floundered in their confrontation with obdurate reality, such as the change to a fascist-like dictatorship in Thailand, the politicization of the civil service under the Commonwealth government in the Philippines, and Dutch repression in Indonesia. These developments were topped by the Japanese occupation and the spirit of war. Militarization, war-time corruption, coups d'état and dictatorship, all-out war against the peasantry of Northern Luzon, and the fight against the Dutch, were not exactly conducive to a civilized discourse and rather led to establish a survival-oriented mentality that prioritizes personal needs. Simultaneously, public morality and the rule of law deteriorated.

A general loss of cultural direction pervaded the 1950s. Under chronic military rule, this could only be expected in Thailand. Confusion and fading ideals were characteristic of Indonesian society after the successful revolution against the Dutch. In the Philippines, a certain smugness—the only Christian nation in Asia, English-speaking, a democracy among dictatorships, special relations with the United States of America—blinded it from its neocolonial dependence. It was only in the late 1950s and 1960s that Philippine mendicancy and colonial education were exposed, and that a student-driven movement evolved demanding equity, justice, and popular democracy in the face of the ruling oligarchy (the communist New People's Army (NPA) was founded in 1969).

In the margin such demands were courageously formulated by certain journalists and novelists in Thailand, but their ideas were effectively suppressed until they burst upon the scene when unprecedented violence drove the dictatorship out in 1973. These ideas would be out in the open until October 1976 when the reaction smothered them in blood. In the Philippines they flourished until Marcos's declaration of martial law (1972). In Indonesia, the fall of Sukarno ushered in a period in which all voices, save for the Left, could be heard, until they were strangled after the Malari event of January 1974.

The ideas that surfaced in the 1960s and early 1970s were basically born in the 1920s and 1930s. They assume that society could be improved, that progress could be made, such as reflected in the proclamations of the People's Council in Thailand in 1932, in the Philippine Constitution of 1935, or in the intellectual heritage of the so-called Generation of 1928 in Indonesia.

At this juncture it is important to reflect on the transition in the intellectual climate that occurred with the change from the 1960s to the 1970s. The people who formulated the founding ideas of modern, independent polities had, during their education, been exposed to contemporary Western thinking, and were familiar with the ideas of equality, the rule of law, humanism, and, of course, nationalism. They constituted the first generation of modern people in their societies. As such, they were a small group, both marginal to and very influential in the social process. They were an advantaged class of people who not only studied to learn a profession but who also took a wide interest in domestic and international affairs. They were both spectators and participants, both idealists and critics. They studied at a time when study was still a privilege. This educational climate with all its optimism and idealism persisted into the 1960s. Nowadays, we find the heirs to this tradition on the NGO-scene: active, and vociferously challenging 'the system.'

In the 1960s, the idea of development took hold. Governments wanted to modernize, to achieve economic progress, to produce people capable of handling sophisticated technology. The capital cities' skylines changed: the first high-rises appeared. This signaled an economic sea change to which the education industry eagerly responded. In 1960, some 15,000 students enjoyed higher education in Thailand; in 1990, 600,000 were enrolled in tertiary institutions, a forty-fold increase! This expansion continues into the present day.

Contemporary higher education is no privilege any longer; it is a necessity. The people it produces are new people, different from the older generation. They are technology- and career-oriented. Politically, they are indifferent; socially, they are inattentive. They grew up in an incipient consumer society. They matured with television rather than with books. These days they constitute the bulk of the middle classes. It is on them we need to focus if we want to chart the evolution of the culture of the public world and to gauge the prospect of the arising of a civil society.

In order to appreciate the vast changes in style of life in Southeast Asia and the new people it has brought to the fore, we need to clearly understand the newness of it all. It is development without tradition or history, without example or culture. At the end of the Sukarno period, Jakarta, with two million people, not exactly a village, still looked like one, save for Hotel Indonesia, the National Monument, and two or three unfinished high-rises. The people who mattered had the idea they knew each other. There was little traffic. Today, the conurbation may count 18 or 20 million people. The height of the skyscraping city overshadows the earlier monuments of pride. Traffic is nightmarish.

We can tell similar stories about the expansion of Bangkok and Manila. Signal to us is the observation that town is, in the main, inhabited by new people who came there from other places. To them, urban living is new, and so is the experience of the city's anonymity and a fully monetized way of life. They have come to a market-driven environment that stimulates individualization and consumerism. They have arrived in an archetypical *Gesellschaft*, that is, a society where everybody strives after his own gain.

The people who belong to the middle classes—in itself a new social stratum—earn their money in government, in business, or as professionals. They are the products of massive education, especially in institutes of higher learning. It should be realized, though, that the quality of their training varies widely. This becomes clear when we note, for instance, that of the approximately one thousand degree-offering schools in the Philippines, only twenty meet official criteria of excellence. The expansion of education at all levels is so rapid that its quality has, in general, dramatically declined. What is clear, however, is that the schooling offered is profession- and career-oriented, and has little to do with the Enlightenment ideals of rationality and mental emancipation.

In urban areas, people are fully exposed to a media-dominated environment that advises on what to buy, how to be entertained, how to dress, what to choose. Perhaps this is a good thing, because many people are at a loss about how to behave in the new environment. The members of the new middle classes are eager consumers who have no experience or tradition of what belongs to their new status. They are literally shopping for lifestyles. They are attracted to Western examples, such as blue jeans, McDonald's, Greek colonnades, and international football, but also invent traditions based on aristocratic examples, such as Thai classical dance or the Javanese royal wedding ceremony. In the Philippines, American models are imitated, such as beauty pageants and musical shows. Altogether, a fantastic hybrid culture is in the making that lacks all direction and that is largely dictated by how much one can invest in its paraphernalia.

Naturally, many people feel confused. They have not been trained for urban anonymity and commercialism. While some prop up their self-respect through lavish spending, most people are not in a position to do so. They are looking for other means of shoring up their sense of self and of finding some security in the fleeting scenes of urban living. As a result, religion offers a very lively spectacle. With people striving for mainstream or sectarian respectability, cults, sects, superstitions, but also orthodox faiths are doing very well indeed. Their emphasis on moral righteousness parallels the ideas promoted through national indoctrination and values education in school. All these seem to emphasize that individuals should lead moral lives, and know their place and duties; they also propagate the example of the modern, monogamous middle-class family.

Religion may also be compensating for the widespread sense of disenchantment with the nation-state. In the confusing, market-dominated urban world, the early promises of national solidarity and democratic citizenship have failed to mature. Apart from religion, a new channel to replace the loss of these great, modern ideals has meanwhile been developing through the timely possibility of participation in an active civil society.

The purpose of this collection of essays is to explore the mental images members of the urban middle classes in Southeast Asia hold of their public world, and to assess the possibility of an active civil society emerging. This investigation particularly aspires to trace the conceptual patterns that structure the social imagination. This thinking is partly conditioned by the teachings school children are subjected to. That is why we shall first of all scrutinize the textbooks concerning the national self-imagination of Thais, Filipinos, and Indonesians. These texts are amazingly influential and mirror what Althusser called the 'ideological state apparatus.' They constitute the subject matter of the section on national self-image, consisting of the first three chapters. In these, as well as in the following five, I chose to let the sources speak for themselves; they are self-evident. At the end of each chapter, however, I shall comment on these texts and the social imagination that informs them.

The second section is on change, its problems, and the hopes it inspires. In contrast to the state-dominated national self-images, the part civil society plays becomes increasingly important. The discussion of change and its problems in Thai school texts in chapter 4 comes close to the substance of the public discourse as reflected in the press. The same applies to chapter 5, which offers both a realistic diagnosis of Philippine practice and clearly church-inspired moral remedies to improve it. The next two chapters fully originate from civil society. The sixth, on the reform debate in Indonesia, introduces the ideas characteristic of the discourse among public intellectuals. Some of these thinkers truly fit Mannheim's idea of a 'free-floating intelligentsia.' These are the few people who are both unconnected and original, and who, because of that, stir controversy and hopefully advance the debates. Most voices, however, originate from a more mundane level, and represent political, business, and civil society organizations' interests. The latter considerations tend to be more expedient, with the sight set towards feasibility.

In chapter 7 three women authors envisage the emancipatory trajectory to be traveled if women are to flourish in and contribute to present-day life. Apart from the quality of their writing, they drew attention because they treat the topic of sex quite openly. They are the first to challenge a situation that has, of old, been put under taboo. In doing so, they possibly reveal an interesting trend in the evolution of Southeast Asian culture.

The novels of four social-critical authors, all of them public intellectuals in their own right, open the section, The Present, which offers various interpretations of the moral predicament of the three societies under discussion. In chapter 8, these novelists sketch broad pictures of the evolution of their societies, and reach alarming conclusions. Whether the social condition is as appalling as they describe is open to question, but their writings do offer most useful diagnoses. In all cases, though, they shy away from giving recommendations about how to promote reform. In that sense they contrast with those who take activist positions.

In chapter 9, the usually critical voices of the public intellectuals will be juxtaposed with the voices of religion and morality. In a way, they seem to agree with state-ideological and schoolbook messages, except that they do not aim at nation-building or civic behavior, but at personal exemplariness and faith. In the public discourse these particularistic messages enjoy a wide appeal, as they seemingly agree with how life in the private sphere should be lived. This stream of thinking constitutes an important counterpoint to the more social-analytical thought of committed intellectuals.

In chapter 10, all this will be joined by reflections on current social practice. People appear to be career-oriented and engrossed in advancing their level of living. They have come to live in a highly materialistic, media-dominated society that delights in consumer culture and virtual reality. This draws attention away from public issues, and may thwart the development of a vigorous civil society.

This takes us to the concluding section, The Public Discourse. In chapter 11, we shall develop a general picture and reflect on commonalities. This endeavor will demonstrate the advantage of comparison, because it will enable us to identify shared characteristics that lend Southeast Asia its peculiar flavor; it indicates a strikingly similar social imagination. The point of departure, however, is the comparative reviewing of the matters raised in the first six chapters. In the sixth, for instance, we present an inventory of issues in need of reform as formulated by Indonesian intellectuals. The problems discussed there, however, and the need for reform, are generally shared by Indonesia's neighbors. While the problem of ethnicity, or minorities, surfaces most acutely in the diversity of Indonesia, it also occurs in the other states. The religious divide between national groups, the position of the Chinese, class conflict, unemployment and poverty, centralization versus regionalism, the disastrous state of public education, the politicization or venality of the judiciary, the exploitation of the weak, the rapacity of politicians, and the ever-widening gap between elites and the rest—these are all shared problems that animate public opinion and demand solutions. So, while the situation in Indonesia is avowedly graver, and while its problems are more fundamental—even threatening the very existence of the unitary state—it makes sense to review them in a comparative perspective.

In the concluding chapter, we shall elaborate the idea of civil society and evaluate whether the trends and images noted throughout the text can be conducive to the emergence of an influential civil society. Have basic conditions for that emergence been met, and how far needs society to evolve to give rise to active citizenship and a civilized culture of the public world? It is as if we are watching a contest between cultural inertia and the market-driven consumerism on the one hand, and the creative-idealistic imagination of social progress and emancipation on the other. Such, at least, are some of the ideas mulled over in chapter 12.

Because of our policy of letting the materials speak as they are, excessive footnoting and referencing has been avoided. Yet, to provide the reader with essential background reading, a bibliographic note follows the conclusion. Naturally, that note is far from exhaustive but indicates some widely available key sources that, in turn, contain extensive references to the recent literature on Southeast Asia and the individual countries discussed.

SECTION I: NATIONAL SELF-IMAGE

CHAPTER 1

THE THAI DEMOCRATIC WAY OF LIFE

Buddhism and ethics have always been at the core of Thai education. Since the introduction of modern schooling, a course in citizenship has been included in the package of value-based subject matter, originally entitled *The Duties of the Populace*. Since the curriculum reform of 1978, these subjects are offered under the less forbidding titles of 'Character Development' and 'Preparing for the Experience of Life' (Mulder 1997a: ch. 1). Meanwhile, the material on 'the democratic way of life' has been added. As always, these teachings aim at creating 'good people,' that is, well-behaving and obedient subjects of king and state.

In this chapter we want to investigate those latest ideas on the democratic way of life that are expected to animate the democratic system of government under the king. In this system, Thai society is imagined as a hierarchical moral order consisting, from bottom to top, of Nation-Religion-King. These ideas are formalized in the national doctrine of the Three Institutions in which nation, state, and society fuse to become an intimate community, a family, in which problems originate from individual waywardness. As a result, propagating the democratic way of life should not only serve to improve the practice of political democracy, but also to rein in the Thai citizen.

THE LABORATORY OF DEMOCRACY

In teacher's handbooks appearing over the past ten years it is proposed that elementary school must take the lead in democratizing the country.[1] With seven million pupils in over thirty thousand schools, elementary education is an omnipresent institution. If it succeeds to exemplify, and to instill in the minds of students, the 'democratic way of life,' other institutions—family, community, nation—will be saturated with that 'way' and its mentality. Elementary schools, therefore, must be the pioneer and the laboratory of democracy.

In the *Handbook for Organizing the Study and Teaching to Promote Democracy in Elementary School*, emphasis is given to setting up groups and student committees. Working in groups should follow democratic procedures such as selecting heads through voting, and reasonable discussions to reach decisions. The students concerned must then see to it that these are enforced 'in order that the rules are lived up to and in order to drill them in so as to lead to personal discipline.' This is proposed as a useful exercise in student self-government, to be practiced at various levels of school life; 'it is more than certain that such decisions will lay the basis of respect for the rules of society and the laws of the state, and will result in a peaceful and happy social life.' Classes can be divided into groups on various occasions such as library work, scouting activities, and preparing for excursions. In the last case, students could decide on how to reach their destination, for instance in marching order, and agree not to play or be noisy. When consenting to such behavior, they should themselves ensure that they stick to it, which will result in establishing ethics and pleasing habits, which will grow to become permanent and ingrained (34–5).

Further on in the text, teachers are offered charts helping them to assess the democratic behavior of their pupils (63–7). The points to observe are divided into three categories: Respect, Cooperation, and Wisdom. Especially the show of respect is very elaborate. Elementary school children have to demonstrate respect physically, in speech, in matters of opinion, for the rules, and for the rights of others. Under the first we find showing respect to the teacher every time the child meets her or him, and to parents before going to and when coming from school; in speaking, people must use pleasing and polite words, refrain from gossip and lying; they should listen attentively to their teacher, not interrupt others and carefully consider their opinions; they must be very serious in following the rules, even when they are on their own, whether it concerns school, society, or state. As Buddhists, they must stick to the basic injunctions; as nationals, they must be loyal to the king; as members of the nation-state, they must seriously respect the law. Respect for the rights of others is demonstrated by not disturbing them, not taking their possessions, asking for permission, queuing in orderly fashion, not hurting others, and not damaging public property.

Under Cooperation, the teacher should watch whether pupils always work together, whether they do so in earnest, finish the work at hand, and use their time efficiently. Wisdom is demonstrated by knowing cause and effect, asking the right questions, discussing rationally, not being guided by temper, feelings, and self-conceit, looking at problems from all angles, while always probing and questing for awareness and knowledge. All these qualities the teacher must observe in the relationships of students divided into working groups that choose their own chairperson—in all other respects it is behavior among equals. In relation to these groups, the teacher is arbiter and adviser. He or she remains the teacher, too, which means that he or she must always be shown respect, be addressed with honor, and be taken seriously. Parents and senior relatives, even group chairpersons, belong to the same category as teachers.

Lest teachers forget the qualities of democratic government, these are explicitly reiterated later in the text (148–9). The highest power is with the people. This is stipulated in the constitution: the people are the holders of sovereignty. Government, therefore, is of, by, and for the people. These elect their leaders, who are organized in political parties. Such representatives take majority decisions while respecting minority positions. In school, these principles can be brought to life through establishing a Students Committee (SC). This committee will represent all the school's students, and deliberate their interests according to democratic procedures. Having an SC occasions campaigning, voting, and suchlike, thus giving substance to democracy. The committee is the discussion partner of the school's administration and the teachers committee, and conveys to these the wishes and intentions of the students. 'Moreover, this will help in cooperating in the organization of student activities, in smoothing school life, and in promoting ethics and good manners.' Of course, the students committee operates within the bounds of the rules and under the authority of the school, which must be stipulated in the committee's charter. Administration and teachers will see to it that 'the students concerned will not engage in activities that are unbecoming or doomed from the outset' (150).

An operational SC affords a good exercise in acquainting students with democratic procedures and in raising good future citizens. It will give them insight, and the opportunity to practice. They will participate in and openly opine about school activities. This will make them more mature and aware, and also aware of their interests in school life. It teaches them to cooperate and plan, and fosters communication throughout the school. In brief, it will serve as an instrument to instill a positive attitude to 'the system of democratic government under the king' (150).

With all this in place, the school can be presented as the nucleus of the democratic way of life that—also because Thais are said to love democracy—will spread out to cover the nation. After all, being in democratic surroundings for six years produces children who behave nicely, who value democracy, and thus constitute a good example for others to follow. This is the indirect manner of spreading the democratic way. The direct method that the school uses to propagate the desired way of life is to impress the people who visit with the school's atmosphere and students' behavior. Subsequently, they will be encouraged to practice such conduct in their own home and community. Similarly, orderly excursions, polite and rational discussions, group work and scouting activities, the atmosphere when honoring senior citizens, and merit making to express gratefulness to elders, will contribute to the democratic transformation of Thai communities (181–4).

The preface to the *Handbook to Promote the Democratic Way of Life* draws attention to the widespread practice of selling votes in spite of the fact that 'most people have a good idea of what electing representatives means.' The Ministries of Interior and Education are, therefore, cooperating in spreading the spirit of democracy in order to make it a way of life. It is essential to let all people participate in decisions affecting their lives. This can be achieved through working in groups, organizing and planning together, on the conditions that ethics are the guide and that people fulfill their various duties. This pairs with a way of life in which people respect each other and each other's rights, do not abuse privilege, stick to the rules, feel responsible, work for the common good, and approach problems rationally. This should be family practice: to listen to each other, to be neither egocentric nor prejudiced, and thus to ensure that everybody is happy (6–7).

The starting point of such a good condition is the individual heart. If people are ethically inclined, family life will be affectionate, and thus engender a peaceful and contented social life, which, in turn, will promote the prosperity of the nation. This shows that democracy begins in the hearts of each one of us. This corresponds with behavior that is peaceful, respectful of law, rules, customs and culture, and reasonable. It shows through in Respect, Cooperation, and Wisdom. These are then filled in in a similar manner as in the previous book to which, under Respect, 'faith in customs, culture and tradition' has been added. Cooperation is summarized as not being self-centered. The practice of Wisdom implies understanding the points of view of leaders and of followers, obeying majority decisions, being willing to listen, and using reason. It is summarized as 'be attentive to yourself and your intentions,' and you will be on your way to democracy (12–3).

Next, under the heading 'Indicators of the democratic way of life,' the text maintains that 'the Thai way of being is the democratic way of life.' This is specified in ten clauses as: be reasonable and well informed; respect each other's rights, duties and freedoms; treat all people equally and without bias; play your part in all activities; develop your own opinion, and show it; be responsible for your own actions, and sacrifice for the common good; be disciplined and respect the rules; consult each other before taking decisions; accept majority decisions, respect minority opinion; appreciate that people depend upon each other, and so had better solve their problems peacefully (14). These points are then summarily brought home by simply repeating nice words. Under 'reasonable and well informed' we find, for instance, 'be open-minded, know to accept other people's reasoning,' which is still followed by, 'be broad-minded, tolerant, and reasonable in problem solving' (15).

This is substantiated by examples of being democratic. About an exemplary family—the father gave up drinking when his wife got pregnant—it is said:

Mrs. Gem represents a woman who fills her part of housewife to perfection. She is full of love, of responsibility, of self-sacrifice and good sense. At the same time, Mr. Bua, her husband, is tolerant, willing to listen open-mindedly to the reasoning of child and wife. Boonma, the child itself, is brave enough to express his points of view, all the while showing respect and obedience to his parents. This family is a model of true happiness (36).

This deserves a prize. When the uniformed teacher comes to present the Exemplary Family Award, he proclaims:

> The family is the very foundation for teaching and instilling responsibility, love, patience and tolerance, self-sacrifice, good sense and mutual openness in its members. These qualities, in turn, will make family life quiet and happy. The stability of any society flows from the way life is lived in each of its individual families (37).

These idealistic observations on the Thai democratic way of life from the teachers' handbooks stand in marked contrast to the practice of democracy as suggested in elementary schoolbooks.[2] There we read that democracy is a system of government that typically belongs to the developed countries and therefore is worthy of imitation. Before it can take root, however, people need to be educated. Without a good level of schooling, the participation of the population in government through voting will be flawed (*6 Country*: 32). This problem may explain why people these days do not appear to appreciate their right to vote; they do not think it to be important at all (*6 People*: 52–3). They elect unworthy candidates to run politics in a materialistic and competitive environment where people take advantage of each other and follow their emotions rather than common sense, and where those who use power or influence to go against the law are held to be honorable (*Experience 5*: 83–4).

Comment

When we look at the total of qualities said to reflect democratic behavior, it appears to mirror what is being taught in the mandatory course called 'Character Development,' and thus to correspond to the well-worn lessons on Thai civil behavior and Buddhist comportment. Such native traditions are said to be democratic at heart, to agree with beautiful customs, and to tally with religious lore. The new things proposed are the method to make children work in small groups on subjects that lend themselves to such a procedure; the slight emphasis on expressing personal opinion, and the possibility of voting. These innovations are balanced—and that is not so new—by a steady stress on respect and obedience, law-abidingness and discipline, ethics and duty.

Elementary school is thought of as the laboratory of democracy. The fact, however, that the schoolbooks offer preciously little information on the underlying principles of democracy, is not so strange if we consider how national life is supposed to be constructed. In elementary, the teaching of the national doctrine of the Three Institutions pervades all social studies. Its salient points can be summarized as, without king, no Thailand; without king and religion, no moral guidance; without self-sacrificing ancestors, no nation. Ancestors notwithstanding, the always fatherly and caring kings brought the Thais together, taught them ethics, and spread religion among them. Because of this, ordinary people are first and foremost morally indebted to the king. They must also be grateful for the boon of religion. These two—primarily the king, of course—established the Thais as a moral, undifferentiated nation.

This moral, familial, functional construction of society informs the teaching of democracy and its way of life. As members of the nation, people are equal. As a result, the equality of individuals or citizens no longer needs explanation, and can be avoided. In a happy family, there are no conflicts of interest. There only exist mutual obligations; people depend upon each other as they form one whole, one community. This thinking equates state with nation and society. It is 'the people' or 'the students' who are represented. This conception cannot inform about democracy as a system in which opposing interests and opinions are negotiated, but explains 'the democratic system of government under the king.' Democracy thus becomes something like a Thai moral way of life, an expression of being nation. The question that remains, then, is whether this community-centered thinking can explain what happens in the wider society.

THE HIGH-SCHOOL REPRESENTATION OF DEMOCRACY

The sociological contradistinction between community and society is radically side-stepped in the text selected by the Ministry of Education for the first year of high school.[3] It even seems as if the authors want to bar the idea of anonymous, businesslike, and individualizing society from the outset. Of course, the word society cannot be avoided, but it is explicitly explained that we had better use the word community 'because the latter stresses the idea of the importance of *people* relating to each other and sharing a place' *(102*: 93).

A little further on we are informed that cultivating a democratic mentality is as delicate an endeavor as caring for a small plant. It takes many years before it grows into a sturdy tree, and much groundwork and attention need to be invested. The environment, so to say, must be fine-tuned to the requirements of its growth. If the family operates in a democratic manner, with opinions and options being openly discussed, it will foster the spirit of democracy. It is the same at school. The point is: can things be discussed; are people open-minded enough to listen to each other, or do they think that not to speak is wiser, in the manner of 'speech is silvern, silence is golden'? Whatever the situation, in a democratic society there is no pigheadedness, no pushing of self-importance irrespective of the opinion of others. Besides, a democratic society respects and fosters originality, and does not stick to tradition. Such originality is the fruit of free exchanges of thought. If the majority agrees, such original thinking and new ways of acting may be accepted (*102:* 110–1).

Be that as it may, people should be tolerant, give in, sacrifice part of their interests for the sake of the public good and nation without asking for honor or compensation. In the final analysis, it is the fulfilment of duty that leads to reward. Such duty-conscious people live up to the standards of society, respect the law of the land and the moral code; they have order and discipline. Mahatma Gandhi and Abraham Lincoln are mentioned as paragons of democracy, but even ordinary people can be democrats as long as they fully live up to the duties inherent in their roles (*102*: 112).

The text for the second year attempts to introduce the notion of basic rights. This is done through a legally correct but awfully technical definition, followed by the seventeen rights and freedoms the constitution specifies. These are then explained in a manner that does not really agree with the ideas behind the Universal Declaration, as may be clear from the way the first right is presented: 'All have the freedom of their body, meaning that we can do with our body as we please; if you want to be fat, nobody has the right to forbid it, but you have to keep your clothes on in public, because people are not allowed to go against our good mores or the criminal code that forbids obscenity' (*204*: 155). Following similar explanations of a few other rights, students are warned not to insist on them, because if people claim their rights irrespective of concern for others or the common good, it can only lead to trouble and confusion.

A little further on in the text, several problems of the prevailing democratic system are reviewed. The first among these is individualistic behavior that indicates that the good values, conducive to a democratic way of life, have gone lost. In line with this comment, it is observed that most politicians are self-seeking, and that clear ideas of what constitutes personal gain and what serves the public interest are lacking. As a result, the country is still struggling to establish Westminster-style government (*204*: 181–3).

In the third year, attention is drawn to the great number of parties that compete in elections. This inevitably results in coalition governments with a reduced capacity for efficiency and stability. A further problem of the democratic system is the practice of vote buying. This leads to excessive campaign spending, which corrupt politicians recoup through profiteering from the office they have been elected to. This is narrowly connected with the fact that most people have very poor understanding of democracy. They vote for the wrong candidates, to wit, those people to whom they are morally indebted, or who particularly care for their home districts. This leads to being biased to favoring the own constituency without considering the national interest. Moreover, people vote for persons rather than for parties. It is asserted, however, that in Bangkok public opinion influences the result of the polls as well (*306*: 238–9).

Voting for individuals instead of for political parties means that party ideology has no meaning, and that parties are mere groups of individual people who happen to enjoy popularity in their districts. In other words, parties serve individual interests, and thus lack continuity. Every single person wants to become a cabinet member, which results in a good deal of infighting and perennially shaky coalitions. These conditions cause unstable governments and the prejudiced behavior of elected representatives. It is hoped that further economic development will result in better income for all and a higher level of education. Also civil society organizations and the coming of age of political parties will be beneficial for the development of Thai political culture. All this will take a long time; as long as the youth continues to acquire a deeper understanding of democracy, however, there is no reason for despairing (*306*: 239–40).

Later on, a text used in the tenth grade summarizes the traits of a democratic society as:

> We could conclude that the democratic system is a system that has very lofty ideals, that it is the best possible model, and that it is a style of life that should be desired by both individuals and society ... This system values individuals by recognizing that they have freedom, and that they are equal in dignity and humanity. Enjoying freedom implies that people must not be under the control of others because democracy is a system of government that holds that the sovereign power is of the people and that the people are their own ruler. In order that people can rule themselves, they must have full freedom ... Democracy recognizes the value of the individual by allowing him political freedom and the freedom of expression (speech, writing, criticism). Political freedom means the freedom to elect representatives ... It also means equality: every individual, whether a millionaire or a beggar, has one vote ...
>
> A democratic society is a society that believes strongly in the dignity of human beings; they trust each other. The people consist of persons who have reason and who know how to think with discretion. They are replete with the desire to compromise and to give and take. They share in the spirit of sportsmanship and concede whole-heartedly that things are always changing. A society that consists of individuals who have a democratic way of life can accordingly be called a valuable society, a society in which it is a pleasure to live (*402:* 21).

In the last year, the great vista of democracy offered in the tenth grade is balanced by a firm dose of realism. Suddenly, in the book concerned, we find information on the Sixth Reign (1910–25) that is in full contradiction with the history taught during the preceding eleven school years. The Great Wise King was not a democrat; by pointing to the disintegration of power in China and the disorder in Russia in the wake of their republican revolutions, he argued that the monarchical dispensation fitted Thailand best. In order to consolidate power in the Ministry of the Interior, he annulled certain decentralizing measures; his toy city, Dusitthani, is not even mentioned (*605*: 50).

The seventh king was too late with the introduction of a constitution; he was overtaken by the events of 24 June 1932 that initiated the democratic period. Now, after many military take-overs—a four-page list gives the details of ten successful coups d'état (*605*: 54–7)—periods of dictatorship, and sixteen constitutions, it is observed that:

> From 1932 onwards, the Thai government still lacks the policy and way of life that concur with democracy, because the method it uses belongs to the style of life and thinking of earlier days, which have not changed among the majority of society. As a result, the destruction of democracy, as far as it is the model of government, does not evoke strong reactions, with the exception of the happenings of 14 October 1973, 6 October 1976, and 17–20 May 1992.

COMMENT

In this chapter, we set out to investigate the ideas that the Ministry of Education disseminates on democracy. We found that democracy was represented as the expression of the will of 'the people,' or nation, and not as the expression of the positions of citizens in their diversity. The idea of society, and concrete evidence of conflicting interests and opinions, were relegated to the wings. There was one fleeting mention of 'public opinion' and one of 'NGOs'; the importance of these, in relation to democracy and active citizenship, was not considered.

Democracy was presented as an ethical way of life in which people give in to each other rather than negotiate. In elementary school, this led to the idealization of Thai ways as eminently democratic. Yet, there were snags in it, namely disinterest among voters, the prevalence of highly competitive politics, together with blatant abuse of, and admiration for, power.

High-school texts also started on a moralistic note, but then drew the starkest possible contrast between an extremely idealistic picture of democratic society and Thai practice. The latter somehow suffered from three afflictions, namely money politics, the persistence of old ways of doing and thinking, and the ego-centeredness of Thai people. At bottom, these ills could be reduced to flawed morality.

The picture developed throughout the course is asociological and highly moralistic. This portrayal privileges the parts individuals play at the expense of structures, institutions, conflicts and competition. Democracy is thought to root in individual ethical inclinations, in discipline and duty. In other words, the success of democracy becomes an individual responsibility.

This moralistic reasoning pervades all social-studies texts. This can only be expected as long as the teachings are forced into the mold of the doctrine of the Three Institutions. This national ideology imposes an idealized, ahistorical picture in which Thai society appears as a well-structured moral community under the benevolent guidance of the king. As a result, a teacher's handbook stated that 'the democratic system of government under the king' will come to life if the Thais maintain, or rather revert to, the ethics that support such a moral order. Whether this is a felicitous manner of thinking about the unruly public world people experience is a moot point.

CHAPTER 2

PHILIPPINE IMAGE OF THE NATION

The idea of being a community, of forming a nation, presents a knotty problem that schools need to tackle in Thailand, Indonesia, and the Philippines. While the first two countries possess elaborate national doctrines, Filipinos avowedly struggle with their national identity. At school, they seek to argue their nationhood through idealistic historical interpretations and the authority of legal facts. The resulting representation is not accepted as very convincing, and supports the unruly images of nation and society that surface in the media all the time.

WHO ARE WE?

If we go by the titles of some of the series serving social studies in Philippine elementary schools such as *Ang Bansa Natin* ('our nation/ country/people') or the programmatic *Isang Bansa, Isang Lahi* ('one country, one people/ancestry'), there seems to be little problem. It is clearly suggested that there exist national community and identity, and special reading exercises are offered under *Diwang Makabansa* ('the spirit of nationalism'), all the time intimating that there is substance to it. The title of the Education Ministry textbook for the fifth grade, *Ang Pilipinas sa Iba't Ibang Panahon* ('the Philippines through the ages'), even proposes continuity through time, over hundreds of thousands of years.

Maybe the titles are mere promises. Maybe it is the school's very purpose to create national community. After all, school texts are a very important part of national culture and promote the molding of a people into a single image by spreading shared myths, history, and common wisdom. In the case of the Philippines, they aim at instilling a shared culture in order to make a national community out of the diversity of '7,107' islands and '111' languages and ways of life.

The fascinating thing about Filipino school texts is that they ooze with uncertainty about what the nation actually is. These texts do not stand alone. They reflect and strengthen a sort of ambiguity of culture, of identity. The question 'Who are we?' is bedeviling indeed. According to a Filipino friend, 'A Filipino is an English-speaking, Roman Catholic Malay with a Spanish name who eats Chinese food.' The Educational Development Decree of 1972 was, among other things, meant to solve 'the problem of nationhood.' But even in March 1987, President Aquino still expressed her satisfaction with Fr. English's *Tagalog-English Dictionary* as, 'This (dictionary) will be extremely helpful in our drive for national recovery since Pilipino is our national language and therefore, a vital element in achieving national unity even as we are the largest English-speaking nation in Asia.'

Is a national community defined by a shared language? And which one is that language, English, Tagalog, or Filipino? Or is Filipino just another word for Tagalog? Who are the speakers of that language? Probably, a national community can be founded on other commonalities than linguistic ones. A shared history may be more compelling, while the idea of community also refers to shared geography. Although the line between history and myth is thin, the modern idea of a bounded territory seems unambiguous. We noted, however, the '111 nations' inhabiting that space.

Modernly speaking, the state defines the nation. Heir to a colonial predecessor state that defined its borders, it legitimizes its sway through a particular interpretation of history that is spread by way of the school system. Possibly it is the state, as shared government, that through its propagation of common knowledge, depicts the image of the nation best of all.

THE PHILIPPINES THROUGH THE AGES

The Ministry of Education concerned does not appear so self-assured when it presents its views of the state. Let us see what happens in the fifth grade when social studies in public school are presented as *The Philippines through the Ages*.[1] This book is divided into five units; the introductions to these are sufficiently revealing.

Unit 1. The way of life of the early Filipinos

There are important events in the lives of people and the nation that need to be recorded. This is history—the written record of the important occurrences in diverse periods. It is important to know the past and its relationship to the present as a secure basis to face the future. That is the purpose of the study of history.

Not all that happened in the past could be written down, such as the way of life of the original Filipinos. In order to know about them, scientists are engaging in research. According to them, people have been living in the Philippines for the past hundreds of thousands of years. They consisted of Itas, Indonesians, and Malays. Strangers came too, such as Arabs, Chinese, and Japanese. They stayed and traded here. The mixing of these groups stands at the beginning of the original Filipinos.

These earliest Filipinos had their own culture. This can be proven by the remains and implements they left behind. It is also proven by the research results of the experts studying the culture of the ancient Filipinos. There are many indications that the culture of the original Filipinos was rich and had reached a high level. This can be demonstrated by the social classes to which they belonged, the method of government, and their types of livelihood. All these illustrate the way of life of the earliest Filipinos ...

The society of the original Filipinos was composed of different groups of people who came from different parts of Asia. Together, they established the settlements of our ancestors. Next to setting up their dwellings, they also molded a system of education. They had ways of worshiping and believing, too, although there were differences in practice among them.

When Islam, the religion brought by the Arabs, arrived in these islands, groups of people in Mindanao changed their religious practices. They embraced Islam. This had its influence on their way of life. Whatever the differences of beliefs among the original Filipinos, their culture remained one and the same. This is the culture that we, up to this day, develop, cherish and take pride in.

31

Unit 2. The Filipino way of life under the Spaniards

For 333 years (1565–1898), the Philippines was under Spanish domination. This brought changes in the way of life of the Filipinos. This, however, did not obliterate the native culture. There were changes in the system of government and in the material culture. Most importantly, the country got a name. From then on, it has been known everywhere in the world as the Philippines and the natives living there as Filipinos ... When Spain was defeated by the United States in the battle of Manila Bay in 1898, its government came to an end ... It was the duty of the missionaries to teach the Catholic religion and to spread Christianity.

Unit 3. The incessant endeavor to reach freedom

(The first part of the introduction to this unit states that the establishment of the various colonial governments caused important changes in the system of administration, in society, and in livelihood. Repeatedly, Filipino efforts to realize their freedom and establish their own government were frustrated, such as when the Americans and the Japanese enforced their dominion.)

The system of government the Americans introduced the Filipinos to was a novelty. They spread the principle of democracy that until this day prevails in our land. They reformed the educational system. Many children could study in public schools. They introduced the values of cleanliness and health. Transportation and communication were improved, which resulted in many changes in the livelihood of the Filipinos ... There is a strong relationship between these innovations and the present way of life of the Filipinos.

Unit 4. The way of life at the time of the Third Republic (1946–1972)

The fourth of July 1946 is a great day for Filipinos. It cannot be forgotten in the history of our nation. That day the Republic of the Philippines was inaugurated ... Be that as it may, it could not hide the poverty of the environment. The war had caused tremendous devastation. That destruction had to be confronted with resolution. Hence, the period of the Third Republic was a veritable time of struggle, too. On that occasion, we had to fight against the poverty of livelihood. Most of all, that time was a period to reestablish the nation.

Unit 5. The incessant endeavor to establish the nation/country

Every period in the history of the Philippines illustrates some sort of serious endeavor of the Filipino people. Many decades have passed since they resisted the Spaniards, the Americans, and the Japanese in order to become free. A variety of problems confronted the Filipinos in their liberation and at the time they obtained their freedom. Among these problems was the slow development of livelihood and peace in the country. Another obstacle is the absence of identity as a free people/country.

A common quality of the Filipinos is their capability to adapt themselves to any problem or crisis. Their reaction gives them the flexible power to overcome any difficulty or challenge. How did the Filipinos face up to the problems and challenges of the 1970s and up to the present?

Comment

In the introduction to unit 1, several contrasting statements have been brought together. It is observed that Filipinos constitute a highly mixed racial group, that, in spite of differences in origin, has mixed so well that it produced one, well-developed, culture. Even religious differences—that resulted in different practices—did not influence the basic way of life. Filipino culture, therefore, remained one and the same from the olden days into the present, which demonstrates the importance of knowing the past for understanding the present way of life.

Yet, there was a snag on that long way. The earliest Filipinos, from deep down in history up to Magellan's arrival, apparently did not recognize themselves as such until the Spaniards gave their country a name. Besides, colonial contact brought about myriad changes in the Philippine way of life although it is claimed that native culture persisted.

The Americans promoted development and progress of all sorts; they brought a superior system of government and policies. When the Filipinos became their own master, they were facing problems, poverty, unrest. They are even said to be lacking identity as a free people.

So, on the way from prehistory to the present, something seems to have gone missing. It has been suggested that people were united in culture—rich, and at a high level—and that colonial contact, especially with the Americans, brought progress. The present, however, seems unclear, riddled with problems, and stimulates absence of concern with the nation.

This weird evolution is difficult to explain. The textbook's authors probably had an idea in mind such as: 'When politics, or the state, were not interfering, cultural community prevailed. Then, in spite of being named and regardless of progress and modernity, life somehow loses its cultural hold. There remains a weak state and a factious society that both miss the integrity to provide identity.' As a result, history appears as the undoing of culture, and with it, of community. Of course, the book devotes its last pages to protest against the degeneration of almost everything valuable in public life. Marcos out. Aquino in. People Power; the New Filipino—rebirth ...

Does this hope for renaissance mean that McCoy's (1993) 'anarchy of families' will be replaced by a strong civil society anytime soon? Will such a civil society bring order to the public world? Will it restore dignity to public office? Or is it that identity as a free people has meanwhile become illusory because the country is more like a market than a nation? Why identify with a market other than as a means of serving personal and particular ends? In fact, people do identify with what really matters, that is, with their families and, sometimes, with their immediate community. Society-wide identification—as in the past—remains weak, and it is only the impositions of the state that define national community and nationhood. The role of the school in all this—generating officially sanctioned confusion, mythology, national symbols, self-doubt, and cultural insecurity—cannot be overestimated.

HIGH-SCHOOL IMAGES

The scheme outlined in the fifth grade is elaborated when the students stream on to the first year of high school. There, in the first unit of *The Establishment of the Filipino Nation*,[2] the origins of the Filipino people are explained, which is followed by chapters on the oppression of

Filipino freedom, and the sprouting and evolution of nationalism. The second unit, 'Towards Independence,' consists of the repression of Filipino nationalism and the delaying of liberty. The third, 'In the Period of Being on Our Own,' presents challenges to independence, and the authoritarian regime. The final unit is on 'The New Filipino' who faces the future with constitution-inspired confidence in a regenerated democracy; it ends on a discussion of the rules of Philippine citizenship.

The very opening sentence of *The Establishment* runs, 'Why were foreigners attracted to the Philippines?,' which demonstrates a remarkable preoccupation with foreigners who, from the third chapter onwards, seem to play an important role in the islands. The other concern is with Philippine unity: the country consists of 7,107 islands, and its far-flung archipelagic diversity is not only a barrier to transportation and communication, but also to the unity of the inhabitants and the evolution of national independence.

Unity and mutual understanding among Filipinos is further frustrated by the many different tongues, customs and traditions that give rise to strong feelings of local and regional chauvinism that are more powerful than the national sentiment. To overcome this impediment, the national language, Filipino, should be enriched and developed in accordance with the Constitution of 1987, in the hope that it may intensify the bond of union among the population.

Apart from calling for unity of language, the text seeks to establish unity through history. Through introducing the old-fashioned, or archaic, Filipino, a unity is created about which general statements can be made, and a precolonial past that should either be idyllic or, contrarily, anticipate the present. This endeavor is colored by the attempt to lend the past some sort of Southeast Asian respectability for which the institution of the state is invoked.

> Historians say that, even in those days, Filipinos had political organization. This is known as the communal state. As a state, the community had a territory, a group of people, government, and sovereignty.
>
> It also had a chief, laws, a judicial system ... The head of the community is normally called headman ... The headman holds authority

and discharges the tasks of government. He is the chief law-maker, executive, justice, and military leader (33).

The coming of the Spaniards means the end of self-government and the beginning of the oppression of Filipino freedom. The widely scattered and independent communal states and the Muslim sultanates did not have the opportunity to unite. Thus the independence of the Filipinos as a nation did not prosper. When the Spaniards came, the freedom of the Filipinos was destroyed before it got the opportunity to arise (38). In the following forty-five pages this line is then explained, devoting some twenty of them to Spanish rule and cultural contributions, that conclude as, 'The Filipinos who were subdued by the Spaniards, received, were changed and enriched by the colonial culture that became a part of their own civilization' (60). Upon this follow the opposition to said rule and an interesting elaboration on the relationship between colonization, and the origin and evolution of national consciousness:

> While the Filipino Muslims were successful, most of the uprisings in other parts of the nation failed. The unity of the Muslims is not something one could ordinarily find in other areas of the Philippines. Many uprisings occurred because of personal interests of the leaders. The Filipino custom of merely caring for oneself helped the colonizer to separate and divide the Filipinos. In those days, the Filipinos were not yet forged together as a nation. With everybody minding their own interests, Ilocanos, Tagalogs, Visayans, Bicolanos, and other groups fought each other. Because of this, it was easy for the Spaniards to use Filipinos to suppress the rebellions of fellow Filipinos.

No matter how much the uprisings were frustrated, the consciousness was also growing that all Filipinos alike were experiencing oppression and maltreatment. They felt the absence of freedom and the low esteem the foreigners held them in. The quelling of the many uprisings cultivated a hatred that slowly awakened the Filipinos to the actual necessity of uniting in order to obtain freedom. Is this the beginning of nationalism?

Nationalism is a feeling for the nation of those people who show loyalty to their own country, and not merely to a single leader or chief. The root of this word is 'nation' which is how an association or group of people is called who have a single desire and purpose in life, and who are tied together by a single race, language, religion, customs, and tradition. It is not enough for people to have a place to live, a recognized government, and officials in order to have the feeling of nationalism. These are important elements, but the most important is the unity of the people who acknowledge that they are members of a single nation, and prepared to defend their freedom. This feeling is not natural to people, but sprouts gradually; it can arise quickly or slowly because it will develop in accordance with the historical experience of the people (63).

The text then acknowledges that the reformists of the 1880s were the first to formulate the separateness of the Philippine nation from Spain; they even threatened that the country could secede from the Spanish empire (71). However radical their vision, they remained a privileged group, too.

> The intelligentsia did not have the determination to use violence in order to obtain reforms. The groups constituting the middle stratum of society reacted similarly. They avoided armed rebellion because it could harm their properties and businesses. While these two groups continued to press for reform, the masses, under the leadership of Andres Bonifacio, grew restless because they lost hope that there would be change (70).

The American and Commonwealth periods are presented as political development. The evolution of culture is treated scantily, although it begins with the acknowledgment that even up to the present the strength of American cultural influence remains a problem. The chapter closes on an interesting question, 'MacArthur abandoned the Philippines and left the management of their own government to the Filipinos. Having been subjected to the rule of foreigners for many centuries, would the Filipinos be already prepared to take care of their own affairs?' (143).

The account of the ensuing presidencies begins with the observation that all problems are rooted in the long colonial past. These are then specified as perennial American interference, frustrated independence, struggle against the Huk rebellion, jurisdiction over the military bases, lack of political will to initiate land reform, corruption, political manipulation and electoral fraud, desirability of foreign investment, irritation at American advice, weak economy, deceit of politicians, and poverty of the masses.

In the section about language and literature that follows, American influence is pointed out again. People seem to be more attached to the borrowed language than to Tagalog. Besides, many people object to the use of the latter because they fear that it will weaken their proficiency in English. Moreover, Tagalog is not representative of the native tongues of the Philippines. In order to avoid this criticism, Filipino is replacing Tagalog as the national language. In any case, the influence of English remains stronger than that of Filipino. On many occasions, English is mixed with Filipino when people are pressed to use the national language.

As if this were not enough, a long list of book titles is given, devoid of any context, of which it is claimed that they exemplify the influence of English on the works of poets and authors, even if they write in Tagalog/ Filipino. Even the subject matter they write about is said to be influenced by the Americans. In fact, many prefer to write in English. Neither do the painters find native ways of expression; first they worked in the Spanish style, and now in the American. The exception is Carlos V. Francisco who works in a style of his own. Foreign music is more popular among Filipinos than their own variety. This compilation of comments is concluded with, 'The Filipinos received, changed, and enriched the foreign influences on their style of life. The borrowed elements became part of their own culture, got a Filipino stamp, and became part of the distinguishing characteristics of the nation' (186).

The last unit, 'The New Filipino,' outlines the political system of the Philippines under the Constitution of 1987, and refers to its Preamble, or list of very good intentions:

> We, the sovereign Filipino people, imploring the aid of Almighty God, in order to build a just and humane society and establish a Government that shall embody our ideals and aspirations, promote the common good, conserve and develop our patrimony, and secure to ourselves and our posterity the blessing of independence and democracy under the rule of law and a regime of truth, justice, freedom, love, equality, and peace ...

COMMENT

By drawing programmatic lines through history, such as from the free Filipino to the new Filipino with an interval of oppression, or by projecting an archaic, idyllic past as the direct precursor of the present, history is seriously distorted. Moreover, it does not provide a framework to explain the current state of the nation, or how it came into being. While the Spanish contribution to native civilization is acknowledged, it has been insufficiently elaborated, probably to avoid admitting that without Spain there would be no Philippines, and that without Catholicism, there would be no nationwide cultural heritage.

The avoidance of certain subjects crucial to national becoming makes it very difficult to account for the presence of certain institutions in perspective. According to the texts, early society was stratified, with a valiant chief as its head. This model makes today's dispensation recognizable: a powerful president, surrounded by his clan/family, and loyally followed by his privileged cronies, relatives, and sycophants; below these special people, one finds the freemen, or the middle classes, who pay the taxes; the lowest stratum is composed of suffering peasants and laborers who provide the better-off with food and services.

It is unlikely that this interpretation of national society is intended. Even so, the implicit model results in the image of an internally divided 'community' within which people identify with class and ethnicity rather than with nation.

Because the national awakening has been firmly relegated to the nineteenth century, the past becomes unimaginable and remains divorced from the present. The idea that the national awakening was a once-upon-a-time event may have inspired the authors to unfortunately omit any mention of the attempts to revive the spirit of nationalism. Yet, it was the recreation of this spirit, in the late 1950s, that partly fueled the resistance against Marcos, and that kept the cultural debate alive into the 1990s when it, again, faded.

The American occupation appears as a watershed event that reduces the history of previous becoming to irrelevance. It ushers in the Golden Age before degeneration and decay set in. With the establishment of the Commonwealth (1935), self-glorifying politicians take over, and 'nation' and 'national community' become unclear slogans. At the same time, the image of the nation becomes political rather than cultural-historical, with the idea of national community safely hidden in a harmless past.

The present has been divorced from its history. This absence of continuity results in a confusing picture of current developments that seem to be more subject to political arbitrariness, caprice and fate than to follow from structural constraints and possibilities. National, then, is the bickering of politicians and, of course, the legal finesses of civics that substitute a state for the nation.

In summary, we found that school takes a legalistic approach to explaining things national, such as the laws on citizenship, the constitution, and the organization of the state. While early on, in elementary school, the nation is still imagined as a family, this image is subsequently destroyed. By disconnecting history from the present, society no longer coheres; government is taken over by politics; the nation disappears. It seems as if the imagining of the nation belongs to a far-off past, to the struggle for emancipation from Spain.

CHAPTER 3

CIVICS À LA INDONESIA

From the first until the twelfth grade, Indonesian students have to study the course on 'Pancasila and Civics.' Pancasila here refers to the five basic principles of the Republic of Indonesia: the belief in one God Almighty, humanity that is just and civilized, the unity of Indonesia, democracy guided by the wisdom of representative deliberation, and social justice for all citizens. Especially under President Suharto, the Pancasila became the basis of an elaborate ideology that justified his authoritarian regime.

Meanwhile, the course has outlived that dispensation and continues to be taught with some concessions to the current transition to democracy and decentralization. Indonesia is still in the process of amending its constitution accordingly, but whatever the changes, it will hold on to the Pancasila as the prime symbol of the nation's non-negotiable integrity. Hence, the Rector of Gadjah Mada University is one among those who presently stimulate the study and elaboration of the Pancasila ideology in order to provide a firm foundation for post-Suharto Indonesia.

Our interest in Pancasila thinking originates from the idea that much of it reflects basic Javanese conceptions about how society is or should be ordered (Mulder 1998). We shall, therefore, trace this imagination through excerpting and paraphrasing parts of the rather repetitious course on Pancasila and civics.[1] Then we shall reflect on the problems that almost naturally inhere in a paternalistic and moral representation of society.

41

THE IDEAL INDONESIAN

Religion

Through all the grades, the course has been divided into chapters that are presented under snappy headings, such as 'Obedience,' 'Concord,' 'Sovereignty,' 'Obsequiousness,' 'Unity,' which often have little to do with the matters discussed. Under 'Obedience,' the first chapter for the ninth grade offers some interesting thinking about religion. There the thesis is advanced that the quality of faith in and devotion to God conditions how much people will obey His will and be benevolent to each other. Religious teachings regulate human life completely and result in most beneficial and useful conditions for social, national, and state life. Religion stresses honesty, hard work, good deeds, and aversion to sin. It is, therefore, good to promote the quality of religious life through devoted worship, social harmony, and service to nation and state. Devotion stimulates peaceful conditions, and participation in national development. Such participation is a valuable aspect of worship.

Faithful obedience to and worship of God is reflected in the three dimensions of religious practice, namely, in one's relationship with God, with fellow men, and with the environment. People praise the Lord, follow His commands, and refrain from sin. The relationship with people, society, and nation and state is shaped by respect for parents and elders, the drive for justice and truth, honor for one's teachers, and obedience to the State. People take good care of the natural environment and exploit it for their common welfare. The social-cultural milieu that fosters the worship of God must be safeguarded. This worship includes respect for teachers and the obligation to honor and be devoted to parents; this is expressed in manners and behavior.

Rights

The chapter called 'Concern' opens on the observation that religious persons will be able clearly to discern rights from obligations. Controlled by religious teachings, they may be expected to strike the right balance in exercising their rights and duties, thus creating harmony in life.

Consciousness of people's equality results in self-respect and awareness of basic rights. Such basic human rights comprise the rights to life, freedom, and property. These rights reflect the state of cultural progress so that, nowadays, basic rights concern private rights, among others, the freedom of religion, of worship, of association and expression; economic rights, such as the freedoms to own, to buy and sell, and to choose an occupation. There is also the right to work, and to receive a reasonable wage, in proportion to ability; the right to equality before the law and government; political rights, such as equality and a voice in decision making, to found political parties, and to propose petitions, criticism, and advice; the rights to education and cultural development, and to be protected against unlawful arrest and searches. These rights belong to people by nature; they are God's gift. As a result, and in gratefulness to God, they are inscribed in the Constitution.

Indonesians take pride in the fact that basic rights were spelled out in the original constitution, which was enacted on 18 August 1945, well ahead of the Universal Declaration of Human Rights of 10 December 1948. What is special about these rights is that people know them to be ordained by God in the recognition of the dignity, value, and rank of the human being as the most perfect creature in existence. Such rights are invested in people.

These rights are circumscribed by certain obligations. All people must respect the law and the legitimate government. The state is there to uphold the law, and to prosecute offenders. This means that people are not allowed to take the law into their own hands. People enjoy the freedoms of association and expression within the bounds of the law. This demonstrates that the state guarantees democratic life. This means that all Indonesians have the right to associate in organizations that strive to develop and educate the nation. Opinions must be advanced through the right channels, such as parliament. This is in conformity with the principle of mutual consultation in order to reach unanimity, which leads to national stability.

Economic rights also entail obligations. The constitution stipulates that economic life is a joint effort, based on the family principle, in which the state must control those branches of production that directly affect the livelihood of the people, alongside the country's natural resources, in order to promote the people's welfare. This means that the economy should be organized in cooperatives. There, the application of the family principle results in the fact that enterprises are run by and for the members, and thus for the common interest.

In the social-cultural field people have the right to education, which the government must provide. This is important to develop human resources. It is crucial to develop national culture too. Indonesian culture is composed of the best things the regional cultures have to offer; they constitute the root of the Indonesian personality. Therefore, people have the duty to ward off negative outside influences that destroy national culture.

Finally, there are rights and duties concerning national defense, and the maintenance of peace and stability. National stability, so important for development and for guaranteeing rights and duties, is not just the army's responsibility. In their neighborhoods, people have watch duty; at school, they must take care of a peaceful atmosphere for study. From all this follows the ideal of shaping persons who are Pancasilaists, who are deeply concerned about all problems that affect the country.

To shape the Pancasila man is an expression of concern about consciousness of being a nation and a state. This attitude is based on the understanding that it is important to maintain the balance between rights and duties, which must be instilled from an early age. Why is this so? Because God urges people to do good and be pious. All good deeds receive God's reward. Human life is not for oneself alone. People must sympathize with the suffering of others, because they do not live alone on this planet. At the same time this attitude expresses how important it is to let duty prevail over rights (*JH 3:* 13–4).

National development

Development, in all its aspects, materially and spiritually, is the necessary condition to reach a just and prosperous society. It requires the participation of all. It also demands the spirit of change in order to attain a modern society. This entails influences from the outside world. Thanks to Pancasila, we can separate the good from the less desirable. Development must conform with the direction, goal, and ideals of our national struggle, such as proclaimed in the preamble of the Constitution of 1945. There it has, among other things, been declared that the country aspires to reach prosperity and social justice. This is not the responsibility of the government alone; all must feel accountable and play their part by caring for the weak, and by utilizing science and technology. In this sense, development begins with personal, familial, and communal development: people themselves are its very subject. This must be paired with the attitudes of service, obedience, and discipline regarding the interests of state and nation.

According to the preamble, the Indonesian nation has been established to realize certain objectives such as prosperity, astuteness, and an orderly world based on freedom, eternal peace, and social justice. This unity of purpose makes each Indonesian feel part of the whole, which results in the spirit of familism. This spirit animates all aspects of life and is reflected in mutual help, appreciation, respect, and cooperation. All this will create harmony, irrespective of religious diversity, because all religions teach self-restraint. It is, therefore, important to promote religious life, tolerance, and national unity. Concord should be the highest aim; Indonesians should sympathize with each other; they should do as they would be done by. This is a mere expression of basic equality sanctioned by religion: God does not discriminate between people. In the same spirit, the Pancasila acknowledges people's equality in terms of rank, rights, and obligations.

Sovereignty—and freedom from foreign interference—is vested in the state. This sovereignty belongs to the people; it is given shape by their representatives. This popular sovereignty—meaning that the people are the source of state power—leads to democracy, which is an old Indonesian custom anyway. This democracy is guided by the values of the Pancasila, which is the national ideology and worldview. This means respect for the constitution and the rule of law, and the rejection of absolute government. Pancasila democracy is further characterized by mutual consultation to reach unanimous agreement that is animated by the spirit of familism and mutual assistance. As a result, decisions will not be in conflict with personal interests.

Parliament decides on the basis of consultation, and its decisions are thus binding on all people in Indonesia. They must obey, respect, and execute the law faithfully. This is true not only for the regulations of the state: in family and village, agreement is also reached through mutual consultation. This demonstrates that people are actively involved—and must involve themselves—in the affairs of state and national development. The last endeavor is nothing else but a fulfillment of the promise of Pancasila, and results in the creation of the Complete Indonesian Man.

Harmony

Under 'Adherence to the Rules,' a cardinal principle is reiterated. People are social creatures. While all of them have their peculiarities, they must live together and need each other; they must cooperate. People going their own way may disturb the harmony and good neighborliness of life. In order to avoid this, they need common norms to hold to. Such norms consist of rules and regulations that bring about order and acceptable behavior. All members of society must conform to the prevailing norms. As good members of the state, in possession of Pancasila morality, Indonesians know they have to conform to and obey the legitimate regulations. Then both personal and communal desires can easily be fulfilled. After all, the law develops with and reflects the social will.

The Pancasila teaches that happiness flows from concord, harmony, and balance in human relationships. People, therefore, need to exercise self-control as members of groups. They should shape their positions in life through awareness. This means that they should be conscious of others and put the interests of nation and state before their own. Since all are equal, it won't do to force one's will on others. On the contrary, people must respect each other and be guided by truth and justice. In that way, they will be able to execute their duties to their own benefit. It will lead to an acute consciousness of group life, to the awareness that private desires are confined by the common interest. If, however, people start to advance their own interests at the expense of others, harmony and the feeling of togetherness will be lost.

To maintain social awareness and responsibility, norms are needed. Knowing and respecting these is to say that people are cultured and civilized, which equates with the ideals that are the foundation of the Pancasila and Constitution of 1945. To live up to norms and regulations results in peaceful and quiet conditions. This begins in the family, then spreads to wider circles of association. This shaping of culture goes together with an ever-increasing self-awareness, and thus with a growing sense of service to community and society. It is, therefore, in the adaptation to the social environment that people can experience and realize their human value and basic rights; true self-realization results in harmonious unity between self and environment. From such respect for order, happiness flows; it results in a dynamic yet peaceful society in which all take an active part.

Worldview

If a nation is to be conscious of its unity and continuity, it needs a worldview that suggests direction and solutions. The Indonesian worldview is the Pancasila; it is the condensation of the national personality. On several occasions, the strength of the Pancasila has been tested by rebellions and separatist movements. Their failure proves that the Indonesian people desire the Pancasila as the foundation of the nation, that it has the power to unite. As the basis of the nation, the Pancasila is the source of its law. It gives purpose and direction. It animates the national soul. Its five principles are forged into one unit, complete in itself; it cannot be broken up into separate parts. It is the noble promise of Indonesia that is contained in the depth of its people's heart. As a result, it stimulates the desire for national unity and sense of belonging together.

Over the years, Pancasila and civics education will result in the Complete Indonesian Man, who is full of belief in and devotion to God, tolerant of others, and who subordinates self-interest to the common welfare. Together, Indonesians constitute one big family. There, everybody has unequal tasks and duties, the execution of which serves the common welfare. The good child must, therefore, always honor parents and elders, refrain from saying whatever it likes, and restrain itself from irritating others. Politeness is mandatory in everyday life.

Being subjected to group decisions is softened by the second Pancasila principle, 'just and civilized humanity.' It boils down to the recognition of human dignity; of justice; of the qualities of creativity, feeling, will, and conviction. Therefore, the individual differences we observe in everyday life only show that there are differences in tasks and duties. This is underlined in law. Indonesia is a constitutional country that respects freedoms and basic rights. These may be enjoyed in a responsible manner, without taking advantage of others, without arbitrariness, and without causing conflicts and cleavages that endanger national unity and integrity. On the other hand, the principle of equality—together with love for nation—is a powerful appeal to eradicate poverty, misery and discrimination.

> Necessity/God's will ordains that people, as social beings, must be ready to sacrifice. Total happiness can only be attained when we experience harmony, smoothness and equilibrium. To attain these, we need to be

ready to sacrifice. This readiness serves the interests of humanity, and of our society, nation and state (*SH 1*: 50).

In the Revolution, patriots went a long way in bringing sacrifices. Many of them even offered their lives. These days, citizens have to pay contributions and taxes, and to help each other in making social progress. They must accept decisions taken in the name of the common good and for the sake of development. Accepting these decisions demonstrates solidarity. This inspired the willingness of the population of Kedung Ombo[2] when they sacrificed their land for the sake of a reservoir, that is to say, for the sake of nation and state.

New Order

The New Order arose in response to the unrest of the early years of independence. In those days, national unity was threatened by all sorts of conflicts; by unlimited freedom; liberal, West-imitating policies; extreme ideological cleavages. All of this led to the political stalemate that resulted in Guided Democracy. Then basic freedoms were suppressed; the country spiraled down into inexorable chaos. The new regime understood the need for a firm ideological direction: if people are animated by the spirit of Pancasila democracy, problems will dissolve and development will proceed. This meant basic political retooling; people's participation; democratic consciousness; Pancasila training; the strengthening of parliament; clean and authoritative government; national stability; elections; the creation of a free and responsible press.

Even though Indonesia has been quite successful on many fronts, it still needs to be on guard to defend independence and attainments. The fight against colonialism resulted in a milieu in which humanitarianism and justice could flourish. To maintain these, and to realize national progress, Indonesians must practice the Pancasila and Constitution of 1945, and be vigilant. They need vigilance in five areas. In the field of ideology, it is important to have a strong worldview, based on the Pancasila that has already proven its potency and sacred qualities. In the political field, they should be guided by popular will and Pancasila ideology. In the economy, they must be on guard against liberalism and the profit motive. After all, the cooperative principle is the central pillar of economic life. In the socio-cultural field, they must cultivate loyalty and solidarity, and be wary of conspicuous consumption, the gap between rich and poor, and jealousy among groups; these three issues can easily cause a social tempest. Concerning defense and peace keeping, it is clear that all have their part to play. People should be alert to everything that might disturb peace and order.

The Complete Indonesian Man

The development-oriented Complete Indonesians, the real Pancasila men, are nation builders. They are animated by the spirit of Pancasila, have been touched by it. They are inspired by the unity and integrity of Indonesia, and are willing to sacrifice for it. They are honest and sincere, not striving after their self-interest, but equating it with the interest of all. Their sense of duty makes them exemplary leaders who inspire other people. Their identification with the group is like the ideal unity of government and people. It results in the stable and dynamic union of economy, politics, the social-cultural field, defense, and peace keeping. If the youth of today, as the successor generation of the lofty, original ideals, shall carry on the good work, they can be said to be Pancasila-inspired nation builders. To create these is the very purpose of Pancasila and civics education.

Naturally, such nation builders have a high sense of discipline. Ultimately, it is from the self-discipline of each and everybody that national discipline, and thus national unity, follows. In the first place, such discipline seems to entail obedience, or obsequiousness, to the normative order of society. At a deeper level, it means the training of one's character in order to be in step with social life. This will result in development. Discipline mirrors civilization: the more mature a nation, the higher its respect for the rules. A developed society is a well-regulated society. Thus, whereas by nature individuals strive to fulfill their self-interest, in society they become conscious of the benefit of harmony and conformity, without yet losing their essential being. After all, mastery of the self leads to the realization of the common welfare, and to the harmonious unity of social life from which individual happiness flows. As a result, as private persons, all nationals fulfill their basic obligations, such as strengthening their religious life; serving nation and state; being devoted to parents, teachers, and humanity. These noble duties are most proper to cultivate.

Cultural considerations

It is recognized that in the modern world, cultural contact is inevitable, and often invigorating. As long as foreign cultural elements are grafted on the national identity that is firmly rooted in the practice of Pancasila, no problems will arise. Yet, next to this main concern, namely the deviation from one's own culture when being led astray by a foreign one, we find two other problems that need to be attended to. The first is the imbalance between ethnic and non-ethnic Indonesians. The second concerns the imbalance between foreign and local capital. The first problem should not occur; after all, Indonesians want to be united 'because basically the government offered the freedom to all its subjects to do their utmost to realize the common welfare.' The second problem roots in the relative backwardness of the population in comparison with the developed countries. To solve this condition, Indonesians must study and learn from the experiences of other nations, at the same time that they 'work for the continuity of the noble cultural values of the Indonesian nation.'

The last recommendation can be realized by developing and caring for the regional cultures. These are deeply rooted and really alive. They contain religious, humanitarian, unifying, and collectivistic elements that should be strengthened. The unity of the nation can be promoted by exchanging cultural and artistic missions. In that way, groups who were formerly isolated can receive new cultural elements. 'Another manner that can support the quest for elements from and the development of regional culture is to collect its art in the expectation that regional culture is a part of the national one.' The examples given concern dances, songs, and tunes.

Pancasila democracy

The last chapter summarizes the idea of the Pancasila state, and it is appropriate to reproduce the main clauses. Pancasila democracy is said to be neither individualistic nor liberal, neither based on the people as a group, nor is it a class democracy. It is not a mass democracy that looks at the people as social beings only. It is 'monodualistic,' which means that people are both individuals and fully integrated members of their familistic community. It is constitutional, too.

The familism principle can still be seen in the villages where the government functionaries feel to be one with the people, always caring for social unity and equilibrium. As a principle of state, this finds its expression in the idea of the integralistic, unitary state that transcends the various group-based views. The theory of the integralistic state does not place the state in isolation from its members as individuals, nor from their associations and groups. Yet, all groups and individuals must be conscious that together they form one system under one government, in which the state must uphold the unity that binds them all.

Thus the essence of Pancasila democracy lies in familism, the Indonesian nation being one big family; in the rejection of individualism; in the discarding of the theory of class struggle. Pancasila democracy is based on the theory of the integralistic state, in which the people, as democratic subjects, have the right to voice their opinion through elections and parliament. This manner of free expression demonstrates self-restraint and a great measure of social responsibility.

Pancasila leadership moves the nation on to its destiny, and is legitimized by the consistent application of Pancasila democracy; this is also expressed in the government's relationships with social and political organizations. Decisions are reached through mutual consultation, not through the application of might; such decisions reflect the totality and unanimity of opinion. In this way, majority and minority groups are avoided, and the problems of opposition and conflicting interests do not occur.

COMMENT

Throughout the course on state ideology and civic behavior, rights are repeatedly mentioned. These rights are said to be God-given, and underscore man's dignity. The constitution, and thus the state, guarantees them. Even so, they do not give rise to individualistic citizenship because, in Pancasila thinking, the morally autonomous individual simply does not exist. The smallest social unit is 'community,' of which individuals are fully integrated parts.

In order to argue this convincingly, the Pancasila state usurps religion. It declares that belief in God—which is mandatory—is the moral basis of the state, and that religious devotion leads to good citizenship. Consequently we have noted the constant stress on duty and moral obligation. The individual must yield to what is more exalted than him or herself. Such subordination implies obedience as a religious act that is given shape by submission to God, state, nation, society, teachers and parents. Implicitly, these are presented as a totality worthy of worship: it is this devotion, and self-restraint, that bring about its harmony.

The underlying premise is that national interest always takes precedence over individual and group interests. This is the meaning of familism, integralism, cooperation, mutual consultation, and the avoidance of conflict and confrontation—in brief, of harmony. In its turn it is said that this idealized equilibrium is the necessary precondition for national development and future prosperity for all. In this way, the state imposes itself on nation and society, at the same time that individuals are explained away. The state equates with them, it is 'the people.'

Problems

The above construction almost naturally implies the existence of certain problems. In the civics course, these problems are not thought to be rooted in the practical and ideological dominance of the state over society. On the contrary, they are presented as flaws of human nature, such as 'the culture of depending on the government,' and the attitudes of pessimism, fatalism, and nonparticipation in social affairs. Dependency, in its turn, easily leads to taking 'short-cuts' in promoting one's self-interest, to bribing one's way while disregarding the law. Other people operate under the protection of powerful patrons, and do very much as they please. Then there are those who take their social responsibilities lightly; they do not care about others and only see their own material interests. In brief, a fine inventory of what is presently referred to as corruption, collusion, and cronyism.

Another cluster of problems centers on materialism. Its spirit stands in the way of intimate relationships. After all, its main motivation is money. Because money makes a person special, it furthers status competition and discrimination. The spirit of secularism is problematic, too. It reflects worldliness. It leads to the separation of worldly and ultimate concerns, to the separation of state and religion. Undesirable individualism is a consequence of the progress of technology and communication. People serve their own interests only, and thus compete, which leads to the situation where the poor lose out. A further undesirable condition is elitism, which means the existence of groups who consider themselves to be much superior to ordinary people because of power, position, and wealth. This gives rise to the spirit of feudalism and exclusivism.

Many of these problems are implicitly presented as originating in modernity and contact with the West. The question is therefore asked whether it wouldn't be better if the nation closed itself off? Well, as a state striving for progress, this is not possible; even if it was wanted, globalization would prevent it. Indonesia has to go along with the times.

In other words, it appears to be recognized that Indonesia is advancing in the direction of an anonymous, modern society in which people naturally care for their own interests first of all. There, community-oriented values—such as propagated by the state—have lost their validity. In the new situation, they make no sense. As a result, people who now call for reform (chapter 6) want to introduce a type of civics education that is more relevant to Indonesia's social evolution. Up to this moment, however, teachers and students have to make do with the durable course the Education Ministry prescribes.

SECTION II: CHANGE

CHAPTER 4

CHANGE AND PROBLEMS IN THAILAND

Disregarding some state-ideological messages, the ways in which the problem of change is discussed in Thai high schools is remarkably similar to its presentation in the press (Mulder 1997a: ch. 5). Following high-school texts, we shall here be especially interested in determining the explanatory frameworks used to elucidate societal events. From these schemes follow the suggestions given to solve certain social problems. We need, therefore, also to reflect on whether these solutions are adequate or realistic. Finally, we will comment on the social imagination informing high-school texts.

CHANGE, PROBLEMS AND SOLUTIONS

Development and its effects

In junior high school, students are informed that, since the late 1950s, all governments have given priority to economic development.[1] It therefore became the task of the civil service to implement this policy. As a result, schooling is now available in every village. Apart from schools, dams, powerhouses, and roads needed to be built. These, and rural development projects, affect the countryside.

Originally, most development projects were initiated by the government, but increasingly these activities have involved the private sector. This had led to rapid progress. This is also reflected in the country's demography. From less than 5 million inhabitants in 1850, the population grew to over 26 million in 1960, then on to 56 million in 1989. This has resulted in a rather high population density, and has necessitated a more productive use of land.

Economic change affects the condition of the population. First of all, economic development means material progress, such as higher levels of well-being and rising standards of living. Nutrition improves, life gets more comfortable, people have more spending money, health services ameliorate, certain diseases disappear, and life expectancy increases. Schooling is now provided up to the ninth grade, and soon it will be available up to the twelfth.

Negative things also occur. The environment suffers badly, and the balance of nature has been severely disturbed, causing all sorts of problems. Industrial pollution, the deteriorating quality of the air, and the suffocating urban environment, result in a lower quality of life and a worsening of mental well-being. These give rise to psychological problems, crime, a general relaxation of moral standards, and new types of illness such as cardio-vascular diseases, cancer, and AIDS.

The negative impact of economic change can be softened, or even overcome, if government and people cooperate in a reasonable manner. Apart from this, people should bring themselves and their livelihood in harmony with changing conditions. The need for such harmony with the new circumstances requires some original thinking about how to bring life in line with the law and morality, because the old ways are invalid now. Ways of working have to become more efficient. Land is limited, and thus needs to be worked more effectively. Increased efficiency will also stimulate ruralites to learn modern occupations.

There is more to this than adapting one's profession to the times. To have a satisfactory life, people will have to increase their knowledge, about hygiene, family planning, drugs, and AIDS. They must adjust themselves, and steady their minds by studying religious truth in order to avoid becoming slaves of materialism and forgetting about ethics. They also need to understand the tensions and anger induced by urban living, and avoid the problems industrial society experiences in Europe and America, such as broken homes, psychological disturbances, and the loneliness of the elderly. It is through understanding the causes and effects of the advance of materialism that a way out can be found. Besides, people should help each other by executing their duties in the pursuit of right livelihood.

People can defend themselves against the problem of poisoning the environment. They should not litter up public places, nor release waste in surface water, or let exhaust fumes and chemicals freely escape into the atmosphere; they must avoid the lavish spraying of pesticides. They should face the problems of rapid urbanization by living in harmony with the urban environment, such as respecting laws and regulations concerning traffic, building, construction, and environment. They should be modest in using public utilities and services. This adjustment to industrial and urban living is really very important.

Positive change

The texts for junior high school classify change as positive and negative. Whether this clarifies the subject, is a moot point, because many things positively rated appear to be rather problematical. In any case, urbanization is desirable, according to the texts: In contrast with the countryside, people in town hold a great diversity of occupations and have to live in limited space. They have to race against the clock, and free time is scarce. As a result, mutual help and cooperation diminish. All people seemingly work in isolation from each other, and thus they experience less human interaction than ruralites. Even so, in the contemporary countryside, relationships are also becoming less intimate and close; in town, they have become businesslike. Everywhere, family life is changing. Whereas Thais used to live in extended families, these days family planning and urban living have reduced family size, which in turn contribute to geographical mobility.

Further on, it is noted that nowadays, people have more dealings with the state and its bureaucracy. Economic development planning emphasizes cooperation among people in the villages and in town, and civil servants help people to organize in order to help themselves. This mentality, shared by government and people, contributes greatly to the development of the country (*sic*; *101*: 103). Public services in the fields of health, education, safety, public utilities, communications, and media have become widely available. Health and education services contribute to physical well-being and promote the quality of human resources, thus stimulating rapid development. Although crime rates are still high, police and civil service are very concerned about public safety; their efforts are reassuring. The government is additionally preoccupied with supplying utilities, such as safe water, electricity, efficient communication and information services, and transportation networks, all of which result in a better quality of life.

The latter developments give rise to an informed population and a thirst for news; mass media are flourishing, and many sorts of information and knowledge are spreading rapidly, giving people the chance to be up-to-date in their decision making. This results in expanding markets and an ever faster pace of development. Although cultural development was neglected in the earlier plans, people are now very interested in that matter. This is so because many people have begun to worry about the speedy adoption of Western ways. Because of this, they now insist that the government takes the lead in spreading Thai culture and traditions. In the recent past, these efforts have already served to increase pride in country and nation, and interest in reviving original values, ethics, and religion. Nowadays, Thai values are widely accepted.

Even so, the students are told that Western culture especially affects them. The new generation appears to be strongly interested in the universal values of consumerism and materialism. For this reason the educational system and institutional religion will have to cooperate more to propagate Thai culture. Many people hope that the propagation of its values will cause a change of heart among the youth.

Because of financial constraints, the restoration and preservation of the national heritage of old sites and objects has been neglected, and many persons do not mind this at all. Several among them even prey on these historical places, considering them their private property. These days, though, government and mass media stress the importance of preservation, and money is being made available, hopefully convincing the populace of the importance of conservation and restoration. This evolution of consciousness must be considered as a positive development, just like the other transformations discussed so far. These developments are often the result of economic change, at the same time that social and cultural evolution stimulates economic progress. When students understand these dynamics, they will be able to support those changes that lead to the real advancement of nation and country.

Negative consequences

Subsequently, the textbooks impress on the students the drawbacks of change. The first problem to receive the spotlight is the jammed traffic. People who grow more prosperous buy cars, but those who cannot afford them take to the road as well, albeit by bus. There are so many vehicles in town that they simply grind to a halt. The stalled traffic keeps its engines running, poisoning the air, and wasting petrol, which means wasting foreign exchange and disturbing the balance of trade. Besides, to be caught in the urban gridlock is bad for nerves and mental health, and leads to short-temperedness and scolding; these, and the bad air, are detrimental to physical well-being, too. Moreover, when the traffic moves it also causes problems. Accidents have become a major cause of death these days, and most of them occur on the roads. The victims tend to be young which drains the strength of the nation. Others are disabled, which means economic and social loss. Yet, defending ourselves against accidents is not that easy, because the Thais are ill-adjusted to rapid social change. The best thing to do, therefore, is to instruct people how to deal with the situation.

Because of population growth, inmigration and rapid urban growth, slums are spreading. The newcomers from the countryside have little education and few professional skills, and thus earn only a little money. They live tightly packed together, leading to a deterioration of health. In addition, slum conditions are the source of crime, prostitution, and drug abuse. Impoverished, without education, and in bad health, the people concerned can neither help themselves nor their communities. The spread of slums is thus a threat to good society yet difficult to solve. The government must see to it that the people concerned have better housing, better income, and, above all, better education.

With this, the students are informed that drugs are a global problem that has penetrated Thai society over the past twenty years. Their sale and abuse are on the increase. Dealers often target the young, thus destroying their future. Apart from the ruinous effects on health, the demand for drugs leads to all kinds of crime. It constitutes a problem that is particularly hard to solve.

It is not only people who are poisoned; other frightening problems are the poisoning of the environment and the destruction of natural resources. Cutting down forest means drought and flood, erosion and the extinction of plants and animals. Garbage and waste degenerate the quality of water and the sea, killing marine life in the process. Dirt along the beaches makes them unattractive to tourists, and their staying away negatively affects the national economy. Apart from dirty water and air, pollution in cities includes excessive noise with all its detrimental effects on mental health. Such degenerated circumstances are purely man-made and threaten to make urban life insufferable if nothing is done about it in the shortest period of time. It is especially individuals and NGOs who campaign for a solution to these problems.

Finally, the textbooks point to a change in values as a cause for discomfort with modernity. The dynamics of economy, society, and culture have influenced the Thai style of life. It seems as if the old morality and good manners have been abandoned, while new values have taken their place. Protest has been sounded that the heartfelt values of the past have been substituted by 'imported' materialism, which in its turn induces changes in behavior among the young. Their drive for unlimited consumption has been criticized; they do not respect those who are older, are not interested in basic—and beautiful—ethics, practice free sex, dress awfully, do not control their movements, and so on. The rapidly changing values of the new generation make the senior generation, which constitutes the foundation of the nation, worry. All seniors fear that the country's progress is merely materialistic, and thus only superficial. All those who wish the best for country and nation hope that more spiritual values will arise. Value change means an important change in culture that affects morality, ethical standards, and the civilizing principle of society. For this reason, well-meaning people are very apprehensive of these developments. This consciousness of the negative aspects of rapid change brings the problems to light. This, in turn, helps in defending society against them, and ultimately, in solving them.

Population growth is also worrying: 'All members of society should behave in a way that demonstrates their responsibility for themselves, their family and society, so as to help each other in solving and preventing demographic problems' (*101*: 128). This personal approach is complemented with the observation that the aging of the population produces many old people. These days, these elderly are ill-understood and not well cared for by the young. The new generation is therefore implored to sympathize with and understand the elderly.

Such appeals to individual responsibility, awareness, and morality are often repeated. 'The problems of the environment are problems of society or problems of every single individual. They must help each other in solving such problems' (*101*: 135); 'Because the rapidly changing environment affects our way of life, it is the duty of every individual to take part in the care for, and the promotion of, the quality of the environment' (*101*: 136).

Frequently, recourse is taken to a simple black-and-white approach to explaining the characteristics of the present, for instance through glorifying the past, when water was clean, fish abundant, and rice grew without the benefit of chemicals. To be part of life in those days was a pleasure of peace and happiness. Degeneration set in with the advance of progress: the comforts of the car are accompanied by sound and stench, and so forth. Ultimately, it all leads to the ecological disasters of drought, flood, erosion, and even global warming. In the final analysis, population pressure, inappropriate technology, rapid economic expansion, wasteful consumerism, ignorance, and greed are identified as the main culprits.

> The degeneration of the environment is, on the one hand, to be blamed on inadequate knowledge or ignorance and negligence. On the other, it originates from passion and prejudices, or the unlimited desires of people who are never satisfied and who accordingly strive to become very rich and wealthy which results in converting natural resources to serve human covetousness. Thus, at least in one way, the destruction of natural resources is related to the problem of the human mind (*101*: 160–1).

Finally, the problem of change is summarized. Private initiative and free enterprise are more effective than the earlier system of state enterprises. Since 1958, foreign investment drives the economy; economic growth is a good thing. Ecological and moral problems crop up, though. Foreign capital benefits from Thai labor and exploits it; it is greedy, tries to dodge taxes, and exports its profits and national natural resources. The towns grow rapidly, giving rise to slums, lack of discipline, and crime. Factories pollute. In the early days the Thais lived together in good friendship and cooperation, but the shift to industrial production even affects social relations in the countryside. Nowadays people compete with each other with only their personal interest in mind. With everybody motivated by money, the gap between rich and poor is widening. To a certain extent, these problems are brought about by the rapid expansion of Western culture. This brings in discotheques, bars, cocktail lounges, karaoke sing-alongs, and other things that do not benefit the young. They begin to spend money and time in those places, ultimately wasting their lives and addicted to drugs. Respect for elders and teachers, alongside belief in religion, is diminishing all the time, while tendencies to egoism are strengthening. It is most worrying to watch how senseless violence and drugs are strengthening their hold. Thus, while economic growth increases people's income, it should not focus on earning more money only; the quality of life, the environment, moral principles, education, and equality have to be taken into account.

Social problems (grades 10 and 12)

In senior high school,[2] social problems are explained as problems that are widely recognized, problems that people feel they must do something about but can only be solved if the members of society cooperate (401: 62–72). In line with an underlying idea of ethics, it is stressed that the working together of all individuals is conditional to solving problems. It is further asserted that social problems arise because of group-based differences in opinion, desires, and interests. They also stem from behavior that deviates from social norms, which results in lack of order. Finally, social problems originate from social change.

The problems of Thai society are then specified as demographic, environmental, narcotics-related, criminal, Western-cultural, epidemical, and poverty-related. In the section on demography, rapid population growth is identified as both a result of and an obstacle to progress. Improved medical and sanitary conditions, together with the general increase in well-being, have speeded up demographic growth, because people are still sticking to the old ideal of having many children. This demonstrates the urgency of spreading knowledge on population questions in general and family planning in particular, because moderate population growth will enhance the quality of life and result in better education and improved chances of finding remunerative work.

The environment has become problematical because of population growth, pressure on resources by expanding industry and technology, and the absence of responsibility and cooperation among the members of society in relation to environmental questions. Solutions must be sought through instilling ecological awareness among the public. This eco consciousness should also be reflected in economic development planning, and expressed in relevant legislation.

A further problem is abuse of habit-forming drugs. Remedies should be sought in loving parental care, in awakening awareness in school, in counseling children with problems, in positive newspaper reporting, in promoting a sense of self-responsibility and straight reasoning among youth, and in taking effective measures against dealers. The government should also provide adequate treatment for addicts.

Crime is troublesome too. It stems from a variety of causes, such as lack of emotional warmth, whether because of broken homes or inter-individual distance on the work floor; degeneration of moral principles; faulty values, such as desire for riches, which results in kidnapping for ransom or dealing in drugs. Other factors that aggravate the problem are poverty, the prevalence of local godfatherism, and the modern value of suicide (*sic*). These days certain people seem to think that it enhances their honor and demonstrates their courage, even though it was never thought to be a value in earlier days.

Social change, such as urbanization, makes crime easy: think of supermarkets and places of entertainment. Besides, media are saturated with Western culture, such as infectious violence on TV, and criminal equipment is readily available.

To fight the problem of crime, it must be tackled at its roots in a degenerated mentality that should be countered by moral education in all schools. The police authorities, upon whom the people depend, must be more serious and efficient. In order to keep abreast of the times, criminal law should be adjusted. Poverty, and the closing of the gap between the haves and have-nots, must be addressed. Finally, local godfatherism should be eradicated.

Upon detailing the threat of the AIDS pandemic, defensive measures against it are advised. The final problem discussed is poverty. It results from rapid population growth that in its turn produces a vast, unproductive population of children and senior citizens. Poverty also roots in low levels of education and skills, and in a shortage of full-employment possibilities. The best way of fighting poverty is further economic development that will follow from the improvement of the national communications network, from land reform and urbanization. Social development, such as fostering education and skill training, should not be neglected either. Furthermore, enhancing the quality of life through the promotion a work ethic of diligence, patience, and originality will not fail in having its effects on the reduction of poverty.

Although not mentioned as a specific problem, it is of interest that the school texts direct attention to deficiencies in the legal process (*402*: 91–5). The public lacks confidence in the judiciary; there are many outdated laws on the books; justice is often delayed. Next to this, there are all those influential enough to be above or beyond the law, which does not contribute to respect for it either. On the whole, the levels of violence and legal insecurity are still high, which is harmful to tourism, the good name of the nation, and the willingness to invest in the country.

In the final school year (*606*: 118–20), Thailand's social problems are summarized. They consist of unemployment of the unskilled labor force and migration that makes for the high population density of Bangkok which, in turn, leads to traffic jams, crime, prostitution, quarreling, slums, etc. To solve these problems, the cooperation of the people is necessary. They should manage their living quarters and environment in a healthy manner, stick to traffic regulations, teach their children, and not litter up roads or pollute water.

Another set of troublesome conditions are qualified as societal and cultural. Important among these is expensive new agricultural technology. Those who cannot afford it lag behind, stay mired in poverty, and finally migrate to the cities as unskilled laborers. It is the elderly back in the villages who have to take care of the young. If the migrants take wife and children along, all will end up in slums where the children have to fend for themselves because both parents must work. Drugs, crime, and disregard for the law are the logical consequences. The government and the private sector must sympathize with these people, reaching them by way of school and media in order to make them aware of the values of family and child-rearing. People must realize the value of helping each other, of sympathizing with each other, of not being egoistic but of encouraging one another in order that the condition of society, culture, and livelihood will be and remain Thai.

The institution of politics generates and reflects some difficulties, too. If the quality of life is high, people are likely to choose good representatives who will act for the benefit of the country. This is evident among the educated urban population that has developed a sound political consciousness: they will not tolerate military coups d'état any longer. In the countryside, however, the quality of life is low, and people there have a poor understanding of democracy. Government and the private sector must cooperate in explaining democracy to them, through direct lecturing and by way of the mass media.

COMMENT

Change is presented as a bewildering phenomenon. In line with the idealized thinking about culture as progress, change is desirable, a necessary condition for reaching a higher stage of civilization. This is very clear from the historical imagery in the texts: beginning with the Fourth Reign, Thai society is brought into line with Western or universal civilization, demonstrating to the world that Thailand is second to none, that it is abreast of the times, that it is progressing. Yet, change also confuses, and brings in undesirable side effects.

When progress, under royal auspices, was still orderly, or at least surveyable, there was no doubt about the course of the nation. That 'things Thai' were lost in the process was taken into the bargain. Problems, however, start cropping up when change, as 'development,' begins to accelerate. Does that make it less desirable? Not really; the point is to solve the problems that accompany the dynamics of the process; the process itself is good. Dams, power-houses, roads, schooling, a vigorous private sector, higher levels of well-being, better nutrition, improved health services, the comforts of the city, public utilities—who is to deny that these constitute progress?

Early in the seventh grade, economic conditions are presumed to fundamentally affect society; the economy is the workhorse of progress. It is voracious too. Somehow it eats the environment, destroying nature; felling forests; polluting land, water, and air; and suffocating towns. These undesirable conditions, in turn, cause all sorts of suffering, from crime to AIDS. Even so, the course in social studies never suggests that economic dynamics themselves are to be blamed for such negative effects. In order to counteract the problems that come with progress, certain remedies are suggested: people need to harmonize themselves with changing conditions. They can do this, firstly, through improving efficiency and professionalism; and, secondly, through bringing their lives in line with the law and morality, increasing knowledge and understanding, studying religious truth, fulfilling duty, and not littering.

Here we should note that the remedies emphasized throughout the course, up to its very last lesson, hint at an individual-centered, moralistic approach to society and its problems, in which personal ethical awareness is proposed as the key to avoid the undesirable. Enlightened people do not create a mess; they are orderly, and refrain from detrimental action. Ultimately, education, or the acquisition of (moral) knowledge, is the solution. Criminals need to be taught right values, and so should the poor, the migrants, the inhabitants of slums, and the materialistic youth. In the final analysis, it is not the economy but individuals who cause problems.

Poverty means lack of education, and thus lack of ethical awareness. The poor should not only learn a remunerative trade, but especially overcome the basic deficiency that is the root of the vicious circle of ignorance - poverty - slums - bad health - criminality and prostitution - hopelessness - drugs - street children: they should become morally enlightened men. This very thinking transforms social problems into personal problems, and structural poverty into individual poor people free from moral moorings. If every person has a strong basis in religion or ethics—the two are presented as identical—society would be orderly.

If the young would respect the older generation, would be interested in ethics, would not practice free sex, would not dress awfully, would control their movements, and would stay away from bars and cocktail lounges, then the grown-ups, the 'big people' would not need to worry. Then, if everybody cooperated, mutually as well as with the government; if there were unity and no differences of opinion; if people were willing to sacrifice their personal advantage; if all played their part in taking care of the environment; if people would go to the temple again; and, perhaps, if the world stopped changing, they would find themselves in good old paradise.

It is not that structural factors are not mentioned; they are. There is even much discussion of ecological and environmental conditions, and industry, urban growth, migration, traffic, inter-individual competition, changing family structure, economic development and housing, are pinpointed too. Yet, such factors are merely listed, and hardly ever interconnected in a framework that would enable the student to develop a firm mental grasp of the phenomena. By directing to individual-centered ways out, and by obscuring the core characteristics of the Thai polity in which these structural factors are embedded, the discussion finally bogs down in drivel. The West, Western cultural influences, modern values, foreign capital, working parents, the police, poor people, broken homes, greed, ignorance—all these are presented as causes, at the same time that more economic development, which means more money, and thus better opportunities for schooling, is expected to solve the problems, and even to enhance the quality of Thai democracy.

Social imagination

If there is any method in the presentation of social studies, it is functionalism. Institutions and individuals all have tasks and duties. If these are faithfully fulfilled, the social process will unfold smoothly. This harmonious condition demonstrates that people are guided by the right values. Such values can be taught and learned. And thus, in the material reviewed, we noted a steady emphasis on, firstly, teaching, schooling, and education, and secondly, on values as guiding people's awareness and, presumably, their actions. This persistent inclination towards functionalism may have much to do with the state of development of the social sciences in Thailand as well as with the period the texts' authors studied. It may also, however, be reinforced by a general religious point of view that highlights the importance of individual ethical behavior. The idea that such action can be learned agrees with Buddhist thought. In this thinking, the basic opposition is not so much good versus bad, but knowledge/insight versus ignorance. A wise person simply abstains from stupid/undesirable action; ignorant/stupid people need education: then good society follows.

The functionalist, and possibly Buddhist, bias leads, by its own logic, to a reification of values: values become causes in their own right. However, the rather one-sided stress on values takes attention away from other Buddhist causes of unwholesomeness, namely, greed and anger. Of course, cupidity is noted as a factor in the rape of nature, and bad temper as a result of urban conditions has repeatedly been mentioned. Yet, values and education dominate the presentation, thus highlighting the part the individual is thought to play—do not litter!—to the detriment of a structural analysis that brings systemic causes and effects to light. This is why suicide became specified as a modern value; where it stems from remained unclear.

All this may also be related to a deep-seated unwillingness to analyze Thailand's own condition critically. It is the West that brings the bad things. Thailand was placid and pleasant; Thai means beautiful traditions, customs, and culture, and the present condition in which people compete for pelf, power, position and prestige, is novel. Such self-deceit leads to the subterfuge in which the dynamics of state and economy as causes of social problems are largely ignored. Interestingly, and in spite of the individual-centered approach, outstanding individuals like directors of politics and business, and their actions, are not considered, and so corruption, profiteering, merciless exploitation, competition, violence, land-grabbing, privilege, abuse of power, authoritarianism, just to mention a few of the usual things one finds higher up in society, are not considered as problematic. They are probably the private concerns of those 'big people' who are seriously worried about the awful manners of the young and the loss of respect for seniority.

With such serious prejudices and omissions, the discussion of social issues at school cannot aspire to a great degree of realism. It remains inconsequential at the level of chit-chat and cheap moralism.

CHAPTER 5

CHANGING FILIPINO VALUES

IDEAS BEHIND VALUES EDUCATION IN THE PHILIPPINES

The Philippines has a long tradition of teaching morality in school, harking back to Spanish Catholic ideas about the relations between God and individual, and between people, and, more recently, to American conceptions of Good Manners and Right Conduct (GMRC), at some schools even called Eugenics, the improvement of the race. Since 1989, values education has achieved the status of an independent 'knowledge and skill' area. This means that ideally every day a period in school is devoted to the subject and that specialized teachers are being trained to instruct it.

The formal establishment of values education can be traced back to a commissioned report, *Building a People, Building a Nation. A Moral Recovery Program*, that is the product of the cooperation of certain public intellectuals, most of them based at the University of the Philippines, Diliman, and the Ateneo de Manila University.[1] This report identified the weaknesses and strengths of the Filipino character, and recommended that people must be convinced that their personal righteousness makes the difference between national advancement and stagnation.

In the fourth year of high school, the preface of the official text, which will serve as our guide in this chapter,[2] reveals that the effort of teaching values education seeks to explain to students who and what they are, how they relate to each other, how to respond to their social responsibilities, and how to attain (moral) maturity ('inner completeness/perfection'). These four subjects constitute the focal points of the course.

The choice of this particular text is attractive because the book is the best by far of the four volumes that comprise the full course. The texts for the first two grades—for twelve- to fourteen-year olds—are very academic and, in my view, suitable for beginning students of sociology. They explain what a group is, and describe a value—the subject matter of the course—as something that is freely chosen from among alternatives, and this in a thoughtful manner. A value is something to be cherished, publicly affirmed, acted upon, and acted upon again. This concept is then substantiated by sets of rules to go by. As a result, the tone of the first two years is dogmatic rather than realistic.

The teachings for the third year are more lively, and often reflect the public discussion in the media. They take their point of departure in the theses of the *Moral Recovery Program* report, that are elevated to gospel truths. This results in the common practice of Philippines-bashing: Filipinos are self-centered to the extreme; their society is unjust and thus at war with itself; its ecology has been destroyed. Similar to the uninteresting two-way moral choices offered in the text, such pertinent statements are at a considerable remove from everyday experience. The book is explicit, however, when it discusses human rights and the problems of the nation.

The inspiration of the text for the fourth and final grade is derived more from moral theology than from abstruse social science. Its tone and wording are different from the earlier material, and the moral-choice situations the students are confronted with reflect everyday life. Implicitly, the focus is on attitudes and orientations. The text benefits from the Roman Catholic Church's moral ingenuity but does not elaborate on liberation-theological issues when these are brought up. Moreover, a little more adolescent psychology would have benefited the discussions of falling in love and sex.

Be that as it may, an important difference in comparison to Thai and Indonesian curricula (chapters 1 and 3) comes to light in the discussion of the individual. In modern Catholicism, the stress is on the individual conscience that roots in man's being created in God's image, and in the love for God and fellow man. Love is the wellspring of good conduct and good society. Because of this, obedience and the duties that group membership entail are not so constantly emphasized. On the contrary, encompassing groups—especially the state—are distrusted in their capacity to provide moral leadership. Morally mature individuals should take their own decisions. Even so—and that is made very clear—they cannot escape from their family membership, its duties and demands of loyalty.

These Roman Catholic tenets are complemented with the parallel vision of then President Ramos. According to the text, at the occasion of launching the Moral Recovery Program in 1993, the president emphasized that the moral basis of the nation stands in need of thorough reform. The nation must renew itself, both spiritually and materially. In order to improve their moral basis, Filipinos need to amend their person-centered values and attitudes concerning honor, conscience, and faith. The present laws are not rooted in the true values of the people, and virtues such as nationalism, integrity, and concern for others are only weakly developed. Self-centeredness and materialism prevail.

> If we aspire to national renewal and progress, we must change the values that constitute the center of our life. We must rid ourselves of the ills that plague social life, such as irregularities, tax evasion, rotten politics, inaction, and indifference. If we consider that the individual capacity for improving life hinges on personal spiritual power and stability, it is not far-fetched to think that the capacity of a community to renew itself is an inner affair. Our experience of freedom is sweet indeed, but what we also need is devotion to duty and self-discipline. Our praying is not enough; we must act up to our values, too (45–6).

Later on in the text, under 'The Moral Dimension of Filipino Culture,' the Moral Recovery Program—the very basis of current values education—is reviewed. After noting some eight positive traits, Filipino behavior also needs to be criticized because people fall short in self-knowledge and moral conviction. They are too self- and family-centered, without discipline and initiative; they do not think for themselves, and are almost completely incapable of analyzing their own lives or what happens around them. Furthermore, many people—because they are spoiled or poor—happily depend on others.

Filipinos are said to live in a very poor society, tainted by a big gap between haves and have-nots, and by inadequate government services. The rich have the power to govern, to exploit the political process to their advantage; they have foreign tastes, and their American orientation is engraved in the educational system and the media. It seems as if the ability to speak English defines a person's self-esteem. Nonetheless, the people are characterized by an inferiority complex when dealing with Caucasians.

The present educational system does not agree with basic Filipino culture. Religious attitudes, however much they contribute to the capacity of accepting life's hardships, also lead to indifference and gullibility. Poverty promotes perseverance and self-sacrifice together with gambling and corruption. The media exemplify a slave mentality and are an opiate for most. Moreover, respect for seniors and leaders easily leads to admiration for all sorts of despicable behavior (173–6).

This negative self-image largely defines the ideas behind the Moral Recovery Program (MRP). Its stated goal is to renew society through cultivating nationalism, national pride, and self-esteem. The intention is to foster the common good, social concern, social justice, and respect for human rights. It also aims at instilling loyalty and responsibility, discipline and diligence, and a distaste for 'irregularities.' It hopes to create people with both self-respect and self-criticism, who value the spiritual and inner dimensions of existence rather than its superficialities (176).

Whether the intentions of the former president and his sister can be fulfilled through teaching values education at school, is a moot point. Many people seem to think so, considering the vastness of the undertaking. In any case, they feel that the present situation is intolerable, and apparently hope that moral restructuring is easier to accomplish than structural reform. Seemingly, they shy away from the latter, and do not want to think too much about any linkage between the two.

The course is obviously meant to remedy certain ills. In doing so, a certain image of society arises. This image is not as much based on the outrageous generalizations of the presidential speech or the pretensions of the Moral Recovery Program, as it is on the practice and experience of everyday life. In this chapter we want to investigate this image, as deduced from the ethical conundrums that the students are invited to reflect upon.

REALISM IN VALUES EDUCATION IN THE PHILIPPINES

In all courses on values education commented upon in this chapter, the input of the state is clear. In Indonesia, this reflects the ideal of the Complete Indonesian Man who is an obedient subject as well. With aims set so high, realism suffers, although it is avowed that there still is much rot in the realm. In Thailand, many problems are blamed on individual moral decay. The two-way choices offered, however, are not of this world. What, for instance, to do with the information that smoking, drinking, frequenting prostitutes, having mistresses, coming home late, and suchlike, are destructive of family happiness? Some children can only reach the conclusion that their father is a devil rather than a saint—which does not appear as a correct portrayal of everyday life.

In the Philippine curriculum, at least in the final year of high school, subjection and obedience receive scant attention. The emphasis is on conscience, and thus on individual choice. In so-called 'situations,' the student is presented with recognizable, most often real-life dilemmas. As a result, the students are being made aware of certain situations they may have always taken for granted. It should be noted, however, that the perspective is entirely defined by modern—post-Vatican II— Roman Catholic teachings, to the detriment of other views, such as humanism; autonomous citizenship; social-structural considerations, or the connection between individual responsibility and democracy.

Just the same, given the age and experience of the students, there is little cause for wonder that their relationships with adults, especially with parents, often receive attention in the imaginary situations they are placed in. The first situation focuses on money and obligation. Si Kuwan (Mr/Miss So-and-so) is treasurer of a school project at the time his father falls ill. The parent is brought to the hospital, despite the family not having any money. The question the student has to face thus becomes whether he would use the project's assets to care for his father. Because it is almost unthinkable that he would not, the problem becomes: 'And what if you are then unable to refund the money?' (43).

Throughout the text, the reader is repeatedly assured that parents always love their children and are full of goodwill towards them. Situational parents, though, do not always live up to that image. We are told of parents who are extremely cruel to Kuwan's elder siblings, so cruel that the eldest plans to run away. For fear that the fierce father would hurt the boy, Kuwan can neither inform the parents of the plan, nor convince her brother to give up. So, what should she do? Since it is almost impossible to give a straight answer here, the next question becomes whether the sister thinks that fleeing will contribute to the personality development of her brother (43).

This last possibility seemingly anticipates the following exposition on 'the true meaning of aging.' Growing older should be a process of maturation, of growing up spiritually, and of carrying responsibility gracefully. A few pages onward, however, readers are confronted with the possibility of less than mature parents. Under the title 'The Family as the Foundation of the Moral Personality,' ideal parenthood is contrasted with the many problems Filipino families are experiencing. With both parents working outside the home, they have little or no time to devote to their offspring and their upbringing. When this situation arises, it makes the children responsible for the unity of the family. They must look for ways of tying the family together, of keeping the home in good order, while cultivating mutual understanding and love. This is all the more important because the wholesomeness of society—at present full of problems—ultimately depends on the firm spiritual foundation of its individual citizens (50–1).[3]

Anyway, problems with parents abound. Some mothers are absolutely unwilling to listen to their progeny and just hit them at their slightest displeasure. Some daughters are so dependent on their mama that they cannot take any decision by themselves. After all, many parents are in the habit of forcing their will—however unreasonable—on their offspring, and the latter are supposed to obey. Often parents equate children with their school results. When these grades constitute the only measure for recognition and approval, children naturally will feel abandoned and of no value. Besides, not all parents behave nicely. In some homes they shout at and fight with each other every day (104–5), while certain fathers are well-known to be less than honest in taking advantage of their position of honor and trust in the community (141). Can a child protest against such things?

Using position, connections, or white lies to one's own advantage is often at the heart of moral-choice situations. The school's advice on fathers who personally profit from the communal development fund is to refuse to accept the much needed pair of shoes bought with that dirty money. Then, what if you lose a contest and father offers to pull his strings to improve your grade? (104). Apart from dubious manipulations in the world outside the home, there can be many domestic problems with parents. Some are so strict as to forbid the simple pleasures allowed to your friends. Would you go against your parents' dictate and yield to the pressure of your peers? (250).

A reason is not always given for bad parent-child relationships. So what to do when father and child are so mad at each other as to avoid each other, even to the point that the child stays away from the family meals? (202).

There are also a few situations about the debt of gratitude children are to feel towards their parents. When the girl in question prefers having a good time to studying, she is clearly in the wrong because her parents have to scrape for every penny to send her to school (173). But what about a mother who, because of the child's miraculous cure, vowed to St. Martin that her son would become a priest, while the boy concerned does not feel attracted to that vocation at all? (154–5).

It is interesting to note that problems with teachers and the school administration hardly receive any consideration other than two cases in which a pupil is cheated on his grade in competitions in which the runner-up has been declared the winner (121). The in-and-out-of-school situations that receive ample attention, however, are the problems with peers. Often the ethical emphasis is on being courageous, willingness to sacrifice personal considerations for the sake of others, generosity towards and sympathy with those who need it, and having the guts not to give in to peer pressure (128–9).

Frequently the imaginary situations in which the students are placed are quite complex, and sometimes even seem to imitate the prevailing person-centered dynamics of politics for which the country is famous. What about the following:

> The girl you're engaged to is certain to win the honor of being the valedictorian of her school. You told her and her parents that you'll be your school's valedictorian. However, the next day you get to know that you'll have to compete for the honor with your close friend. The two of

you will be given a special examination in order to know who's the winner. Your friend, who is of a very poor family, absolutely needs to win if he is to enter college for free, and thus at all. On the other hand, your family is quite well-to-do. What if you are not going to finish first? Wouldn't you lose face with your betrothed and her parents? What are you going to do? Now, in case you are the poor student, would you propose to your well-off friend that if he pays you, you will let him win? Explain your answers (43–4).

The issue of smooth interpersonal interaction is regularly discussed. After all, 'to know how to get along with others' is and remains an important asset if one wants to be accepted. So, what to do if you have been orphaned and then accepted into the household of your aunt? This aunt is almost never at home, and your cousins flaunt the most reprehensible of manners: watching lewd movies, drinking with their friends, and always noisy. Of course, they invite you to join, but you, because you feel disgusted, cannot bring yourself to go along. As a result, they get angry with you. They take your refusal as an insult to their friends and a shaming of themselves. This is the message they convey to their mother, who does not even ask for your side of the story. 'If you cannot get along with your cousins, you had better find another place to stay.' What will you do? (91–2).

A related argument is presented in the case of a young adult who, because he's handsome, infatuates many girls. He himself, however, is not interested, and spends most of his free time chatting, discussing, and drinking with a close friend. This is understood as a show of disrespect for the opinions of his relatives and neighbors. As a result, he is advised to break with his 'sissy' friend (92).

Apparently, people often need to tread the narrow path between individual common sense, taste and desire, and the expectations of others. Moreover, when being a newcomer, a person should first achieve security through cultivating amiable relationships. It is not really possible to give sensible advice if that runs counter to the opinion of an established group. The latter may simply feel insulted, or irritated at the very least (118).

People do need to associate pleasantly with each other. Some fellow students, though, are simply abandoned, apparently unable or uninvited to join in the activities of the majority. This is no fun for them, and Kuwan is advised to extend sympathy to the loner, who may be a newcomer or be stigmatized. This becomes more delicate when the person concerned is the butt of sly digs and suchlike. Would you dare to side with him or her, and risk the contempt of your classmates? (129; 154).

This lesson on lack of consideration for others can be extended to the discrimination of the Ita ethnic minority, or the tolerance of corruption. To side with the 'silent majority' is apparently safer (141). Yet, students are repeatedly reminded to consciously take their own decisions, to the extent that girls are encouraged to let career prevail over (early) marriage (252–3), and that in a society that exercises considerable pressure to the contrary.

Apart from these general problems in the relations with peers, there is also the problem of love. When the girl Teri assures Kuwan that she loves him too, the boy feels great, and more committed to make the best of high school. Soon after, however, he meets Teri in the company of a former rival. Kuwan gets so jealous that he even misses a day of school. He confronts Teri saying that he is the only boy to accompany her and that she must stop seeing the other. Teri protests and advises Kuwan that if he insists on such a restricted relationship, he had better find another girlfriend who is equally narrow-minded (92).

Love not only leads to untamed feelings, it can also be exploited. The boy complains to the girl that she is very intractable, even to the extent that he doubts whether she really loves him. Being afraid of being abandoned, the girl wants to know how she can prove her devotion to him. 'If you really love me, you must be willing to give yourself to me even though we are not yet married' (92).

Other situations reveal the possibility of aggressive and unreasonable behavior in emotional relationships, whether between lovers or between parents and their offspring. Whatever the source of trouble between parents and children, it may well affect the minds of the children concerned. Such is the case with Baby's boyfriend, who proposes that they have sex so that he can forget the problems with his parents. In order to do that safely, he even advises that she start taking the pill. What is Baby to say or to do? (97–8).

The way community life is problematized points to a near-absence of civic action, indifference (147), and exploitation. We have already encountered corrupt local officials—people who are supposedly there to act for the common welfare—who have the power to allow a karaoke bar to noisily and drunkenly destroy the night and the good order of its neighborhood (122). What steps can ordinary citizens take to defend their surroundings, or what can they do against the inconvenience caused by irritating and abusive out-of-work youths hanging around at street corners? (119). It seems that people can only complain, and that no action is ever taken. Besides, those in power routinely abuse their workers and servants (118; 119; 141; 146–7), and it takes a lot of guts to protest. 'Do not provoke the other, do not build yourself an enemy' seems to be the prevailing wisdom. So, if you want to keep your job, do not ask the boss for justice.

The rich seem to favor their narrow self-interest above being a good boss or initiating civic action. The reasoning of the members of Kuwan's family is interesting. A flood has struck the area where they live, and especially the poorer people have been hard hit. Kuwan's father is a rich and prominent member of the community who should be expected to lead the relief effort. He does not feel like it. 'If we start helping, nobody else will lift a finger.' The mother does not agree. 'What will the people say about us if we do not step in?' (129).

Next to indifferent and sly haves, we are also presented with the less virtuous of poor people. Some of them seem to really cultivate their dependence on do-gooding, alms, and government, and have no inclination to take personal responsibility, let alone action. Besides, they appear to be insulted when they are reminded that there are things they can do themselves (147).

The difficulty of appealing to law, civic spirit, or consideration for each other—do not vex thy neighbor or the powerful!—is a theme that runs through many 'situations.' Of course, people should dare to advance their opinion, to confront others about their antisocial behavior, and people must even have the courage to face themselves (201), yet, in the final analysis, they are no more than ants in a big world full of evil, controversies, noise, anger, and confusion (200). So what to say to or do about those who dump their garbage anywhere, who make a lot of noise, who cause grave environmental problems? (181–2). What about a neighbor who likes to fire his gun, especially when drunk? People are already afraid of him, so it becomes a very delicate problem (202).

Apart from such instances, corruption and getting away with dubious action almost seems to be part of the culture. Would you just say no to a good opportunity because you are under age? It is so easy to up it by a year or two, and boss or coach will see to it. Is tampering with statistics not a normal thing to do? Who would abstain from copying from a classmate if that helps you to pass a test? Aren't the newspapers hiding the truth because of tea money or a bribe? Isn't it true that those in power are always right? (211).

This last instance is elaborated in various examples. It may be seen in the controversial position of the rich versus the poor—and as long as it lasts, there will be no justice and thus no peace (200). It appears as the protection of illegal rackets by the authorities. Would Kuwan support this by also gambling in the perennial underground lottery? (250). You witnessed a rich man's car hit a poor fellow. The car ran off. You know the number of the license plate. What do you do? (173). Then, closer to home: you know of a murder committed by someone high up who is rich and well-connected. He needs you to cover up his crime. Because you refuse, he causes you, and even your relatives, all sorts of trouble. What are you going to do? (254). Similarly, your superior in a road-building project appears to be masterminding the use of inferior materials and the upping of the budget. If you shut up, you automatically become his accomplice. Well? (254–5).

COMMENT

Throughout the text, there is considerable emphasis on overcoming one's own limitations, and developing personal judgement and conscience. These ideas also surfaced in President Ramos's advice. If people are guided by their responsible conscience, and act accordingly, society will be orderly.

This idea of the individual being the wellspring of good society seemingly corresponds to the moral conceptions we noted in the Thai and Indonesian curricula. There, however, the emphasis was more in the negative: individuals have the capacity to damage the good order of society, and the teachings particularly stressed that they should submit to group and hierarchical relationships. This stands in stark contrast with the course of conduct the Philippine curriculum advises. There, even in situations constructed around imperative of cultivating smooth interpersonal relationships, the ethics course stressed demonstrating individual independence and personality rather than going with the flow. As a result, rule following and obedience received little attention.

In practice, this contrast with the ethics taught in Thailand and Indonesia is not as stark as it appears. In the Philippines, it is as important as in the neighboring countries 'to know how to join,' to smooth in with one's fellows, not to (openly) oppose, to guard and save face, not to rock the boat. In the Philippines, too, people see themselves as part of groups and identify strongly with them. This belonging, or the possibility of doing so, is much more important than the development of an 'autonomous' conscience. The ethical advice advanced by the study materials for the fourth year of high shool reflects hopeful developments, future ideals, and still stands at quite a remove from the way life is lived. It does realistically reflect problems of everyday practice and morality, though.

Image of society

The image of society as a whole remains, because of selective presentation, rather disorderly. Sociological considerations of structure and process remain vague, and are not elaborated. In one paragraph about liberation theology, unjust structures are mentioned (144), but the meaning of that phrase is not explained. There are haves and have-nots, rich and poor, exploitative bosses and subservient laborers, but how it sticks together is never illuminated, and social oppositions are simply reduced to ethical, and thus personal, questions. Interestingly, school-based moral situations that involve its vertical relationships—pupils versus adult personnel—are totally absent, while the statement we found in both the president's speech and the Moral Recovery Program, namely that the present educational system does not agree with basic Filipino culture/values, receives no clarification at all.

The image that has been presented in the president's and MRP's analyses is one of trouble and strife, a kind of negativism known in wider society as Philippines-bashing or self-flagellation. Filipinos are no good; they are family-centered egoists, exemplary of what in anthropology has become known as amoral familism. Such behavior is strategic and understandable, because it is a way of coping with a basically unjust society presided over by a weak government.

The clearer picture is that based on the experiences of the students. Fifteen- or sixteen-year olds are, according to the hypothetical situations given, fully aware of the corruption, hypocrisy, abuse of power, and the general absence of civic-mindedness that surrounds them. To counter these negative tendencies, they have to go through values education. They need to reform themselves, or at least to strengthen their personality and dare to go against the flow. Putting so much responsibility on individual shoulders may—though not necessarily—reinforce the negative image of social life. After all, the magnitude of the social chaos—to which people are well adapted in any case—is such that a sense of despair easily leads to widespread indifference and cynicism. Most people certainly are men of good will, but individually they are powerless against problems that are deeply rooted in unjust hierarchies of politics and exploitation.

Students also appear to be rather fully aware of 'love' and its consequences, of sex and birth-control pills, and a few of them seem to already have made up their mind about who will be their life's partner. The way the situations concerned are presented is rather realistic: sex is a male preoccupation; love leads to jealousy and strong emotions. What is called 'love' is represented as a most egocentric drive, and it is unfortunate, certainly so for the students, that the text leaves it at that.

The overall image of Philippine society that emerges is unpleasant. Although there are many well-meaning individuals—and one meets them practically every day—their society itself is ugly, messy, and hard to cope with. This image is, sorry to say, fair.

CHAPTER 6

INDONESIA: THE CALL FOR REFORM

Ever since its inception, Suharto's New Order regime has gradually but persistently attempted to superimpose the state on society. This was necessary to achieve the peace, stability, and national unity that would allow for economic development. In practice it meant the violent suppression of the political left, the muzzling of critics and press, government control over political parties and labor unions, the reduction of parliament to an assembly of yes-men, the 'normalization' of the universities, and the imposition of state ideology on all organizational life, including religion.

Of course, some voices of conscience expressed themselves all along but hardly allowed for anything resembling a public debate. For a very long time, official repression of dissident voices was quite effective while many people seemingly believed in the messages of nationwide indoctrination. To them, there was nothing wrong with the state ideology. If things on the ground turned out differently, they were seen as aberrations and 'excesses of development.' In this way, Indonesia turned into a closed society, enclosed in its own web of official lies in which dissent, criticism, and conviction equated with the foolishness of heroism.

The more oppressive, paranoid, and Suharto-centered the regime grew to be, the clearer the cracks in its facade, such as the impunity of the army, the arrogance of Suharto's children, the currency of Suharto jokes. That there was something evading the grip of government became clear as early as 1992 when Abdurrahman Wahid called on his followers to convene massively in Jakarta. Although the rally was not a great success, it demonstrated the indomitableness of certain segments of the Islamic community. On the other side of the political spectrum, the star of Megawati Sukarnoputri began to rise. In 1996, the government, in the run-up to the next year's elections, felt uneasy about the number of people pinning their hopes on the first president's daughter. It came to a head with the officially sponsored rowdy attack against the Democratic Party's headquarters on 27 July that year. From then on uncontrollable restiveness has been the normal condition in Indonesia. The culture of violence with which the New Order maintained itself had obviously taken root.

In 1997, we saw the last New Order-orchestrated 'Festival of Democracy' election campaign. It was the running up to Suharto's umpteenth mandate to continue his rule in March 1998. His new, nepotistic cabinet demonstrated how much the president had grown out of touch with reality. At that time the Asian monetary crisis was really hurting the people, and the 'Father of Development' suddenly stood in emperor's clothing. It meant demonstrations, more violence, topped by the days of rage in Jakarta in May. On the twenty-first of that month, Suharto stepped down. After thirty-two years, the New Order, born of violence and confusion, ended as it had come. Full of hope, yet still horror-struck, Indonesians entered the 'Order of Reform.' All at once, everything was possible—or so it seemed.

This chapter is not written to recount the history of deceptions, setbacks and advances of Indonesia since the second president released his grip on power. We are all familiar with the civil wars raging in various parts of the country, the unreliability of the army and police, the unclear scheming and maneuvering of interest groups, and tendencies toward national disintegration, aggravating poverty and the economic mess the country is in. This chapter is about the ideas that are suggested and discussed by the country's foremost intellectuals.[1] I do not think that there is anybody among them who is not daunted by the challenge of reform, yet all of them agree on its necessity.

REFORM

Some analysts reflect on the principle of reform itself. They point out that the New Order was basically totalitarian, call it fascist or feudal, and that it prioritized the state over society. Ideologically, it equated the state with the nation, even with society and its individual people. In the same way as Sukarno legitimized Guided Democracy in 1959, it found its justification in appeals to the Constitution of 1945, the Pancasila national ideology, and the principles of state. The latter highlight the unitary nation built on the ideas of familism and integralistic state in which the president presides like a father over the national family. There is no opposition and no tyranny of the majority: all decisions are reached through deliberations aiming at consensus. This widely opened the road to presidential dictatorship, over-centralization, and an excessive emphasis on unity and stability. While traveling on that road, the complementary founding principle of the nation, Unity in Diversity, was conveniently forgotten.

Other victims of the direction chosen were the principles of popular sovereignty, separation of powers, basic human rights, and the rule of law. To justify all this, first President Sukarno cooked up his *ad hoc* ideological statements. The New Order regime was more systematic in its approach, and gradually developed its Pancasila philosophy of state in which the regime is always triumphant, and society and individuals are perennially at the receiving end, in addition to being grateful for the protection and blessings of the Pancasila.

There can be no cause for wonder that the edifice of state grew to be a web of lies, that corruption, collusion, and cronyism could flourish, and that very much attention was given to the systematic indoctrination of the population in the state ideology. This, and the continual stress on economic and technological development, led to generations of New Order babies, students grown up during these times, whose minds are blank, who have not learned to think about history and society, who are uncritical and socially inattentive; they are career- and consumer culture–oriented at best. If they protest, it is owing to frustration, and not because they have reached clear conclusions about what is going on.

All this poses formidable challenges to the few people who have maintained a critical mind. They have to face the results of forty years of brainwashing, of unlearning to think, of following. As they see it, the legacy of the New Order has to be dismantled totally. Its ideological justifications must be exposed for what they are: humbug to legitimize dictatorship. The ideas of familism and integralistic state stand in the way of the principle of popular sovereignty. It is the people who should, through parliament, control the executive, not the other way around. Such people have rights, they are equals, and must be equal before the impartial law. They should run the affairs of state democratically.

Dismantling the old order and establishing an open, democratic society is a very ambitious undertaking. Whatever the rejuvenated order of things is going to be, it inherits the civil and military services that maintained the New Order for so long. These cannot change their ways of thinking overnight, even if they are willing to do so. There are many vested interests that can only feel threatened by any attempt to revamp the system. They will certainly fight back. Besides, there is a great deal of conservatism among the people themselves. They are not in the habit of thinking critically, and for everybody concerned the word 'democracy' may have a different connotation. As a result, visionary ideas—many of which hark back to the Generation of 1928—are difficult to connect with the experience and imagination of most.

So, whereas the call for total reform sounds eminently reasonable, Indonesia is stuck, for the time being—a time of economic crisis to boot—with a thoroughly corrupted infrastructure of state, a rapacious system of crony-capitalism, and vast masses of people not accustomed to asking questions. How to substitute a judiciary that has grown fat on the manipulation of the law with one that seriously upholds it? How to rewrite, or reinterpret the principles of state as they have been intended against strong currents of Javanese and Islamic conservatism? These two examples are telling enough. Where to find new personnel who have sound ideas of what a constitutional state and the rule of law mean? How to change ideas that not only acquired the status of sacred mantras but that are also rooted in venerable traditions that are basically autocratic and repressive? After all, the dictatorship did not operate in a cultural vacuum.

Consequently, the necessity of total reform, no matter how well-reasoned, runs counter to stubborn realities that cannot be circumvented. Because of this, there are respectable public intellectuals who do not see the necessity of a Constitutional Assembly to deliberate the legal fundamentals of the state. They opine that the hastily written, preliminary Constitution of 1945 is basically sound and only needs to be amended. This is precisely what happens these days, with the Consultative Assembly formulating and enacting a series of amendments while avoiding consideration of certain sensitive issues, such as the Islamic nature of the state.

UNITY IN DIVERSITY: FEDERALISM?

Certain public intellectuals, among them Mangunwijaya, Magnis-Suseno, and A. B. Nasution, disagree with this order of priority. According to them, unrest and disintegration are the products of the obsession with unity and uniformity of the previous regime that suppressed the country's characteristic diversity and that did not allow for the open negotiation of the many cleavages that naturally run through the society. By tabooizing differences, these came violently to the fore during the closing years of the New Order in which all sorts of minorities became targets. Christians turned against Muslims, Muslims against Christians, laborers against factory owners, the populace against police, against Chinese, against ethnically different groups, against migrants, in brief, against any target available to vent pent-up frustration. The economic crisis aggravated the rage. Chinese-owned shops became a target-of-course. Impoverished peasants plundered government go-downs. Symbols of authority were attacked and burnt down.

Naturally, diversity, and respect for it, became the topic of serious debates that spill off into various directions. One of the driving forces behind these discussions was the late Mangunwijaya (d. 1999) who made diversity, and thus respect for the individual, the basic point of departure of much of his thinking. He thus became one of the foremost advocates of the knotty problem of federalism. Indonesians united in their desire to expel the centralizing, exploitative colonial dispensation. Their shared suffering also made them want to stay together with due respect for the multifarious differences among themselves. What they got was an ever more centralizing government, preoccupied with unity and integrity, intolerant of diversity, as well as highly exploitative. The regions were simply bled dry of their resources, while spectacular wealth accumulated at the Javanese center. The Dutch had simply been replaced by even more rapacious native masters.

This is in flagrant contradiction with the principle of unity in diversity, and an arrogant show of disrespect for the variety of peoples and traditions that constitute Indonesia. As a result, certain regions, such as Aceh, Papua, and East Timor, try to break free, while all and sundry want to have more say in affairs they perceive as their own; they clamor for a fair share of their often rich resources. Consequently, if Indonesia wants to survive, the principle of unity in diversity should be sincerely implemented. This means far-reaching decentralization, respect for the provinces' cultural and other peculiarities, and a great measure of autonomy. In order to prevent future usurpation of power and resources, the best way of guarding the integrity of the country is therefore to reconstitute it on a federal basis, which has proven to be quite successful in, for instance, India, Germany, and North America.

Obviously this advocacy goes against the idea that, for fifty years at least, Indonesia has been a unitary state, and however reasonable and well-argued, it will be very hard to find many supporters of the idea of federalism. While it was good for Indonesia's international reputation to let East Timor go its own way, many fear the breaking-up of the country if more than a modicum of autonomy is granted to the provinces.

CIVIL SOCIETY

Whatever the constitutional shape of the Indonesian state-to-come, this much is certain: the country needs to build a civil culture of the public realm. To do so, the lies of the previous regime need to be exposed. For instance, is there such a thing as the cultural uniqueness of Indonesia that justifies authoritarian government and distrust of human rights? Such myths have been created to perpetuate the position of power-holders, and serve the interests of the elite. But even if people realize this clearly, the task of building a civilized political culture is intimidating because, under the New Order, civil political traditions have gone missing. The only valid political culture was the law of the ruler.

What needs to be built up now goes against the grain, not only of the Suharto years, but against many aspects of (Javanese) Indonesian culture. For instance, all know about the importance of appearances, form, formality, and face. These not only guard reputation, but have made people callous to hypocrisy. Hypocrisy has become part of the way of life, and exposing it is bad manners. Individuals can never be held personally responsible; they hide in the maze of hierarchy and bureaucracy—which they manipulate to their personal advantage—while blaming others or circumstances for all things that go wrong. So, at least, it was under the New Order when opposition equated with 'communism' and 'obstructionism.' Under the cover of 'Indonesian values,' all meaningful exchange of ideas was smothered, which strengthened an old trait, namely, the incapacity to criticize, let alone the tolerance of being criticized. Yet, in the absence of critical exchanges, truth easily vanishes, and all that democracy stands for cannot be realized.

Laboring under the double heritage of forty years of dictatorship and Javanese cultural restraints on equality, it is difficult to see where a modern civil society and a democratic environment might hail from. Many public intellectuals, among them Muhammad Hikam, Arief Budiman and Jakob Oetama, are convinced that a strong civil society is needed to realize the principle of popular sovereignty and to establish real democracy. In Mangunwijaya's view, civil society should function as the conscience of society that protests against all forms of abuse, whether they originate from the state, economic development, or consumerism. The latter three impose themselves on the freedom of thought; they shackle people into subservience.

Although this thinking is basically sound, the prospect of a viable civil society arising—and thus the prospect of democracy as it is hoped for—is not that clear. Can it arise from 'the people,' the vast, uneducated masses? Can it be expected to issue from the crowd of poorly educated college graduates? Or is it the very limited group of public intellectuals themselves? The call for civil society somehow takes it for granted that justice and prosperity for all can be realized, that structures will change because of ideals and ideas, and that a civilized society is in the offing.

If I understand them well, Jakob Oetama and Aristides Katoppo are among the careful optimists. Considering their professional positions as publishers and newspapermen, they are in the hub of the public debate, and are naturally convinced that such debate must be open, that all opinions be heard, and that a critical press is indispensable. But is it realistic to call the present dispensation the Order of Reform that will be driven by a 'strong and effective civil society'? The editor of *The Jakarta Post*, Susanto Pudjomartono, is not that sure. While agreeing on the vital role of a free press, he is not really optimistic about the rapid development of a broad critical public. Students may protest, and that is a good thing, but can it be expected, in view of the confusion of ideas, that they present parliament with feasible projects, and if they do, that there is the political wherewithal to implement them? It still seems difficult, despite all the open trouble going on, to discuss the so-called *SARA* issues of ethnicity, religion, race, and class in a rational manner; they are easily clouded by emotion.

ARMED FORCES

There is near unanimity, however, that the armed forces have no place in the political affairs of a democratic society. They were one of the pillars of the New Order, not only strongly represented in parliament, but also claiming a civilian role in government and economic development. Yet, since the beginning of the Suharto period, the people have recognized the military as the instrument of their suppression—and not as the popular freedom fighters as myth has it. Besides, an army with its hierarchical structure of command is, by its very nature, an undemocratic establishment that should, for its own and everybody's good, be under the control of civilian government. While the debates agree on these points, there is divergent opinion on how to rid society and politics of army influence. A situation that has grown over many years, which is reinforced by military interests in vast sectors of the economy, give the institution considerable clout that can only be phased out slowly. Moreover, and this unduly complicates the problem, the armed forces appear to be split in many factions that are in practice often not under the control of the center, with some groups even behaving as so-called 'lost commands,' more as independent warlords than as instruments of state.

Even so, no matter how unpopular, the armed forces may be needed to guarantee the unity of the country, not by defending it against outside aggression but by subduing all those who think that the first sentence in the preamble to the original constitution is also meant for them. That sentence stipulates the right to independence and self-determination of all nations, which, of course, sits awry with the claim of a unitary Indonesia comprising the territory of the former Dutch East Indies. But then, is keeping the country together through the force of arms an acceptable prescription?

DIVERSITY

Mangunwijaya did not think so, and developed a vision in which a new culture would transcend, first, regional differences and then, narrow-minded nationalism. For instance, Javanese should become Indonesians in the first place, adding a new dimension to their existence, and Indonesians should evolve into broad-minded citizens of the world. At that level of culture, the integration of the nation would no longer be a problem. We noted already his advocacy of federalism as the solution for the time being.

Looking at Indonesia over the past few years, however, we must note that New Order policies have resulted in strengthening the forces that tear at its fragile social fabric. Prejudice and emotion keep people separated. As long as government was strong and the economy performing, the *SARA* skeletons of discord remained safely in the closet, but afterwards ravaged the country with a vengeance. As a result, public intellectuals recognize the need for diminishing the power and emotional force of prejudice by appealing to reason and dialogue. Some even call for transcendence when they argue that the dialogue should not be based on differences between religious faiths, but on the fact of having faith itself. Again, this seems visionary, and the present situation offers not much hope. Part of the heritage of the New Order regime is the intensification of fissures: those who spectacularly profited from national development were Suharto's Chinese cronies. The forceful indoctrination of the national ideology smelled of the Javanization of the land. So did the massive program of transplanting Javanese throughout the national territory, and the overrepresentation of the Javanese in all higher ranks of army and civil service. The emancipation of Islam has put it in a competitive position vis-à-vis the other religions.

The accumulation of wealth and privilege in the hands of the happy few exposed the underdog position of most. As a consequence, ethnic, religious, racial, and class differences became more acute, and the demand for identity in a vague nation in a globalizing world became stronger, almost inevitably so.

There are two ways of overcoming these and other clefts and fissures. The self-defeating nature of the first, namely the strong center that forcefully imposes itself in the name of unity and integrity, has been abundantly established. By suppressing differences, frustration could simmer on up to the boiling-point.

The way out of the impasse the New Order led the country into is the democratic way of dealing with diversity and oppositions. Indonesia, however, has preciously little experience with democracy, and has only just been freed from forty years in which the state attempted to impose itself on society. So, whereas the option for democracy is reasonable, there is little in place to shape it.

EDUCATION

Educators like Mangunwijaya and Mochtar Buchori have since long pointed to the opposition between the New Order ideal of the Pancasila Man, or the dutiful Complete Indonesian, and the free, responsible citizen needed to animate democracy. According to them, the current system of school education is not conducive to the creation of citizenship and a vibrant civil society. Firstly, the quality of the education the state provides has degenerated to the point of 'training for stupidity.' There are many reasons for this. The very rapid expansion of the system ever since the end of colonial days eroded its standards. Teachers needed to be trained in a hurry, and teachers trained in a hurry then trained new teachers in a hurry. With the expansion, the Ministry of Education and Culture also grew rapidly, and with its vast budget it became corrupt to the marrow. Since the beginning of the New Order, the system expanded again very rapidly at all levels, with quality steadily declining, while swelling the mass of confused graduates who know many outlandish words and who cannot get a sentence straight. The books used, both in school and college, are half-baked. Because the reward for teaching is minimal, the teacher-training courses attract the less competent and the rejects of the more prestigious faculties. All this results in an appalling low level of teacher competence.

This sorry state of affairs is complemented by a second cluster of factors relating to purpose and method. Under the New Order dispensation, education was seen as the handmaiden of national economic development. The aim was to produce technocracy-minded, disciplined people who would be loyal subjects of the state to boot. To this end, the humanitarian aspect of education was fully replaced by the indoctrination effort aimed at creating the Complete Indonesian Man. Gradually, the ideas of the state ideologues pervaded all social-studies' materials. Whether things made sense or not, to pass the test students had—and still have—better memorize the answers, and this is what prevailed: rote-learning. Thus, students and teachers knew the answers, and nobody knew the why's. Competence and creativity became antagonists of a system that fostered authoritarianism on the part of school principals and teachers, and confusion and disinterest on the part of students.

As a result, there is a painful deficit of originality and creativity in Indonesian society. The New Order babies were trained to be meek and to unlearn curiosity. Intellectually, generations of Indonesian youth have been wasted. Mangunwijaya's original way out of this bad situation was to pin his hopes on the drop-outs. Those who have not been stupidified by the system would possibly be mentally free. More serious, though, were his attempts at educational reform through connecting schooling with the life-world experience of the pupils, and through stimulating them to be creative and search for solutions. Schooling should not be drudgery but fun; it should open horizons instead of closing them. In his view, it was not only the purpose and method of teaching that were at fault. Javanese authoritarianism and cultural conservatism could be at least as disastrous in creating mentally caged people. People should be made to think for themselves and be able to sort out their moral dilemmas.

All critical educators have come with their diagnoses of the system of education, and many agree that it stands in need of a total overhaul. Yet, where to begin, and to what purpose? While there are some private pilot projects, the system, no matter how unsatisfactory, is there, and it is very slow in responding to initiatives for change. What the purpose of education should be is perhaps easier to answer. According to some critics, education should aim at developing the talents of individual pupils. It must respect the individuality of students, stimulate creativity, responsibility and moral consciousness. In brief, it should breed the ideal citizen, the active, autonomous member of civil society. Naturally, this sounds much better than can ever be expected, and goes against the grain of all recent experience.

Mangunwijaya's emphasis on the individual, and individual diversity, is well-taken, however. While in his discourse the focus is on the method of education, others stress the necessity of building a sound civil society as critical opponent of the state and watchdog against vested interests.

What I have not come across in the debates is a sociological perspective. Pancasila education stressed obsequiousness and bred, for a variety of reasons, cynicism about politics and the way society is run. It did not provide realistic guidelines on how to act in the public world. In that public world, people have to fend for themselves: the experience of modern society, like it or not, individualizes. School education should therefore train for individual moral autonomy and conviction; it should shape the will to participate responsibly. Currently, however, people experience too much untamed individualism in a market-driven society. In order to civilize that society, people should learn to see themselves as citizens first of all. In whatever way it is argued, the obstacles to this transformation seem formidable.

INSTITUTION BUILDING

This was also apparent in the discussions on and in parliament, and on the state of national leadership. After the July–August 2000 confrontation in the Assembly, people had to agree that there was no alternative to the incumbent president. He might be controversial, confusing, and often headstrong, but there was nobody capable of replacing him.

Over a long period, people have not been trained to lead, and especially in the divided party-political arena there are few who have the potential to qualify as national leaders. Such figures are much needed, because people, accustomed to depend and follow, are looking to them for direction. In the absence of credible institutions, personally trusted leaders carry extraordinary weight.

Many would like this to change, and much of the reform debate is about institution building. The executive, the legislature, and the judiciary should be mutually independent, strong establishments. An invigorated civil society must develop that, in its turn, gives rise to a panoply of watchdog and activist groups. The rule of law has to be established. Political parties are to do more than to strive after their own narrow interests; they should serve the nation. A truly democratic society strives for securing the common welfare, and does not tolerate privilege; it respects law and regularity. It cherishes and protects human rights and civic freedoms.

In the debates it appears that people are aware of the interrelatedness of these issues. It often seems that law and regularity are recognized as very basic to the desired-for institutional development, whether it concerns the separation of powers or the emergence of a viable civil society. All these are based on respect for rights and legal guarantees. But for forty years, at least, there has been no legal development, and popular political culture has been killed in the bud. As a result, the cancers of corruption, collusion, and cronyism could flourish and became, no matter how debilitating they are, the axis around which affairs revolve. And thus, if people call for reform—let alone total reform—these cancers have to be cut out. So far, there has been very little progress on that road.

ENVIRONMENT

Such have been the main issues raised in the public discourse. They appear to be fundamental but are not exhaustive. Next to them we frequently find two other debates, about the environment and the place of women, and like so many other things, they have been very much inspired by policy and practice under the New Order.

While the forest fires of 1997 drew worldwide attention to the ecological disaster brought about by Indonesia's 'development,' insiders have since a long time been aware of the basic issues. They point, for instance, to the practice of land acquisition which resulted in vast tracts falling into the hands of the privileged few while more and more farmers and residents lost control over land they rightfully considered theirs. Compensation was always below market value, and the army was there to intimidate and push through whatever had been decided. But well apart from the display of arrogance regarding the common people, the projects involved often were inconsiderate of the environment. Enormous tracts of primeval forest were cleared in the hope of creating rice land or of becoming vast oil-palm plantations. Mining concessions were notorious polluters. Foreign trawling depleted the resources of local fishermen.

This list of ecological problems can be lengthened at will. The point is that greed and rapacity have been unleashed, and that precious resources, whether timber or land, can be exploited, siphoning off actual and potential provincial wealth for the benefit of the Jakarta elite. The problems are thus more complex than just environmental. They have crucial structural dimensions, and the interests of the elite do not sit well with the call for reform.

WOMEN

The gender issue has been out in the open since the middle 1980s. By then, because of its sexist ideology, the women-unfriendly nature of the military-dominated regime revealed itself through the tenets of the compulsory associations of the wives of civil servants and army personnel. Such wives were supposed to serve their husbands and to devote themselves to their families. The husbands, in turn, were expected to be 100 percent loyal to the regime. The support of the wife would free her husband from worry, and thus enable him to devote himself totally to his task. If he was lowly paid for that endeavor, wives were allowed to earn some supplementary income. Apart from this, superiors were to monitor the marital situation of their inferiors. It is therefore safe to say that civil servants and army personnel were considered to be some sort of state property, with women lowest in the pecking order.

Whereas this arrangement sounds 'traditional,' it is not. Ordinary

Javanese women have always been very active in economic matters, and were more than mere props for their husbands. Moreover, in their market and agricultural activities, they enjoyed considerable autonomy. The ideology propounded, therefore, was a New Order invention in line with the propagation of Western middle-class family ideology, housewifization, and social regimentation. The counter-emancipatory nature of this thinking is clear, and contrary to the trend of more and more women enjoying higher education. Consequently, the feminist demand targeted New Order thinking, and is now aspiring to gain access to all sorts of positions. In a reformed Indonesia, one half of the parliamentary delegates should be women!

ISLAM

The issue of the place of Islam in state and society is less obvious in the general discourse. This situation will certainly remain so as long as so-called fundamentalism and the demand for an Islamic state remain as weak as they are now. The debates that take place are inner-Islamic affairs. When focusing on these, the diversity of and within the Muslim community becomes immediately apparent. Almost everything is conceivable, ranging from the modernist position of desacralizing all those aspects of Islam that are man-made accretions, through the revivalism that sees religion as an identity marker in opposition to Christianity or the West, to the transformative position that sees Muslim society arising from justice, tolerance, equity, and democracy. This last position agrees with the current call for reform.

This relatively calm picture of Islam at the national level is belied by sectarian unrest that sets Muslims and Christians against each other. There can be no doubt that this antagonism is aggravated by the dire straits in which an increasing number of Indonesians find themselves. Their problems and frustration easily reinforce narrow-mindedness and sectarianism. Having been left behind by progress, and disgusted with the spirit of materialism, secularism, and contempt for the ordinary people that dominated the public world for so long, they may seek recourse to 'fundamentalistic' or 'revivalistic' movements that have no democratic potential and threaten to tear the nation apart.

CHAPTER 7

THINKING WOMEN'S EMANCIPATION

In this study tracing ways of thinking about public life, it is of interest to note what has become possible to publish and discuss on the subject of female sexuality. The books we review by women authors envisage the freedoms of work, political activism, and individual expression; they claim social and sexual equality. It is especially this latter demand that is revolutionary, clearly expressing what has, until very recently, been thought of as unspeakable.

This chapter's focus on the claim to sexual equality is certainly no substitute for the debates on gender in the three countries concerned. So far, these debates still center on practical women's issues such as discrimination in the workplace, political representation, livelihood, officially sanctioned 'housewifization,' prostitution, family planning, etc. Culturally and theoretically, however, the public discussion has not yet advanced beyond the appeals for fairness, liberation, and emancipation made in the following books.

The first book to be reviewed is *Saman* (1998), by Indonesian author Ayu Utami, which garnered first prize in the 1997 Jakarta Art Council's novel-writing competition. For the whole of the following year, Utami's award-winning book was reprinted every month. Yet, to be honest, it was not the book's excellence and sophistication that made it sell edition upon edition. What attracted the public was that a woman had something to say about sex and, possibly, love. Consequently, she became the target of heaps of invective. Polite society was shocked, and awfully curious.

The second book hails from the Philippines. It is Lualhati Bautista's Tagalog-written *Child, child... how have you been made?* (1983). It is a singularly frank novel about a woman who claims the right to sex, to her body, to earn a living, and to a career of her own—in brief, to be the equal of men without compromising her femininity. This very entertaining tale won its author the much coveted Palanca Award, and has ever since been in print, which is a remarkable feat in a country where people do not read books very often—let alone in Tagalog. To my knowledge, the novel did not cause a scandal when it appeared: it is simply too humorous, and achieved lasting fame because of the movie based upon it.

The Thai work to be reviewed is a collection of short stories, *As if dancing with the kapok flower* (1993), by Suchinda Khantayalongkot. As a minor author, she is not as renown as the first two novelists or as certain other Thai female writers. She builds her reputation on stories that revolve around love and sex, that obviously relate her own experiences without a trace of embarrassment, reluctance, or shame. This exhibitionism does not sit well with most members of the Thai reading public, but is yet attractive enough to warrant a steady reprinting.

The three authors concerned are pioneers who have brought the female side of sexuality out into the open. In their treatment, they have gone far beyond what any respectable male author has written on the subject. Speaking frankly about sex is rare, and if it does occur it merely focuses on male lust. Men's licence in relating to market and village women, to mistresses, prostitutes, dancers, singers, and entertainers, has always been taken for granted and is firmly part of the culture, even though the said culture is awfully prudish about lovemaking; this, of all things, should not be out in the open. These attitudes have now been challenged by women who are solidly part of respectable society. Let's give them the floor.

AYU UTAMI, *SAMAN* (1998)[1]

Saman is a sophisticated, magnificently composed novel that offers a kaleidoscopic mix of points of view situated in different times and places, often transgressing the threshold between fantasy and fact, between dream and reality. By no stretch of the imagination is there any obscurity: the language and similes Ayu uses are enticing and crystal clear.

The bulk of the story is familiar fare, certainly the parts set in the late 1990s when the atrocities of the Indonesian regime had been fully exposed, and common knowledge was vindicated. The army, the police, paramilitaries, or security guards are only there to repress and intimidate the population, in the name of the state, of power holders, of agribusiness, of concessionaires, of golf links, of development. Demanding justice or recognition of rights equates with subversion, rebellion, and opposition. It endangers harmony, it insults the powers that be. It invites terror and trouble.

When *Saman* opens, Laila is sitting in New York's Central Park. It is the mating season. Birds do it, bees do it, even the apples on the trees do it. Are they sinning? Of course not. They are part of creation, and this is creation's law. 'Soon, I'll be doing it, too.' She waits for Sihar. It is a little over a year ago since she went to bed with him. She is still a virgin, however.

Sihar is a Batak engineer she got to know when doing a photographic report on an oil rig. She was intrigued because he was the only one not paying any attention to her, the only woman on that all-male island. The overbearingness and arrogance of the Javanese company supervisor led to the accidental death of Sihar's closest comrade. Laila convinces him not to destroy himself by avenging this personally, but to seek redress in court. It is a preposterous proposition. How can one take on an oil company? How can one fight somebody who enjoys official protection? How to deal with the power of money in court? But Laila uses NGO-style reasoning: 'We'll seek publicity and keep the press interested in our case. I'll introduce you to a highly motivated human rights activist.' Laila presents Sihar to Saman. The victim's family, who lives in the Sumatran rubber growing area, goes along. Laila also involves her friend Yasmin, an activist lawyer.

In between we read some interesting considerations. Will Sihar take an interest in Yasmin who is svelte and beautiful? What is that strange feeling for Saman, on whom Laila had a crush when he was still the seminarian, Brother Wis? Later, when Sihar and Saman get down to business, Laila feels excluded. Anyway, now she waits in New York, where Sihar will be far from his wife, and she from her parents, far away from all the obstacles and feelings of guilt that prevent them—or is it only Laila?—from enjoying the fruit of infatuation.

> He will be my first—it is mating season. We shall be free from elders and friends, free from sin. We shall tell each other how much we waited for this moment. We'll kiss. Perhaps we'll do it here, right among the bushes in the park. Later, in bed, I'll feel his skin. He'll be everywhere. (20)

Why doesn't he show up? His plane must have crashed. There is no such news in the paper. Something must have happened. She phones Jakarta. 'Sorry. Here it's four in the morning. Call again tomorrow. Thank you.'

Shakuntala, whose father calls her a whore because she enjoys sex with quite a few men, is Laila's host in New York. To her, life is dancing, is having a body, is enjoying it. She is a heavenly nymph whose body is not subject to lowly drives but to the lust for life, to the libido. She watches as Laila emerges from a subway entrance headfirst, her body next, her feet last, like a newborn baby from the womb. Yet, there is nothing new as far as Laila is concerned. She is laden with anxieties. After all, Sihar challenged power and privilege too big to take on. 'He has been killed,' she thinks. 'It took revenge.' Hiring a hitman or ordering soldiers to have their fun—aren't those minor considerations in Indonesia? Take the killing of Dietje, the flight attendant, or of Marsinah, the courageous woman labor leader. But will they get to Sihar, too?

> 'Do you have any news, Laila?'
> 'No.'
> 'Sihar is not dead. He is at the Days Inn. Together with his wife.' (79)

The reasons why Saman had to change his identity from the innocent, idealistic Father Wis to that of a human rights' activist, are recounted in the second chapter. On a visit to the house where he grew up—a house haunted by the mystical adventures of his mother who delivered a ghost child, stillborn or unviable, almost every year—he is drawn to a subhuman, deranged girl. His pursuit of her leads him deep into the rubber gardens to the hamlet of her relatives. They usually keep her in a pen to prevent her from running away. (When she does break out, people see her wandering through the streets, satisfying herself on poles and posts, and being taken by certain men).

Full of compassion for the animal-like girl, Father Wis decides to make her a decent cage, equipped not only with a latrine, but also with a bar-shaped object to soothe her urges with. In the time it takes to build, the girl, Upi, casts a spell on him as it were; the hamlet and its people become an obsession. In order to visit as often as he can, he initiates concrete measures to better their livelihood. The rubber gardens are improved, and in time a measure of modest prosperity prevails, expressed in lighting and a generator.

Then, trouble starts. Like in other hamlets in the far-flung area, the people are approached by unpleasant types who propose that they sign papers. Their land will be converted into a vast oil-palm plantation; the rubber trees must be cut down. Organized and brought to subsistence level through the endeavor of Father Wis, the villagers refuse to cooperate, which sets off a train of intimidation. First of all, women are raped, including Upi—who even may have liked it. Then the generator is wrecked, very much like in Orwell's *Animal Farm*. More physical violence follows. Father Wis is taken away. The description of his incarceration and torture, desperation and loneliness, stands as a powerful image for the regime's tactics of dehumanization.

At the end of the chapter, Wis is a fugitive, not even secure in the embrace of the Mother Church. The priest disappears, must disappear—is there a God?—and Saman emerges. He flees the country with the aid of Yasmin and Cok. To flee is to be under threat. Yasmin breaks down. He tries to console her, but soon finds himself in the role of a child, burying his face in her breasts. They have intercourse, then Yasmin masturbates herself before mounting him again. Father Wis/ Saman is totally befuddled, helpless, shamefaced.

In New York, he starts e-mailing Yasmin. Both hanker after each other. Yasmin's married life has become routine, sex a mere physical exercise. For Saman it is still an unfulfilled and confusing promise.

> 'But I couldn't even bring you to a climax.'
> 'Dear Saman, just thinking of you makes me orgastic.'
> 'Come. Teach me. Rape me.' (132)

In between these final sentences and Wis becoming Saman, the four female characters are portrayed, from their common school days up to their early thirties. Yasmin is the gifted girl who has everything, and a 'normal' marriage. In America, Shakuntala, the dancer, is at long last out of the way of the father she despises. Laila is the romantic dreamer, who thinks that the enemy is male opportunism. Then there is Cok, who was shipped off to Bali to finish high school after her parents found a condom in her bag. Later on, she needs the protection of her family against the fury of some of her jilted lovers.

The friendship of these four characters offers the opportunity to survey female sexuality, its experience and fantasies. Often the stories are hilarious, such as when Laila goes off to a hotel with Sihar while being monitored over the phone by her three friends. When Sihar is in the bathroom, she calls to tell where she is. Meanwhile the three women place their bets. Will it finally happen? The loser will have to buy polka-dot condoms in a crowded drugstore. Yasmin still believes in male love without penetration. The two others totally reject that idea. Yes, when a man loves his child, or his dog, he will abstain. For a male, 'love' and lust are one. Laila phones again,

> 'So, it happened?'
> 'What?'
> 'Well ...'
> 'No, not to that point'
> 'Did you come?'
> 'He came.'
> 'And you?'
> 'I don't know ... Tell the others that I am fine.' (86–7)

Now, what that does not answer, is: who lost the bet? Who is going to buy condoms? What is sex? Penetration? Coming? After all, you cannot deny that masturbation is sex. And then, after a few weeks, Laila starts complaining that her period is late. 'How come? What did you do really?' But Laila is incapable of detailing what happened. Anyway, a urine test, in Yasmin's name, is the end of it. They join each other for a meal of noodles, as they did when they were at school. But since they have grown up, the noodles have lost their flavor.

Apart from such delightful stories, the book is full of interesting snippets and metaphors, often plainly sexual, or merely alluding to sex. What about the simile, 'Father's tears trickled down his face, very slowly from the two corners of his eyes, as if he was restraining his scream at the point of orgasm. An extraordinary relief' (36).

Comment

The intriguing quality of the novel is the convincing mesh of two unlikely themes: the brutality of the New Order and the sexual preoccupations of four women friends. Thanks to Ayu's choice of words, the sex is never crass, yet always explicit. To the Indonesian public, this came as a shock; women—even men—are not supposed to be open about their intimate urges. According to New Order doctrine, women are to serve male needs, and should shut up. Anything else is scandalous. None the less, Indonesian women have begun to claim the right to their own bodies and to their sexuality, and they will probably run way ahead of men who still need to emancipate themselves from the golden cage of their privilege. After so many years of stultifying patriarchal rhetoric, it is most refreshing that Ayu Utami's voice can be heard.

LUALHATI BAUTISTA, *CHILD, CHILD... HOW HAVE YOU BEEN MADE?* (1983)[2]

As with *Saman*, Lualhati Bautista's story is set against a background of unsavory violence. Presidential detention orders, a military run wild, truncheon-wielding police, systematic crimes against humanity, 'salvaging,'[3] and even the killing of Aquino provide the backdrop for the novel's main character, Lea. The abuses of the Marcos days impelled protest—and thus emancipation. Still, she has more to protest against, as becomes clear from the preamble to the book, which was added as an afterthought.

These first pages, which she edited out of her earlier *Dekada '70*, treat 'The Meeting of God with Amanda Bartolome.' Upon leaving this world, Amanda knows that nobody will remember her as she is or was, because she does not even know herself. So, when asked who she is, she can merely answer by her name. This annoys God. 'You do not even know your name! Bartolome ... that's your husband's.' Yes, that is true. It is Julian's and our children's name, 'and now that I'm dead I feel as if I am an outsider to the family I left down below' (iii–iv).

'But Sir, everybody knows me as Amanda Bartolome.'
'If you will not say your name, I'll send you down!'
'Yet, why is it so important? When I was born, they called me Amanda. My family name was inherited from my father. Why, for once, not from my mother?'
'Well, dear, that is how it should be. You see, it's a man's world. And to be a legal human being, you need your father's surname.'
'Suppose, though, that I am somebody else's child? Then I shouldn't have the right to the name of my mother's husband!'
'Now wait, do you believe in that gossip?'
'I'm not spreading gossip ...'
'In your mother's time, there were no women having children by other men, right?'
'Of course there were. Only, women did not acknowledge having somebody else's child. These days, we are more straightforward.'
'Now, that will be my thought for the day.'
'Perhaps you think that women in the past had no sexual fantasies?' (iv–v)

At this, God blushes as Julian would do, and directs the exchange back to the subject of the name, whereupon Amanda replies:

'What's so important about that name? When you made me, you made me a second-rate being without a mind of my own, without essence, without guts, without conscience!'
To this God protests, 'You are aware enough. You know that you know nothing!'
Talk about male chauvinist pigs! (v–vi)

Male chauvinist pig or not, it does show that God is right: it is a man's world. Besides, God is always right, and does not need to consult anybody when he decrees his presidential commands. He is the very symbol of brains, guts and power, and cannot but be male. That is why he set apart the roles of men and women.

God's son, Christ, is the kind of man who drives you crazy. He is brave and heroic, prepared to die for the country. Meanwhile God's spouse, the Virgin Mary, is of unequaled goodness. She does not contribute anything to history but kneeling and praying. The girlfriend of God's child, Magdalena, is credited by the church as the woman who washed Christ's feet—and not just with water but with scent! And the kerchief of that stray woman, Veronica, with which she wiped Christ's sweat, is carried along in every procession. (vi–vii)

Can it really be true that women in those days did not think or get angry? That they did not protest when their men were 'salvaged' by the military? Did they only weep and never scold? So much is certain that, beginning with the story of Israel, it has been propounded that women cry only when their men suffer, that they wipe sweat, that they comfort and console. There is nothing against their doing these things when appropriate, but women also think, get angry, and have things to say. Perhaps they have even more to say than men, given that they have been oppressed and bullied for so long.

The story begins at little Maya's graduation ceremony—she has just finished kindergarten. The tots are suffering in the heat, dressed up as they are in gown and mortarboard, and appear to be far less serious about the affair than their parents and teachers. The function continues with the 'Miss Kinder' pageant. Lea is not in favor of such things, but since Maya insisted on participating, she was allowed to do so. Lea's philosophy is that people, and this includes children, have the right to make their own choices in life. Then again, at Maya's age children are still dressed by their parents. Thus: no make-up on a child's face; no elaborate frilly dresses. Just be yourself, that should be good enough. And when her turn comes, Maya recites

> Mother's stomach is big and round.
> 'What's that,' Ojie asks his mama.
> 'A ball? A basketball?'
> 'No. Something else'
> 'Can I play with it?'
> 'No. But it is quite something.'
> 'What is it then, mama?'

'A surprise. A surprise.'
When the surprise came out, it was me!
'How can a ball become Maya?'
To which mother promptly laughed,
'When you grow up, Ojie, you'll know!' (8)

Ding, Maya's father, is startled. The school principal exclaims, '*Que barbaridad!*,' but the audience applauds and laughs. Therefore, Maya wins the pageant, not only as an honor student, but as the only one who behaved as a real child, yet full of pose and conviction. Ding is overjoyed.

Ding was the first man to show some sympathy—easily mistaken for love—when she and her son, Ojie, had been left behind when her husband, Raffy, took up a job at a mine in a remote area of a faraway province.[4] Not much later, she was pregnant. In that way she became Mrs. de Lara as Ojie's mother, Mrs. Gascon as the mother of Ding's daughter Maya, and Lea Bustamente all by herself, which, throughout the narrative, leads to some riotous confusion. Yet, unlike Amanda Bartolome, she knows full well who she is, and disagrees with the 'men's world' idea.

The experience of sexuality, and the confusion that occurs when love enters into the matter, is an important theme throughout. It is squarely faced when, after the celebrations of Maya's success, Lea feels hot and horny. Why, so all of a sudden? Perhaps it is Ding's hovering about her. In contrast to Raffy, who would be all over her like an octopus, Ding just becomes very quiet. He is always that way when he wants sex, yet the signal he sends out is so clear you feel it inside. Anyway, isn't it nice to have somebody around to do it with if you want to?

Still, why is Ding so shy? There is nothing to be ashamed of. When you are man and wife, then say what you want. It's not difficult, is it? 'Come on, up to the bedroom. Let's make love.' So simple. It is not as if you are declaring war. But Ding does not take any initiative. So Lea proposes, 'Shall we lie down?' 'Mama wants me to come home' (23–4). What a man—still so tied to mother's apron strings that he won't even give it to me when I need it.

After many years—Ojie is eleven—Lea is called by Raffy at her office. All at once, she feels nervous, worried, afraid, happy, eager ... How many years has it been since they last met? About the time she got pregnant with Maya. They broke up because each of them had their pride and self-respect. Each of them wanted to develop themselves first, which reflected on their relationships.[5] Yet now, over the phone, their last meeting comes to mind. She had to explain that she was with Ding, that she needed to make love. 'I must do it with him because you left me!' (41).

At their first meeting, they immediately get involved with each other again. They will meet once more, with Ojie. Then, hesitantly, 'Lea, I also have a spouse. Three months pregnant now. We're happy' (47). Lea's world collapses.

Does lovemaking have anything to do with love? It is a necessity, a force driving us, connected with all sorts of fantasies, and sometimes a means to let the adversities of the day evaporate. In meeting Raffy, she muses whether he also remembers those evenings they undressed each other, often down to each other's soul—those days that they were necking and petting and caressing and clashing and bickering and yelling ... but in the end making love (44).

When you go by novels, making love is imagined as the most artistic scene in the world, while in practice—let's be honest—it is done in the most awkward positions. When they describe the feelings, it is all about happiness, completeness, fulfillment, while all of us should know that having feelings for somebody else has little to do with good sex. Sometimes, often, it is a mere craving of the body (69).

When Lea is back from meeting Raffy, she makes love with Ding as a kind of revenge at Raffy for making Elinor pregnant. With Ding all over her, she thinks about Raffy going all over Elinor, about his kissing her hair, her eyes, her mouth, her neck, breasts, stomach, and lower still. Then, while they are still nestled together, Lea cries silently; Ding also is soundless. 'How come that man is so quiet?' Then Lea chides herself, 'Can't you think anything nice about Ding? Because Raffy is around, you belittle him. Haven't you ever been happy with him? After all, without Ding, no Maya. Then, I could have had a child with somebody else, perhaps even with Raffy! I'm the sort of woman who will look for a man when she is without.'

'Do sleep.'
'No—I want, one more.'
'Whaaat?'
'Like with beer. One more please!'6
Ding laughs, and they begin making it one more. But like a while ago, again she does not come (71).

Ding is unreliable as far as the children are concerned. He's simply not there when needed, spending much time at his mother's. He is argumentative, a whiner, and often a bore. Little cause for wonder, therefore, that Lea starts fantasizing about Johnny, a colleague with whom she takes the occasional business trip upcountry. She begins to call regularly to ask for his assistance around the house. Then a golden opportunity seems to arise: the two of them are included in a fact-finding mission that is to stay overnight in cold and fanciful Baguio City! Lea is excited, and in her daydreams scenes of romantic fulfillment unfold. She wants to know how Johnny makes love, what it would be like with him. She doesn't feel guilty at all about this. She is not ashamed of her feelings; she accepted them. She is a woman, neither black nor white, neither bad nor good ... she is a woman free from the chains of inhibitions and pretensions.

In the morning they will leave for Baguio, Ding is not there. Who's going to take care of the children? She rushes to their school, gets them out of their classes, drops them off at Elinor's, who cannot but accept them, even though she is nine months pregnant. In the taxi to the office she fantasizes. 'Who of them will open up to the other, who will be the first? They will be far and free from their family lives in Manila ... she will be free to proposition him. And is Johnny ... is he also thinking about how he will seduce her? Perhaps he'll say, 'Lea, I love you,' because men cannot just invite a woman to make love. He has to flatter her first, and even risk being slapped because of it.' Arriving at the office, all are about to board—save Johnny. He is inside, working on some reports.

'Aren't you coming?'
'Why? Sister Ann will fill in for me.'
It is as if heaven and earth close in on Lea (157).

Lea's ruminations are delightful. Upon meeting Elinor, she cannot avoid comparing. Elinor is not a striking beauty. Her skin is lighter, yes, and she is bigger. More importantly, she does not look like Lea at all. That can't be possible? 'I am Raffy's type.' She feels unsettled at the thought that Raffy could be attracted to her for her own sake. Similarly, in the case of Johnny, she tries to understand the situation from her own point of view: Johnny avoided going to Baguio. He is not just after sex; he thinks about the consequences. Basically, he is honorable. He does not want to take advantage of my weaknesses. He does not want to betray a fellow man. Again, the idea that she plays no role in Johnny's fantasies is disturbing, thus needs to be rationalized. Perhaps she has lost her *appeal*. Indeed, she is over thirty, with two children, and not too beautiful. Well, still attractive, but not like an eighteen-year old. Besides, her stomach shows many scratches. 'I am pitiable. My husband has a new spouse. The one I live with is seemingly through. The one I targeted is not interested. Yet, I want sex.'

On the way to Baguio, she challenges Sister Ann,

'Do you ever think about love? I do not mean the love for God. Neither for mankind. I mean real love. The love a man feels for a woman, a woman for a man. Those who do it together. Even though you are a nun, you're a woman, too. Why would you consider natural acts as sin? Sister Ann, when I am lonely and sad—and I feel very sad when there is no man in my life—then I am very conscious of men. I watch them all. With almost all of them, I'll consider what kind of lovers they are. The only one I am not considering is my father.' (161–2)

After a minor accident, Ojie and Maya need to spend a night at the hospital where their respective fathers meet each other. It does not take long before the two of them team up in castigating Lea's shortcomings as a mother. Why are men like that when women who share a lover fight each other tooth and nail? Lea decides to leave the children with their dads at the hospital. When she gets home, and just when she needs a shoulder to cry on, Johnny rings. Lea wants to meet and discuss her frustrating experience.

Those women of two-timing men are justified in fighting. They not only imagine themselves with their lover, but they also imagine the other woman doing the same thing right before their eyes. That's intolerable. But Johnny seems to agree with Raffy and Ding. What's wrong, really? Anyway, being disgusted with her two 'husbands' makes Johnny all the more attractive to Lea. 'I want to do it with you' (193).

This startles Johnny, who wonders whether Lea has gone crazy, or lost all sense of shame. Challenged, Lea tries to explain herself, but Johnny shouts her down. This makes him feel bad. He wants to console Lea. He puts an arm around her shoulder. A little later they kiss. A little later still, they find themselves at an hotel—after all, Lea is a woman ... Johnny is a man (194).

While sex and its fantasies play an important part throughout the narrative, it is especially rich in the descriptions of Lea's often passionate feelings for the two most important men in her life. Being with a man is no simple matter. Being a single-mother's child is no easy matter either. Besides, educating children 'freely,' acknowledging their rights, personalities, wishes and decisions may be vexing for everybody concerned. In a final meeting with Raffy (Ding has already left her for somebody else), Lea vows that she still loves him but that, at that time, it was necessary to leave each other, 'If I had submitted to you, I would probably have lost myself. Will you be happy with a woman without a self?'; 'Yes, I also love Ding. Without the two of you, there would be no Ojie and no Maya'; 'No, I have no new partner yet. But when I do, rest assured that I'll love him' (230).

> 'Can you love me one more day? Perhaps we'll never meet again ... let me borrow one more day. To celebrate our crazy, our wild days, that time that was full of hopes and without truth. When I was a present for you, and you a gift for me.' (231)
>
> It's exhilarating to play the dangerous game. It's walking on the edge of melancholy and gloom, too. 'Thank you (Raff).' They embrace again, kiss each other again. The eyes, the nose, the mouth, the neck. One more. There is still time. Don't leave me yet. It's still early. Let's go on. Some nights should not see the dawn. (232)

Comment

The author presents the picture of a new, modern woman. Lea ('Lioness') is both very feminine and a go-getter; she needs men—'for us women, men are the most delicious partakers of the body, the mind and the heart' (vii)—as much as she needs to unfold her talents and personality. Besides, she is very aware of what she wants. She separated from her husband when she was threatened with becoming a full-time housewife, merely serving in bed and in the kitchen. To her, her work at Human Rights Watch is at least as important as being lover, wife, and mother. Perhaps even more so. Time and again it is asserted that a job outside, being part of society, is the highroad to self-realization. You have to will it, to consciously choose for that fulfillment.

From beginning to end, the novel is a cornucopia of fine observations about Filipino life that gain clarity through their juxtaposition with prevailing hypocrisy, customs, and pretense. These observations concern the legality of children, prevailing morality, the family name, what children are or are not supposed to know, the construction of the men's world, women who derive their whole identity from their husbands, empty gossip, and parents who appropriate their children by staking their own standing on school results. The author chides the twin tendencies of avoiding real-life issues by hiding in ceremony and empty talk, and of upholding taboos and norms for the sake of peace, quiet, and personal safety. Children should be brought up freely, and be respected as personalities in their own right. Yet, the question implied by the book's title is never answered: one day they'll know. You cannot understand everything at once, and in spite of Lea's drive for openness and honesty, her relationship to men and to her body remains fraught with emotions and irrational enigma.

SUCHINDA KHANTAYALONGKOT, *AS IF DANCING WITH THE KAPOK FLOWER* (1993)[7]

The enigmatic title of this collection of short stories contains a subtle hint to the most powerful symbol of adultery in Thai underworld mythology. There, in hell, all those who took sexual liberties are supposed to be punished by being forced to climb the thorny kapok tree known as the *ton ngiw*. This scene is very familiar to most Thais since it is often vividly represented on temple walls.

The use of the word *ngiw* would be too obvious a reference. The words in the title do not refer to a tree, but to a flower, and its genus is not the *ngiw* but the *nun* (pr. 'noon'), not the red but the Java cotton tree. Yet, the association is clear and has been commented upon by the author in the preface to the third edition. A free translation of the title could, therefore, well be read as 'dancing with sex.'

In three prefaces—one to every printing—the writer explains her intentions. The original introduction explains that the text is driven by a suffering from loneliness. Writing the stories of her first collection, *The lonely heart*, had not yet soothed the author's pain, neither does she expect to be cured by her present writing. Still, she refuses to see herself as being confined to herself, as if being secluded in oneself were the normal condition of existence. There must be hope for all those lonely hearts out there—and then, when loneliness has been vanquished 'we can talk about another subject that is equally boring.' For the time being, though, the book is dedicated to 'the lonely girl.'

In the second prologue she reiterates that she sees writing as a means to sort out private matters. Why write about sex, and why so openly— why tempt the limits of morality—as if sleeping with men, or sex for that matter, were the simplest thing in the world? There are no trivial things in this world. Everybody suffers, and she happens to find fulfillment in being engrossed in her suffering. It helps her personally, and even if the conclusions reached have been reached by others a thousand times over, for her it is a confrontation with her own experiences that she has to face by herself, like any individual has to. In facing the problems of sex and the distress of a cold and lonely heart, writing and explaining herself is the right medicine.

The third exposition states that travel is a means to escape from the boredom of routine and of being tied to a certain place. But does it solve the problem? No, upon coming back, we will be tired again, nauseated by ourselves. The same seems to hold for love and sex. The more you are preoccupied with these, the more unsolvable the problem becomes. And still, the key to fulfillment lies there. Love and sex have everything to do with relating to each other, with happiness. Just don't say that being obsessive about sex is bad. All of us are rotten; all of us stink. And the *ngiw* tree, she maintains, is different from the *nun* flower: the first is about adultery, the second about enjoying sex.

After these heavy-hearted considerations, one would not expect a light read. She is at her best when focusing on the sexual act and associated fantasies. Apart from that, most stories are strained and artless. They are about lust; loneliness; whether to have sex when you have your period; having two, even three lovers simultaneously; casual sex driven by solitude; spontaneous meetings far away from home that inevitably lead to the mattress; contemplating the flow of melancholy ('blue river'), then being temporarily relieved in bed with a foreigner whom she knows she will never meet again; fantasies about such meetings that, alas, do not lead to passionate sex; the refusal to sleep together when the party is over; Thai women who are amazingly free when with white men; the hatred originating from being refused and dismissed; the bachelor who prefers liquor to a wife, being unable to reach out to anyone and depressingly handicapped; a man being raped by a go-getting woman; an intriguing fantasy in which images fuse with reality. So, let us pick from the stories that I found most interesting.

The collection opens with 'Lust.' For unclear reasons, the story's protagonist drops by her former boyfriend who has stopped tidying his room since she left him. The place is in a mess and very dirty. This tickles her housewifely urges, and by the end of the day she is so tired that she decides to sleep there. To sleep, and definitely not to make love. When, a little later, he gets on the bed, too, her resolve dissolves in a jiffy. He crawls all over her like a boa, slowly and tenderly. Why hurry, it's as enjoyable as the first time, and yet so familiar as if they never broke up.

He holds her firmer, pressing their bodies together, fondling and kissing, again and again—everywhere, in all places, tenderly like the flow of water, refreshing like a breath of wind. Embarrassment and objections, the past and her self-defenses, all flow away, and she can no longer tell right from wrong. Why bother?

> He bares her top and kisses her nipples. He remembers that she likes it, although not always. Yet, this time, it's fine. In the past this caressing and kissing became a bore after we fell out of love. Intimate contact

became a nuisance when it happened too often, but now, for people who have separated, it is not bad at all (26).

Now she thinks of it, he really is a good lover. 'He is better than all the men I made love with.' She pulls off his sarong, feeling the refreshment of the water of love. He is always wet in this sense, always willing, and today, she is willing, too.

He now fully undresses her, and his mouth moves down her body until she stops him. She, on her part, will not even touch his weapon. She knows that it is quite unnecessary because, when horny, he ejaculates readily. He handles her powerfully yet tenderly. Has she ever found any other man to make love with so nicely? He knows that she dislikes roughness. She hates pain, and while there are some women who fully enjoy it, 'I, for my part, I don't like that today's pleasures spill over into feeling all sore in the days to come.'

He is ready for it—but is she? Well, OK, but she cannot help fantasizing about the other men with whom she did it. Meanwhile, he penetrates her, little by little, in order not to hurt her too much. He starts groaning and purring with pleasure. Does his abandon mean that he gets much deeper satisfaction than she does? Is she envious because of it? Of course not. It is fine that her body can give him so much delight—she lends it to him for a while, but keeps her heart to herself. Still, she enjoys his lovemaking, and to reciprocate she decides to get on top and play the active role. As she does this he seizes her and presses her forcefully to his body. She wants to push him off, but he holds her firmer still until he comes and relaxes. 'Before she was suffocated, he came, and she felt relieved.' "I am happy that you came back." She does not tell him that she did not come back at all, but when he keeps kissing and embracing her, she cannot refrain from asking, "How was it?" "Tops!" 'Well, it's fine that he still has good hopes even though she does not' (27–8).

The narrative perspective is reversed in 'The story of a young man.' A very go-getting female colleague has succeeded in carrying him off—drunk—from the party, and he is amazed to wake up in her bed. 'This is not what I want. Luckily, I'm still dressed, so nothing has happened.' Well, nothing has happened yet, because she is also awake and set on kissing, cuddling, and undressing him. Being very experienced, she knows how to get out of him what she wants, and if his little brother is still reluctant to rise, she sucks him with great appetite, as if it were the most delicious thing in the world. He remains convinced that he really does not want her, and keeps thinking about his girlfriend. 'She has never touched me below the navel, she is most reserved about touching, let alone sex' (183). So, while his abductress gets her share, he does not really feel part of the proceedings. As a result, when his girlfriend is back in town, he can honestly answer her question on whether 'they were sharing love when sleeping together' with 'No.'

Her most convincing story is 'Deceptive image.' At a flea market, a lone woman finds a full-length mirror for her apartment. A wrapped picture gets thrown into the bargain. The chauffeur she buys from is a friendly, obliging man who is her age. He helps in taking the things to her flat, then leaves.

She is happy to have such a big mirror. 'How would it be if I could enter it? What world is on the other side of the mirage?' When she unwraps the extra, she finds that she has come home with the framed, drawn portrait of a young man, naked to where the edge cuts through his body. 'Who is he, pictured in the past? The present?' 'Wouldn't it be nice to have him as my sleeping partner?' Her mind racing, she masturbates. The portrait is alive, he is there—on the other side of the mirror? (162–3).

Then she recognizes the naked young man. It is that driver who helped her. She searches the streets day after day—he must be somewhere. It is as if she is chasing a breath of wind. Then, one day, she is greeted, 'Hello, *tyay*,[8] what are you looking for today?' It's him. She becomes excited, then bashful, because she has always been thinking about him in the nude (165–6). Later on, she invites him home to make sure that the portrait in her room is really him. After a long hesitation, he answers with a smile—like the one in the frame.

At her place, he starts caressing her, until she pushes him back, 'Yes, he is like the portrait!' Even more so when he undresses—he's great. After a first round of lovemaking, she makes his weapon iron-hard again—and he admonishes her not to be so rough. He fondles and kisses her all over, and invites her to reciprocate. Tenderly, his tongue starts running through her mouth. 'Your mouth has the fragrance of a milk toffee.' Smoothly, he slips into her. 'Wow, how nice to be inside you, *tyay*.' 'Would the young man in the picture do it the same way or is he one and the same?' 'Tell me that you are the man in the portrait' 'Whaaat?' Turning around, he looks in the mirror. 'Look in the mirror—that's where we are together. The fellow in the portrait is still in his former place. I am the one who is real,' upon which he thrusts into her again, but she fails to respond. 'Don't you feel anything, or are you thinking of that fellow?' (169–70).

He gets up and stands in front of the picture, smiling at it while extending his hand. The two men fuse, become one. The picture is no longer a picture. She feels excited and confused, almost unaware of herself, and when he enters her again, she fully relaxes in the flow of making love—that cadence—melting and diffusing, becoming one flesh, one person, one voice, one orgasm. Fully at peace, she glances at the picture—it has changed into her portrait.

Comment

Often Suchinda's stories are bluntly erotic, bordering on pornography. The way she treats sex, with the notable exception of the delightful fantasy I described above, is businesslike. 'Borrowing each other's body'; 'It's like food, you have to eat'; 'It is a medicine against the malady of loneliness.' In many stories, sex is a lonely venture, a one-partner affair, the other being inhibited, reluctant or passive while letting the other have it. And anyway, always, in the end you are alone again. Basically, the tales are an endless lamentation about life's unsatisfactoriness, about the human condition. Love is elusive and intimately linked to sadness, or, as she puts it in the story 'The unfinished tidying up,' 'There is an intimate relationship between nightmares, sex and death.'

This depressing conclusion may have to do with her being a Sino-Thai Catholic. From early on, she was taught that the body is the temple of God, according to whom—as the Church says—all forms of sex excepting one are sin, and virginity is a virtue. On several occasions, Suchinda presents the view that, once desecrated, her sleeping with another man makes no difference any more. The only thing that remains the same are the problems—nothing is easy, suffering prevails, and sex does not offer an escape. The 'dancing' of the collection's title resembles the *danse macabre* most of all.

Even so, her writings have a certain impact. They challenge the prevailing moral complacency in a society where illicit affairs apparently fall beyond the scope of ordinary ethics, escaping as it were from its measures. This is precisely the point of the back-cover blurb of Suchinda's collection:

> With these erotic short stories, Suchinda pulls, softly and with tender hands, at the moral nerves of those who are serious about the ethics of Thai literature, that is to say, the ethics of Thai society—a closed society. Some will experience this soft pulling as rough jerks because of the masks we wear to cover our minds, to hide and keep ourselves from the scrutiny of others while probably never showing our true selves. Perhaps those who are serious about ethics oppose those who are honest.

COMMENT

The three books reviewed here constitute a challenge, not only to prevailing morality, but also to the widespread culture of machismo—and thus of male privilege and treating sex as a commodity—in Southeast Asia. As such they are emancipatory, liberating literature. They open up discussion, and go against the grain of the officially or religiously propagated American-style, middle-class 'family values.' The authors belong to that class, that much is certain, but they definitely do not buy the arguments for monogamy, housewifization and female subservience that are popular in state ideology.

Interestingly, we do not find a trace of Western-style feminism and its basic suspicion of anything male. When they problematize and explore love and sex, its pitfalls and deceptions, they do it open-mindedly while explaining that it is as much a part of the life of women as of anybody else's, and that we had better live with it as a prominent part of our nature, to which all of us have an equal right.

Both Ayu Utami and Lualhati Bautista have situated their stories in extremely violent environments. Their expositions on violence may have been induced to demonstrate its ordinariness, but also the need for females to tackle it. It is no far-fetched hypothesis that women, being lowest in the pecking order, are the ultimate sufferers of violence and oppression. In Lualhati's novel, the protagonist's drive for emancipation has a clear relationship to the brutality pervading national life. In Ayu Utami's book, the link is less explicit, but the setting of the Indonesian segment in an atmosphere of fear and abuse, arbitrariness and callousness, provides a very convincing backdrop for the message of women's liberation.

Incidentally, the three authors are all Catholic. In Indonesia these constitute a small percentage of the population, and in Thailand they are a tiny minority. Catholicism, on the other hand, is part of the Filipino way of life, and an aspect that does not need elaboration. Lea's ways are just a protest to bring that way of life into focus. But in the first two cases, intriguingly, it is Catholic women who are the first to explore sex and love. In their formative years, the load of sin and guilt is such that they simply have to face it if they want to struggle free from its impositions. This is clear from Ayu Utami's opening passage where Laila muses about the birds and the bees, and how something natural can possibly be sin. Then, it is also made clear by Laila's reluctance. To her, virginity remains a treasure. Or one goes the way Suchinda depicts it: once the sacred barrier has been broken, one man follows the other. Laila still wants to believe in pure love, while Suchinda's protagonists have given up on that.

The elaboration of the subject is as divergent as the quality of the narratives. Lualhati Bautista received a well-deserved shared first prize for her rather straightforward, witty novel. Her Lea has been squarely pictured, cast after the model of a modern woman. Ayu Utami's first prize was the reward for a very complex narrative in which not only time and place perspectives are juggled, but in which we also find four female views on the subject of love and sex, combined with a generous dose of humor. Both authors pose a challenge, or rather, address a complex of problems. They enhance reality by enlarging, distorting, and adding to it. They open the subject by making it imaginable; in doing so they offer their readers the fantasizing they need to escape from the cages of their prejudices.

Suchinda will probably never be awarded a prize. Her straightforward and humorless descriptions of sex as a commodity focus inward on the loneliness and suffering of a single woman whose attempts to free herself result in ever more depressing incarceration. Without love or passion, sex becomes a neurotic experience that, like imbibing too much liquor, leaves one with a hangover. However, she has opened a few more windows on the exceedingly complex role of sex and love in our lives.

Of course, it is not my task to engage in literary criticism. The purpose of this chapter is to draw attention to the fact that in Southeast Asia—as anywhere else—things are changing and in flux. What was unspeakable not so long ago has come out into the open. Fascinatingly, the initiative to pioneer the subject is with women who are, expectedly, suppressed in the machismo-dominated cultures of gender in Southeast Asia. They assert the right to themselves, not just to their bodies. However sweet they may smile, they want to be and are more than the adjuncts of men. The books, certainly those by Lualhati and Ayu, may therefore also be read as cultural criticism, or as criticism of the morality that precludes honesty. By piercing the prescriptions of culture, all of them arrive at the body and its drives. In doing so, I noted to my satisfaction that at that level women are no less sexist than men.

SECTION III: THE PRESENT

CHAPTER 8

SOCIETY DIAGNOSED

Authors of social-critical novels can be extremely carping of their societies. They highlight tendencies in social life they are displeased with, and want to open the eyes of their readership to see their condition for what it is. Often, however, the images they evoke are exaggerated and one-sided. This notwithstanding, the pictures they paint also hold truth, and may pinpoint particularly worrying developments that should, in one way or other, be attended to by government, corporate business, or civil society. The authors to be discussed steer clear of giving advice on how to remedy the sick body politic they diagnose, yet hope that a shock of recognition will bring people to their senses so that they start clearing the mess they are in. In this sense, such novels may serve as appeals to bring civil society to life.

The first novel to be discussed is by Wimon Sainimnuan. Since publishing his *Snakes* in 1984, he has gradually built a reputation of 'piercing and destroying the deceptive mask Thai society presents these days while fully exposing its despicable figure' (cover blurb for *Khokphranang* (1994)). For the time being this 'piercing and destroying' culminated in the monumental *The Lord of the Land* (1996), here to be reviewed.

In the Philippines, national artist Francisco Sionil José holds a very comparable position. His many works, written in English, tend to have clear historical dimensions. They invariably address both the flaws of Philippine society and the Filipino's quest for a just and moral order. The book to be scrutinized here, *Viajero: A Filipino novel*, was conceived as a kind of *magnum opus*, which is also clear from the dedication of its second edition (1998) to 'the memory of Jose Rizal, on the centenary of his martyrdom.'

For Indonesian society, two works will be considered. The first, with the enigmatic title *Not Waiting for Your Applause; Without Condolences* (2000), is by Sindhunata. This prolific author is an Indonesian Jesuit priest who has been trained in German philosophy. It is this combination that may explain his predisposition to moral evaluation. To a certain extent he shares this inclination with Umar Kayam whose analyses, however, tend to have more historical and sociological depth; so too his *Deviations* (1999), the sequel of *The Priyayi* (1992), that together span the length of the past century.

WIMON SAINIMNUAN, *THE LORD OF THE LAND* (1996)[1]

> Power is the most spectacular, beguiling
> and central manifestation of Thai life ...[2]

This 957-page novel is, according to the cover blurbs, 'a novel of these times' and 'an account of power and the victory of the new way of life.' It promises to reveal the nature of power, to deal with false power, and the falsehood of power itself. The book's subtitle reads, *(The Medium 2)*.

The Medium, together with some other of Wimon's stories, is set in the subdistrict Khokphranang that serves, according to the author, as a microcosm of life in Thai society.[3] This life is not beautiful; it is ugly. In introducing his earlier works, Wimon explains that writing about it is his means of keeping his sanity in these crazy times in which people abundantly demonstrate that craving is the root of suffering; it leads people ever deeper into the condition of greed, anger, and misguidedness/delusion. In *The Lord of the Land* the author wants to expose this through a narrow focus on the craving for power.

The story begins five years after the events related in *The Medium*. That short novel deals with the struggle for power between Headman Thongma and Kham, the medium of Chaopho Phra Sai. Ever since Kham became the servant of that powerful deity, he could bank on the respect, and the offerings, of his fellow villagers. Toward the end of the tale, he has outwitted Headman Thongma who leaves the subdistrict to escape the possible vengeance of the relatives of the man he is suspected of having killed through an intermediary—his half-witted, illegitimate son, Bük. With his foremost rival out of the way, Kham exclaims, 'I am the *chaopho*!!!'

Five years on, Kham appears to be doing very well. His modest farmhouse has grown to become an impressive complex of big, stone buildings, with a vast, concrete parking lot in front. At the entrance to the compound, we not only find a Roman arch, but also an obtrusive sign reading 'Residence of Chaopho Kham.' The source of his wealth is clear: many people believe in Chaopho Phra Sai and seek the deity's advice, tonics, cures, and blessings. Not just the villagers honor the powerful spirit in their midst. His reputation has spread far and wide, and people come from all over to be present at the regular trance sessions at the residence. Most of them come from the city; they are civil servants and businessmen, army officers and politicians, Chinese and Thais, men and women—and all of them bring lavish offerings to the *chaopho*.

Kham is not the only religious entrepreneur in the subdistrict. The temple, too, is thriving ever since Venerable Father Nian took over as abbot. He was clever in enhancing the reputation of the main statue, 'The Man-eating Buddha.' This strange-sounding name refers to a temple thief who disappeared without a trace, save the blood on the lips of the effigy. When Abbot Nian discovered this awe-inspiring occurrence, he did not want it to happen again. He nailed up the image's mouth with a conspicuous tag.

The villagers themselves are not impressed. They need the temple to make merit, for cremations and other indispensable rituals, but they are neither proud of the temple's blatant prosperity, nor happy about it. The Venerable Chandra, its secretary, is a sly loan shark who justifies his rates as 'merit making.' Venerable Father Nian is well known for his ambition to become the subdistrict's biggest landlord. As in the case of Kham, the temple's many glittering additions mainly derive from well-to-do urban patrons.

When the story begins, we encounter Kham's former antagonist Thongma, this time as Venerable Uncle Thongma. He is on his way to pay Kham a stealthy visit in the dead of night. He has good reasons to drop by, because his wife and beautiful daughter Nongphanga live in the compound as Kham's protegees ever since he fled the scene five years ago. For the time being, however, he does not need to see them; he wants to come back to Khokphranang, and thus needs to know whether it is safe for him to do so. In other words, he needs Kham's, or rather Chaopho Phra Sai's advice in this matter.

The confrontation between the two adversaries is a fine sparring match with prestige at stake. It has already begun when the priest Thongma is confronted by the huge, defiant monitor lizard (symbol of baseness and bad luck) that lives around Kham's place, and then by Kham's self-appropriated title *chaopho*. The title is ambiguous. In ordinary Thai, a *chaopho* is a supernatural, a seat of 'sacred' power, and the title may thus indicate that Kham cunningly identifies himself with the deity people believe him to be the medium of. As a modern colloquialism, *chaopho* is also used for godfather, for locally powerful businessmen-politicians who can be extraordinarily influential in all affairs taking place in 'their' territory.

Doubtlessly, Kham has established himself as a most influential fellow who commands vast pecuniary resources and considerable sacred power. Does the Venerable Uncle believe in that power? He would rather not, but he is not so sure. He'll need to compromise if he wants to return to the subdistrict; he needs Kham's blessing. Upon meeting any priest, a layman is expected to pay respect, which Kham, as *chaopho*, squarely refuses to do. This is the more painful to Priest Thongma, because the former headman is about twice Kham's age. But then again, shouldn't any priest steer clear of that thriving world of animism and supernaturalism for which modern Thailand is famous?

When Thongma reveals his intention to seek residence at the local temple, Kham, unhappy with that prospect, warns him that his life is still in an inauspicious phase. To undo his bad luck he should sincerely pay respect to Chaopho Phra Sai. By truly submitting to the deity, it may 'wash off' Thongma's fate. Yet, such submission is not possible for a man of the cloth. Then, if you do not truly believe, and thus honor, the *chaopho*, how could he help you? Humbled, irritated, and vengeful Thongma takes his leave. The temple is his next stop.

At the temple, he meets with its secretary, the Venerable Chandra, to whom, in spite of their vast age difference, he must pay his respect. The secretary and the abbot are not really keen on having the former headman in residence. They change their tune, however, when they become aware of the Venerable Uncle's potential for acquiring land. They can exploit his rancor against Kham—who vies for the same plots—and the sense of obligation of Kamhaeng, Priest Thongma's driver and companion, who happens to be an expert broker in land.

Kamhaeng owes his life to Thongma since the latter rescued him after a gangland assassination attempt. Kamhaeng, therefore, has a heavy debt of gratitude to Thongma, and promises to assist him in trying to buy a certain plot in the subdistrict. Among themselves, they agree on sharing the brokerage fee, which at three percent, could amount to a considerable sum. Prices have skyrocketed because of Kham's persistent attempts at buying a plot of approximately one hundred hectares from the villagers who live in the fields at some distance from the subdistrict's center.

Kham has been successful in acquiring vast tracts of land stretching out from both sides of the river. Still, he wants more; he wants one unbroken estate, with a free view to the mountain range in the distance. To him, the small village in the fields is an eyesore. He is set on owning its land. He not only aspires to be *The Lord of the Land,* he also hopes to corner the market in order to eventually sell out to Thai and Japanese businessmen who want to develop a golf course there.

Both the temple and Kham approach the villagers, or rather their leader Khamplio, to talk about selling their land. Kham offers hefty amounts of money. The temple offers even more, half of it payable as a prestigious kind of indulgence 'of which future generations will be proud.' Under Khamplio, and with the wise advice of Old Man Khong, the villagers are neither interested in buying religious merit nor in selling their ancestral lands. They are a close-knit community, and because they may be threatened by closure of their only road link if either the temple or Kham can lay their hands on a certain piece of land, they have opted for a stategy of self-sufficiency to safeguard their independence.

With Khamplio and Old Man Khong, the village is a stronghold of virtue and all that is good in Thai rural ways. The people there are not given to superstitions, and thus do not honor seats of sacred power, such as a *chaopho.* They do not fall into the trap of Buddha business, and stay clear of the glittering grounds of Venerable Father Nian. Most of all, the money offered for their land does not impress them; they are so old-fashioned as not to be greedy. Even so, they are told that they will have to defend themselves against modernity. If they do not sell, others who surround them may. Then factories will be built that will pollute the water to the point that their agricultural way of life will be made impossible. Real estate developers will build suburban housing estates, and the area will eventually be foreclosed. Noise and stench will become unavoidable. Moreover, the District Officer is said not to like the villagers' policy of self-suffiency: 'You people are an obstacle to development.' Khamplio and his crowd are not fazed by these arguments, and thus, when Venerable Uncle Thongma confesses to priest Chandra that he has not made any progress in buying the land, he is advised 'to use other means.' Kham, too, has reached that conclusion.

One evening, Khamplio is seriously threatened by an unknown character: 'You sell, or else ...' Soon this becomes the talk of town. Kham, of course, acts the innocent party and proclaims his solidarity with his fellow villagers. So, whereas the priests seem safe in their saffron robes, they remember Thongma from the time he was the headman, and they know Priest Chandra as a ruthless character. Most villagers, therefore, point to the temple.

It turns out that this suspicion is justified. After the Venerable Chandra advised 'to use other means,' Thongma instructed Kamhaeng accordingly. The latter thought he could organize threats, and perhaps more, at a price. In case the gangland needed to be mobilized, his commission would be upped considerably, and Thongma's share would not be increased accordingly. Besides, an advance mobilization fee needs to be paid, which Venerable Uncle Thongma must negotiate with Priest Chandra first.

Then, one evening, Kham's bodyguard Lek ('Steel') shoots Khamplio at point blank range. Before that happens, they talk at length. During this conversation, Lek gets more and more upset and irritated by Khamplio's stoic calm, virtue, goodness, wisdom, and willingness to sacrifice. To understand why Lek can act as a cold-blooded murderer, we learn that he was commanded to kill in battle at the Laotian border. That was his duty. His conscience became like cold steel. After losing a leg, he became part of Kham's retinue, and his boss commanded him to execute his duty. By doing so, he hopes to strengthen the bonds of patronage and be rewarded with a plot of land in the future. 'All of us have to fight for ourselves. Being soft on others is stupid.' Kham is fully aware of what happened.

At Khamplio's cremation rites, Kham, for the first time in many years, shows up at the temple. It is a demonstration of power. With six cars, among them two Benzes, he makes a spectacular entry. He is impeccably dressed up as a brahmin, as the medium of Chaopho Phra Sai, and accompanied by a full retinue of dependents, among whom his wife, Kalong, and his suite of female assistants, stand out. They are the most prestigious people in the crowd, and attributed honor accordingly, stealing the limelight from the assembled clergy. While basking in their glory, they are careful not to behave arrogantly. 'We are all fellow villagers. We are friends.' Kham expresses his condolances to Sida, Khamplio's widow, and gives her a contribution to the rites that far exceeds expectations. His plea for her to accept it is moving. Kalong also feigns intimacy, and objects to Sida's sitting at her feet: 'We are all the same. Sit next to me.'

Everybody is impressed with Kham's demonstration of good neighborship. More and more people suspect the temple, especially Thongma, to be behind the killing. This feeling is enhanced by Kamhaeng's hiding from the police. Then, in a verbal contest with the clergy, who are there to perform the rites, Kham emerges as the winner. As the medium of Phra Sai, he proclaims that he knows the identity of the killer, but that Phra Sai will reveal this at a more opportune moment. The only one to see through Kham's bluff is Old Man Khong.

Understandably, the Venerable Chandra and the abbot are not amused. They advise Thongma to seek residence at another temple, to make himself scarce. His misadventures confirm the fate he carries and so, in saffron robes and all, he is finally willing to submit to Chaopho Phra Sai—or Kham, upon whom a henchman of the Venerable Uncle attempted to shoot that very morning. As expected, the *chaopho* is in no mood to forgive or undo the fate of the headman-turned-priest. The next day, Thongma has killed himself in his monk's cell.

Meanwhile, the villagers have elected new leaders. They vow to be as steadfast as Khamplio—to sacrifice their lives for their land, if necessary. The seeds of doubt have been sown, however. Besides, in a meeting with Kham, very interesting propositions are made, and in spite of his idealism, the new number one is not impervious to flattery and expensive inducements. Then, at night, the village cooperative storage is set on fire by two sinister types on motorcycles. Upon this, Kham shows his generosity and sympathy with their fate—and reiterates his offer of relocation. This breaks the resolve of most of them. In the following days, they dismantle their houses and start moving out. The only ones to remain behind are Sida and Old Man Khong. Kham is satisfied. He has broken their solidarity and knows that he can do so again to reclaim the territory that he has ceded them 'for generations to come.' He has become *The Lord of the Land*.

Ever since becoming Phra Sai's medium, Kham has developed into a very competent and cunning manipulator. He knows when to be friendly, when to flatter, when to be generous and, through his other manifestation, when to threaten, or have his way with women. He is acutely aware that all depends on credibility, on what people believe. What they believe is their truth. On that credulity, he builds. The villagers in the middle of the fields were hard to force into submission because they stuck to virtue, solidarity, Buddhist wisdom, and refused to accept the nonsense about supernaturals. Once they began to doubt, they were finished. The only one to see through Kham's game was Old Man Khong. All along he suspected Kham to be the evil genius—and he is certain after confronting Lek. Upon meeting Kham, it is clear that he indeed knows the facts of the matter. Kham is not impressed: 'OK, so be it!' He challenges the old man to tell everybody. 'Will they believe you, the voice of virtue?' And Old Man Khong knows that Kham is right, that Kham can speak with the voice of 'sacred' power, that he has all the money and insight to manipulate, that people want to believe him, that virtue is no match for might. 'It is not the truth that matters. What people believe to be true is true' (871–2).

Apart from land, Kham is after women—and in that endeavor he does not always get his way. In contrast to the impression conveyed by *The Medium*, his wife Kalong does not always accept his arguments. Deep down, she does not fully believe in the two personae. She knows her Kham too well, and in spite of her wealth, her jewelry, her status, she is vexed by Kham's open desire for young women. Of course, this Kham always denies. It is the *chaopho* who wants to be served by his female retinue and, in the secrecy of his possession chamber, the *chaopho*—or is it Kham—gets what he wants. Many women are even eager to be in the privacy of that chamber.

Outside that room, Kham does not enjoy that liberty, being watched and pestered by Kalong. When Kham dreams away while his feet are rubbed by an attractive girl, Kalong sends her off, and claims the right to massage her husband for all days to come. In turn, Kham grows very irritated. He is obviously better at manipulating the public than his wife. He says that the *chaopho* has ordered that his bodily vessel be well-treated and pampered—if not, the *chaopho* may grow vengeful up to the point of them being restored to their former poverty. Kham already thinks he has won, but Kalong remains obstinate about treating Kham's feet.

Toward the end of the narrative, Kham, for the first time, loses his cool. He wants to damn Kalong to hell—but then needs to be the *chaopho* rather than the irritated husband. Yet it is the husband who gets furious and who, in that state of mind, transforms himself into the *chaopho* who indeed threatens that Kalong will fall back into poverty, and who asserts his right that the young thing will massage his feet. We are not told what happened next, but as far as the dislocated villagers are concerned, 'The evacuees turned to see Kham leave in awe of his goodness and kindness, and in the certainty that from now on they could rely on him, and him alone, in their hour of need' (953).

Message and image

Wimon's writings are meant to stand as metaphors for life in present-day Thai society. They are also intended to illustrate Buddhist wisdom and point out how far current religious practice, and the monkhood, have strayed from the Noble Eightfold Path. In the introduction to *The Lord*, 'Power and Swindle,' he explains this position. In its first sentence, he maintains that in this world people find power the most fascinating of subjects. The presence of power as such, as a force pervading nature, is not in itself problematic. It becomes interesting when it inhabits individuals who may, as a result, do the most inane and bad things or, contrarily, do good. However, whether bad or good, all things that happen in this world are caused by power.

All people want power because they believe that it can get them what they want. Some people even believe this means that power equates with freedom. Anyway, if people want to have and exercise power, they need to accumulate it. This very drive is the cause of turmoil in this world, whether in politics, in the competition for honor and rank, or in establishing the pecking order of interpersonal relationships.

When power inhabits people, it shows its true colors. People who have it want more of it. Obviously, power is addictive. To this comes the illusion that people who are driven by power think that they are acting according to their own will. They plan their strategy, and are proud when they achieve more power because of it. What they do not realize is that they have become a means of their own scheming: they simply follow the logic of power. As a result, power does not afford freedom; it determines our actions. It chains us; we become its servant.

Why do people not recognize the true nature of power? Because they are stupid, they are ignorant. They do not even recognize the obvious. The drive for power originates in craving, and when that craving is in the heart, people will turn greedy and wrathful; they will be guided by false consciousness. As a result, they'll often demonstrate uncanny behavior. Guided by delusion, they are unable to tell true from false. They do not know the nature of things, and it is well nigh impossible in their condition to cultivate wisdom. Consequently, we need to probe what greed, anger, and delusion really mean if we want to escape from their fetters. In spite of all the knowledge in the world, we only have a most superficial understanding of what life is. Our schools only teach how to make a living—which just makes us greedy, wrathful, and ignorant. This very condition keeps us from ever reaching true happiness. It thus makes sense to investigate the real nature of power. Then we'll find out that it is mere illusion, *maya*, and delusion.

The story of Kham's unbridled desire to always acquire more land, to be the greatest in the subdistrict, has been written to bring these points home. In the narrative people are driven by greed for money and power; that is what modern times are all about. People are increasingly unaware of themselves and indulge in manipulating the gullibility of others even as they pull the wool over their own eyes. According to Kham himself, he is a good man. His dealing in land, whatever the means, is just buying and selling. His manipulation of others as the *chaopho* is merely helping people who suffer, who need a cure or advice. In a way, he not only feeds delusions to his patrons, but also to himself. In doing so, he is resisted by Kalong, his wife, who is less easily taken in—perhaps because she is jealous and, worse, because she does not fully believe in her husband's alter ego.

With the exception of Khamplio's villagers, every character in the book is a crook, and if not, extremely naive. The priests are no less wicked than Kham, and the degeneracy and Buddha business of many members of the venerable brotherhood of monks are, as seen in Wimon's earlier novel *Snakes*, among his favorite targets. The fact that such degeneration is possible roots in ignorance, delusion, and foolish beliefs that are held as truths.

Because of this insight, Wimon chides the Thais for their credulousness. They are everybody's dupe, and even seem to cultivate this trait as modern times take their toll. The worship of all sorts of venerable fathers (old monks), amulets and other seats of supernatural potency is visibly increasing these years, at the same time that more money is available to buy blessing. People easily attribute miracle-working powers to certain long-time monks, and their eventual cremations, often under the auspices of royalty, draw people in their hundred thousands.

Altogether, the author seems to underscore two points. The first concerns false consciousness. What people believe is true, and if they are inclined not to believe, you manipulate them until they do. The villagers from the middle of the fields are finally persuaded to enter modern life, and walk into Kham's trap to boot.

The second point is about the qualities of power. Power is the subject of its own logic, and that logic is amoral to the bone. It does not care how it is used or applied. It always drives those possessed by it to seek more, as money, as influence, and as associated honor and prestige. It is the driving force of modern times, of Buddha business, of money politics and Buffet Cabinets.

Power seems to be opposed to good sense, to morality, to justice. It pervades 'the new way of life'; its ever increasing influence assures the victory of that way. As a result, ordinary people will be more and more oppressed, humanitarianism will be replaced by ostentatious consumerism, 'the good, the true and the beautiful' will vanish. What remains are glittering temples and majestic residences whose inhabitants scheme and manipulate to obtain the objects of their greed. They compete, and because they always want more, they are never at peace. When power has its way, happiness disappears from this world. It bulldozes over morality. Against power, goodness cannot win. As in so many Thai stories, in the end power is triumphant and the good people are subdued, killed, of no consequence. In the end Kham celebrates victory, 'I am the lord of the land!!!'

F. SIONIL JOSE, *VIAJERO: A FILIPINO NOVEL* (1998)[9]

The traveler of this narrative is a Filipino orphan, the quintessential Filipino, journeying and questing for identity, searching up and down the length of history, migrating to all corners of the globe, looking for social justice and moral order. All of these are steady themes in José's fiction, and *Viajero* is an epic attempt to weave them together. The book, therefore, constitutes an exploration of Filipino-ness and the foundations of Philippine society.

The orphan, the traveler, is uprooted in the Second World War under Japanese occupation. His mother has disappeared; his father has probably been killed by soldiers shooting randomly into the crowd at the procession of the Black Nazarene in Quiapo. A kindly old man picks him up and takes him far away, high up the slopes of a mystical mountain. It is sheer Arcadia. Then stragglers rape and kill his new mother, Inang Mayang—who cannot hear, see or speak—and the old man. A black American captain rescues him and takes him to California where he grows up. The parallel with Philippine history is obvious.

In the far-off past, the islands were more than a pristine place often engulfed in warfare between its various townships and tribes. The people were great seafarers too, raiding and trading as far as China. Commerce with the Chinese flourished. There were astute headmen capable of making peace, of uniting people and territory. A civilization flourished. Spanish colonization obliterated it, raped it. Did America come to the rescue? No, it alienated the Filipinos further from their roots. Is there a living memory of the old days? Do people care to reminisce at all? Now, modernization is threatening to drive out the last vestiges of authentic Filipino being.

It is these thoughts that preoccupy the orphan Buddy—Salvador dela Raza—a prodigious scholar with a haunting interest in the history and evolution of his country and its people. It is a quest for origins, for memory, for identity. How is it possible that Filipinos can be so radiant with smiles when 'beneath their brown skin is lacerated flesh and a bleeding heart for their lives are truly melancholy and harsh'(7). They appear as hapless, uprooted wanderers everywhere in this world, fleeing their unhappy country to be able to make a living, no matter how perilous and demeaning. They are heroic.

Discovering, or is it untangling, history is an exciting endeavor that brings Buddy to all sorts of scholarly destinations, in the States, Mexico, Japan, Europe, and Spain most of all. Three centuries of Spanish rule have deeply affected the islands. The pursuit of history has its pitfalls, however, because 'all of us who are not white are imprisoned in the concepts that the white man made' (60). So, be alert and critical.

For example, what is the most enduring legacy of Spain? The Spaniards are a cruel people, and that is what they left behind, a tradition of cruelty, hypocrisy and greed. If some might think that Catholicism was their contribution to the Philippines, be aware that they are mistaken. Philippine Catholicism is an outrageous charade of worshipping wooden images. What passes for piety, penance, and prayer is the expression of having been viciously subjugated, of a people overwhelmed by force. As a result, people became infected by it, as exemplified by the elites who usually inherit the vices of their erstwhile masters. To a very large degree, these elites are mestizos who disdain the Indios, the ordinary population—yet, the latter are willing victims. They accept the prejudice against themselves. Filipinos are a vanquished people indeed (117).

Because of this, hypocrisy and posturing became part of the culture, best exemplified by the Propaganda movement of the wealthy *mestizo ilustrados* (students, intellectuals) in the 1880s in Spain. Later on, they appropriated the revolution and nationalism, compromised with the Americans. More recently, they expressed themselves, safely in America, through anti-Marcos rhetoric, to justify themselves and to seem sufficiently patriotic. Most of them were clear fakes, quasi-intellectual rejects mouthing revolution, professing nationalism, and blaming foreigners, especially America, for everything gone wrong in the Philippines while gorging themselves on American handouts. To be leftist, to espouse a cause, to be anti-Marcos, it became an opportune and happy profession.

The sham of it all! Is there honest-to-goodness nationalism, or is it just posturing? Is there any unity among Filipinos? Do they consider themselves a nation? It is big words, an exuberant inauguration, then lassitude and decay. When they organize, they soon split up because of their vaulting egos and competition for status. They are at their best when they just take care of their own affairs. Then they are willing to sacrifice and suffer, as modern-day drudges in the Saudian desert, as maids in Hong Kong, as seamen on Norwegian merchantmen, as nurses in the States, as entertainers in Japan. They are everywhere, from the fish canneries of Alaska to the brothels of Italy, fleeing their country, destroying their families for the security of the money their country is unable to provide.

The ruling class has a history of frustrating all initiatives to achieving cohesion and strength as a nation, as a society. It allies itself with whatever master is coming along, and grows fat on the sweat of others, mere peons. Why isn't the Philippines like Japan, or China? Is it because of the lack of a continuous tradition? Is it because of the havoc wrought by colonization? Is it because Filipinos have forgotten that they belong to Asia, that they have thrown away their past? All this is possible, but most of all it is the oligarchy, the real enemy of the people, that is to be blamed. The nation has been destroyed by fellow Filipinos.

Sometimes people argue that the absence of progress is due to the worldwide diaspora of Filipinos who, in their migration, have become the proletariat of the world. Yet, there is something even more debilitating going on. Look at all those at home whose talents are rotting and unused because they do not have the right connections, who are ignored by those in power who prefer to be served by their incompetent relatives and friends. Such is the tribal nature of Philippine society.

The tentacles of the powerful reach throughout society, spreading patronage and corruption. Even school teachers—shouldn't they be exemplary?—are corrupt. They pass students in return for a gift. The school principal plays favorites. Such is the nature of the immoralities that have crept in everywhere and that are destroying the country. Besides, to what use is all that distorted education? Enroll in any course, but as long as you are not connected, you'll end up among the 'educated unemployed,' fit to pursue the Filipino dream in America at best. Then, if you return to visit your country of origin, you'll be jumped on by thieves in official uniform, by all those bloodsuckers who feed on overseas workers.

Who wants to be back in a country that denies its little people honor? (185). What is the attraction of the poverty, filth, and corruption of the homeland? To be abroad is better, and Filipinos are masters of adaptation. They marry foreign misfits, not for love but for their money. They entertain the sons of the Land of the Rising Sun. They run away and try to prosper in illegality. No wonder they are discriminated against, no wonder prejudice has taken hold. 'All Filipinos are thieves. Like their leaders. Their women are prostitutes!' (186). Of course, the truth is to the contrary, but why can't Filipinos use their talents to build their own country, why are they deprived of dignity and opportunity at home?

A revolution is needed. But how to get rid of the oligarchy that has condemned the country to penury? Getting rid of Marcos was one thing: it also meant the restoration of the elite caste. Of all Philippine institutions, they appear to be the single strong one. Only revolutionary nationalism, such as the Americans encountered in Vietnam, can resolve the internal contradictions. This can banish the inequities that prevail in Philippine society.

If people set their sights on changing the type of democracy that exists in the country, they are mistaken. Externally, it is the cosy relationship with the United States of America that matters, up to the point that the fascist Marcos could plunder the nation with Washington's blessing. Democracy in the Philippines serves those in power. It is a means to seal the status quo to the detriment of the ordinary people.

Toward the end of the Marcos period, the *viajero* of the title, Buddy, finally returns to where his roots lie. He comes from the comfort of America to a place riddled by crime, violence, poverty, oppression, and a vicious dictatorship. Why does he bother to go back to a country where all that people hope for is the opportunity to leave it? Why trade San Francisco for Manila, that hideous madhouse in the debilitating tropical heat? Its policemen are touts and thieves, it sidewalks choked with weeds, its streets cratered, its people listless, and slums and squatters and beggars are everywhere. Well, not in the fenced-off enclaves of the obscenely affluent elite, of course. But from the Manila Hotel, one does not need to go far to be confronted with the city's stench, its squalid bay, and the smell of perdition, decay, and filth.

Over the years, Buddy has grown accustomed to the easy confidences and casual friendliness of Filipinos. In seeing Manila, he understands why they are this way. It must be their poverty that propels them to be ingratiating and fawning (210). They are a dependent people. They have been perverted, brutalized. Hypocrisy has become a way of life. Their hearts and minds have corroded through frustrations and unvented anger (215). How people arrived at this appalling state is no secret: the nation was colonized by its own leaders, who met with little resistance because the Filipino masses are apathetic and ignorant; they are incapable of seeing the elite as their exploiters. As a result, the few who are conscious of their condition take up arms, wage war. Their revolution is inevitable, and justified (216).

Even so, can they succeed? If they win, can they patch together the nation? This is probably at the heart of the problem. There is no nation, no tradition, no culture; there is no foundation to build on. There is an absence of purpose, so what can Filipinos be proud of? Their society, almost naturally, brought a man like Marcos, somebody with no scruples, to the presidency. And so it will be as long as the antiseptic Makati precincts of the rich accentuate the gap between their and the common man's life among the malodorous smells of the city, the uncollected garbage on the sidewalks, and the sweaty effusions of the early rush hour.

Filipinos often are their own worst enemy. They are vengeful, unproductive, and imitative. They are petty, take pride in trifles, and are boastful. They are a nation of show-offs—epitomized by a character like Imelda Marcos (242). What is needed is not just a physical revolution to replace the elite that impedes all development, but a cultural revolution that frees the people from the manacles of their dependent mentality.

Could the country really expect change when Cory Aquino replaced Marcos? It merely brought the encrustation of the system of privilege and power to light. Thus, no land reform, no democratic influence on government. Once more, civil war erupted, sparked off by the massacre of demonstrating peasants at Mendiola Bridge. The military ran wild, subduing the countryside with unspeakable violence. The landlords came back, and if they postured as nationalists in Congress, it merely showed their frustration with the Americans. These people really have no idea about the revolutionary nationalism needed to reconstruct Philippine society and make the nation viable.

But then, can you expect an impulse from the masses to this end? Look around, see the dilapidated environment with its endless impieties of soft drink signs, its overcooked food, its abominable coffee, its asinine movies. People living in such drab surroundings can only clamor for escape, for membership in the Iglesia ni Cristo (chapter 9), or for the romance and comedy provided by Filipino films in which the heroes are normally played by mestizos. Filipinos are racists! You see it among the powerful: the higher you go, the whiter they become. Spanish white.[5]

Being so distorted, so out of touch, so colonial still, explains why middle-class Filipinos keep wondering about their identity. They are uncertain about their culture, suspended as they are between East and West. It is their luxury, so to say. It is definitely not the problem of the masses. They are absorbed in the struggle for survival, and they know who they are: it is their life, and you may ask yourself whether it is really worth living. It is like Imelda's owning three thousand pairs of shoes in a country where millions go barefoot. Yet, in this accursed land, the malignant leaders and the stunted masses are yoked together (262).

Message and image

The picture José paints of his society is striking and shocking. It is a wretched land deeply afflicted by its colonial past, history of oppression, submission, and exploitation, which keeps repeating itself long after the colonizers have left. The degraded life of the common people has become routine, people are conditioned by it, and they cannot, at least not in their own country, see or reach beyond it. They are imprisoned in misery. They accept authoritarianism and cruelty as a part of life itself. According to the author, this is the very legacy of Spain, of the Spanish Inquisition—a most successful institution of mind control, to which the present-day Church offers no way out. Philippine Catholicism is a mere cover-up of moral decay. How often Cory Aquino goes to church, and how much she betrayed the people! (265, 270).

Such remarks are reiterated in the last few chapters where José more or less summarizes his ideas about the Philippine condition. He points to the sham that passes for democracy and free press. These exist formally only, in practice they are rotten and corrupt. As a result, the country is a tragic place where having conviction is an act of heroism. Besides, there is hardly anybody who gets excited about it any more. It is as if people have been lobotomized by their own obstinacy. They are married to their degradation and do not want to see beyond it.

According to the author, this condition is bound to continue, because people have no memory, no sense of history, no morality, no identity to take pride in. Thus traitors are elected to office. Exploiters and torturers are forgotten. The powerful are admired: they are Spanish mestizos who do not intermarry with those Indio mongrels whom they consider incapable of creativity or leadership. It almost appears as if the country in its modern condition is beyond redemption.

F. SIONIL JOSE, *CADENA DE AMOR* (1979)[6]

The cadena de amor is a vine that, in the way of vines, conquers obstacles by overgrowing them. The word may also be translated as 'the chain of love' or, rather, love affairs. Both ideas fit the simile José intended.

With *Cadena de Amor* the author wants to present a sketch of an archetypal Filipino politician. He does this through the fictional biography of Narita, a woman whose ambition is to reach the very top of the system. This gives a physical form to the 'oligarchy' or 'elite' or 'leaders' that were held to be at the root of failed nationhood and merciless exploitation in *Viajero*.

The story offers some interesting parallels with Imelda Marcos as one of the icons of Filipino life. She is born in humble circumstances; the house she lives in is a kitchen, the only remains of a mansion ravaged by war. As the child of a minor sugar grower, she is snubbed by her fellow students. Being cold-shouldered fires her ambition; she is set to outsmart the self-absorbed and haughty Negros elite. To do this she has, apart from her uncompromising drive, four assets. She is an extremely beautiful mestiza—and willing to use her looks to her advantage. She is a talented singer, and likes to perform her signature tune, *All of My Days*, on stage. Third, she is totally amoral. Besides, and this sets her apart from Imelda, she is very perceptive and intelligent.

While politicians are often compulsive talkers—a quality occasionally shared by the protagonist—she can also patiently listen to even the loudest braggart. She knows how to give the impression of being attentive to pretentious nationalistic twaddle as if it were pearls of wisdom. As a child, she already demonstrated her character when she fed live mice to her cat, or when she tricked a friend to stand on an anthill. To her, this illustrated the ways of the world: the strong tear the weak apart, and she relishes the sight. She also takes pleasure in ridiculing taboos and sacred cows, such as when she led the singing of the national anthem at school when her white gala uniform was smudged red as if she had started her period. It was on purpose! The stain was pig's blood (8–9).

Her future career was kick-started by her beauty. Winning the school's pageant, she was crowned by Senator Reyes—a very rich and influential politico—whose thirty-year-old son was infatuated by Narita. After a thorough investigation, the senator agrees to the match, but not before stipulating that the girl should finish college first. Senator Reyes had not been very lucky in establishing a political dynasty. His other sons were dead, or disappeared, and his hand-picked sons-in-law did not develop as expected. Narita, however, obviously embodied the most important quality needed to survive and triumph in the political game: brains.

The marriage with Lopito is an unhappy one, he is very jealous and possessive, but he prefers making love to boys. One day, after being thoroughly embarrassed by Lopito's flirting with a male guest at a party, Narita decides to leave their house in Forbes Park. She only returns there after Lopito's suicide. Yet, through the five years of her marriage, she was close to Senator Reyes, and she chose to go by his name. This identity agreed with her popularity as a society figure, her beauty, and her vast wealth. Besides, by passing on the senator's name to her children (not Lopito's), the possibility of a dynasty became real.

She had her first child by an aide to then Senate President Reyes, a colonel who introduced her to the pleasures of sex—for which she was very eager. Even so, she always dominated him. She was so independent that her macho lover never got the chance to consider himself her master. When in New York, where she goes to be freer and to improve herself through study, her stud is dumped for a relationship with Ambassador Iturralda—a man of Senator Reyes's generation—by whom she has a child, too.

While she totally dominates the ambassador, he is also a most useful lover, introducing her to all sorts of important American politicians.

Because the ambassador lives in Washington, and she in New York, she enjoys a lot of freedom. She has no intention of marrying the ambassador, even if his wife would consent to a divorce. She knows that she will leave him when it is opportune to return to the Philippines, all the lavish tokens of his love notwithstanding. Moreover, she has love affairs on the side, with live dildos, as she calls it (35). She knows what to get when she wants it, 'love' being a means to her purposes.

Basically she is driven by the desire for power; she wants to enter politics, to follow in the steps of Papa, of Senator Reyes. Because of her training, she has clear ideas about modern means of politicking. She wants brains in politics, think tanks, polls—not just bribes, backslapping, buy-offs, and vote buying. Of course, she also uses the old methods of bribery, intimidation, and rhetoric, but cultivating a modern image will certainly impress the voting mob. Her Washington relationships have taught her a lot or, as she has it, 'For as long as we are an American colony, we should know how our colonial masters operate. And, brother, this is where it starts' (38).

She expects to inherit the Reyes mantle, and her immediate aim is the Senate. But why? When probing her motivations, the far-off fact of being snubbed by the children of the sugar magnates of Negros comes up again. She wants to get back at them. This also spells her program. She desires power, for its own sake and, locally, to dismantle Negros's sugar industry which, after all, is colonial and has tied the country to the United States. Let them find out whether they can do without the quota system. She also wants to change the country's mores, a kind of sociocultural retooling, and to develop normal relationships with China. According to her, the real danger is Japan to which Filipino businessmen and politicians are selling out the country (39). She can permit herself not to jump on that bandwagon; she has vast wealth.

Being rich allows her to set up a think tank in order to make new ideas sweep through the cobwebs of complacent, traditional politics. She wants to project a modern image, or rather, she wants modernity to reflect on her. This is precisely what some members of the predominantly youthful think tank experience. They identify many bottlenecks, injustices, and obstacles to progress in the Philippine system, but feel that their work only serves Narita's strategic interests on her way to the Senate. They begin to feel that they have been bought, and it is very hard for most of them to deny themselves the privilege of some solid spending money.

Apart from feeling abused, the members of the think tank are insufficiently aware of Filipino politics to translate their proposals into feasible projects. In the Philippines, it is idealism against cheating, violence, intimidation, pork-barrel funds and blackmail—and in whatever idealistic way young people want to see the world, they had better reckon with these stark realities. Politicos shape the state in their own image, and they are conscious that that image is ugly, even evil (52). On the stage they boast about their nationalism, their fine intentions to uplift the people, and their concern for the masses. Yet, practical politics is not in the limelight. The real decisions are made in the shade, from where also public opinion is manipulated through the instrument of the highly corruptible press.

As a result, Narita's campaign proceeds with the customary envelopes of money. She banks on her beauty, with people eager to possess her Japan-made campaign poster on which she figures so endearingly. Before entering new areas, she does painstaking research on the local pecking order, and thus knows whom to befriend. On the platform issues are not really of great concern: the crowd wants to hear her sing. And although, because of her background, she is familiar with the degradation of poverty, her drive against it is not based on moral outrage but on aesthetics. Slums are unsightly, poverty is ugly; it should be covered up through cosmetic measures. Moreover, in her campaign, especially on her old, provincial home ground, she does not shy away from a murder or two. Violence and the drive for power go hand in hand.

Inexorably, all this lands her in the Senate. Now that she is in a position of power, her think tank expects action on some of their reformist proposals. When confronted with this, she simply maintains that there is no conscience in politics: 'Then let us be pigs. Conscience, duty—my duty is not to God and country. It is to me—to myself first' (61). Because of that conviction, she is not interested in changing anything. She thrives on the tradition of corruption. What she wants is to reach the top, the presidency. Therefore she has to build herself up in the public view, and her stint in the Senate is the means. Her think tank should thus focus itself on the next election. To enhance her chances, she has become the incumbent president's secret lover, which is, of course, no obstacle to other discreet affairs.

Narita is the best student Senator Reyes ever had. He has made her fully aware that what counts most is what people believe at the same time that one should not be deluded by oneself. One should know one's limits, and the limitations of power (67). One should constantly work at one's image, and endeavor to establish a reputation that is beyond narrow party loyalties. If one succeeds in doing just that, one becomes a national figure whose rhetoric about nationalism, anti-Americanism, the underdog, and the common good will carry weight while providing cover for the real action. Feed the people what they want to hear, what they want to believe, then go your own way. Politics is a game, of compromises and accommodations, in which there is no place for idealism. After all, government is not a vacuum; it is human relationships, and these you have 'to play' (69).

Message and image

The author's ideas of what drives Filipino politics are crystal clear, and not nice or comforting. He paints a stark picture of what is known as traditional politics, and despite having written it some twenty years ago, things have not changed appreciably. If there is a message at all, it would seem that the ordinary people are simply too good to be ruled by rapacious and self-seeking politicos, but as observed toward the end of *Viajero*, both are yoked together. This then apparently means that there is no end in sight, and that harsh political and economic realities will dictate people's lives. Idealism may be interesting for the young, but good ideas and morality are no match for money and expediency.

SINDHUNATA, *NOT WAITING FOR YOUR APPLAUSE; WITHOUT CONDOLENCES* (2000)[7]

> Almost everything we call 'higher culture'
> is based on the spiritualization and intensification
> of *cruelty*—this is my proposition; the 'wild beast'
> has not been laid to rest at all, it lives, it
> flourishes, it has merely become—deified.[8]

Sindhunata is a Javanese who, as such, writes for a Javanese readership, and who thus revels in allegory, symbolism, and tropes. Events and phenomena are always liable to multiple interpretations; they are buried under layers of meaning that cover each other like the lighter and darker shadows on the screen we hold for reality. In brief, he draws on theater, on Javanese *wayang* shadow theater. He loves to pack his images of society, whether they concern the suffering of the masses or the degeneration of the New Order era, into powerful metaphors. The present book deals with the bestiality of the self-indulgent Suharto regime, and how its twin spirit of covetousness and egoism extends into the present. Its symbol is the wild boar.

Like his earlier *Semar's Quest for a Body,*[9] this new work is inspired by a series of paintings and a shadow play manual about the boar. Its main character is the painter. In creating the paintings, he releases the boar into the jungle of civilization. He is pulled into that jungle himself, and has to wander until he finds the water of truth that will free him from his misadventures. The parallel with the Dewa Ruci story is obvious. In between, we also glimpse many images of Indonesian life.

These life circumstances are, in the main, ugly and threatening. The exercise of power is arbitrary to the extreme. It is self-serving and callous, criminal and oppressive. It is a burden, weighing especially on the lives of the common people. They are evicted from their homes, they are chased around by the police, it is impressed upon them that they are of no value, and almost powerless to oppose their oppressors. How is it possible that these people can still smile, dance, and enjoy themselves in the darkness that surrounds them? How is it possible that they maintain their dignity? That is because, however adverse the circumstances, they still have hope—the only thing they have left to cling to. One day, a Just King may take over; one day, justice may prevail; one day, there might come an end to these crazy times that reward criminals and punish the virtuous. That hope must not be mistaken for optimism. It is not naive; hope is the force that keeps people going. For the time being, though, they suffer from the boundless cupidity of those in power.

The first major canvas to inspire the narrative is the painting by Djokopekik, 'The Nipples of the King of Boars' (1996). It is the symbol of the power we must, with the force of our hope, oppose. Yet, how?

The painting shows a gigantic boar. It is fat, but in spite of having eaten more than it needs and with its breasts swollen, it still forages, feeds, and stuffs itself. There is no end to its appetite. It stands on earth soaked in blood. It is watched from a distance by a vast crowd that does not dare to approach. The boar can be comfortable; it will not be disturbed. Its six nipples will quietly feed its six children.

The people watching it seem innumerable. The nearest of them stand just a little in front of the massive pillars supporting an elevated highway, probably a toll road, that symbolizes the Indonesian idea of progress, namely progress for the rich. These can afford to fly their cars over the vast masses of ordinary people who are streaming, on foot, from the sky-scraping city in the distance. Because they keep their distance from the boar, we cannot discern their faces. They constitute an anonymous mass.

The date of the painting and the reason for it are interesting. It was done in 1996 when it still seemed as if the New Order regime was going to perpetuate itself. At that time, its means of doing so had grown excessively brutal, such as the blatant intimidation of the PDI leadership and the subsequent attack on its headquarters by officially backed thugs. The culture of violence was as firmly established as the avarice of the power holders.

The painting itself was Djokopekik's contribution to an exhibition in honor of the eight-year jubilee of one of Yogyakarta's 'traditional rulers.' Its theme was 'Mirroring the People's Heart,' and the contributions were expected to reflect the artists' feelings about government and power. In our case, the painter chose a negative example. 'If you want to rule, you become a boar.' He, therefore, decided to expand on the mendacity of power in order that people would know the truth. 'Do not take the "throne for the people" lightly. To be the king is not easy. He has to be responsible because he must lead all of the people of the land. If he does not take that responsibility, he will merely become a king of boars' (36).

The second painting, 'Indonesia 1998 Hunting the Boar,' was done after Suharto stepped down from the throne. It shows an even vaster mass of people streaming from the high-rise city in the distance through the spaces between the pillars of the toll road—it seems empty—and all the way to the boar that is hanging from a pole carried on the shoulders of two obviously poor men. The animal does not move and is safely secured, its feet and muzzle tied with rope. In the procession preceding the two men we see people dancing; they are happy. They have hunted down the boar; for the time being, they may be safe. When we look into the crowd, we see many banners, but we cannot read their messages. Probably they read 'Democracy' and 'Reform.'

In contrast with the first painting, many people are clearly visible. In the main it is a festive crowd that has finally brought down the arrogance epitomized by the skyscrapers in the background. They are not the people who are living or working in those high-rises. Most of them are just poor, struggling to make a living. Still, their spirit brought down the king of boars, and they celebrate merrily. They feel that they have won, and are quite emotional because of it. They have to be careful, though, because their ignorance and emotionality can easily be exploited and lead them into directions they are unaware of. They are honest, but simple.

There are also other faces in the crowd. Some of these are serious and skeptical. They are not shining with happiness. From their clothing we can tell that they are white-collar workers. Given to being cynical, they are less inclined to emotionalism; they think rationally. Some of them expect that the momentous happening of catching the boar will blow over, that either nothing will change, or that no good will come of it, that optimism will eventually be strangled by worry and fear.

We see professional dancing women. They are not just there to stimulate male lust. They symbolize ordinary women who, like them, have to work hard. They not only excite men, but they also know how to handle them when they are drunk. They subdue men under all circumstances. Many people believe these dancing women to have magical power.

The painter expresses his anger in depicting the moment when innocence and honesty are attacked and humiliated by power. We see some crew-cut types dressed in uniforms and boots, one of them stealthily squeezing a dancing woman. In this way, he stains the happiness and simplicity of the people. As a result, there is much in the painting that mitigates unqualified hope.

One reason why this is so is the doubt whether the boar has really been finished off. According to legend, a dead boar can be revived if he is touched by his loving wife. At present, she keeps her distance, but she may change her mind. It is as if dark forces pervade life, forces that can possess and animate even the picture of a dead boar. Accordingly, the painter is not filled with hope. The future looks dark.

Why is it that the painting seems to prophesy a gloomy future just when the boar has been caught? Worse than that, it seems to have come upon us already. At a time when all people sing that a new era is dawning, they still live as they did before. Many people are agitated and confused. Uncertainty reigns. People express their dissatisfaction by doing all sorts of terrible things. Threats and violence have become commonplace.

The condition of social life is worse than before. It seems as if catching the boar has opened the door to all sorts of crime, duplicity, passion, and hypocrisy. People only seem to agree on one thing: 'Life must go on, even without truth' (54). Apparently nobody is interested in seeking the light anymore. We wander in darkness indeed.

'Indonesia 1998 Hunting the Boar' is a huge canvas, to be exhibited all by itself. The painting was to be unveiled by the 'traditional ruler,' but three hours before the ceremony, he had a change of heart. Perhaps he had remembered that the painter had been blacklisted by the government in a dim past, and that any association with such a person could have unpredictable consequences. Besides, the ruler was a candidate for the governorship of the province, and should thus avoid any action that could irritate the authorities in Jakarta.

The official explanation was that the unveiling coincided with a mandatory ritual in commemoration of the death of the ruler's father. The ruler's younger brother, however, only went to that ceremony after attending the opening of the exhibition. Obviously, and in spite of the boar having been brought down, the shadow of the New Order still hung over the land, and the ruler on the people's throne knew that his hands were tied. They were not free to do the opening gesture: to knock an earthenware boar to pieces, from whose belly would then spill automobiles, airplanes, agricultural products, cloves, and oranges.

As a result, the boar remained unbroken. Bringing down one leader does not mean that his power has vanished. It was clear that his influence still hovered over the state, and that this was far more pervasive than people expected. Instead of crushing it, you could spit at it or extinguish your cigarette on its earthen skin, such as a disturbed woman did.

Apparently, the boar was still alive, was whole. It was giving birth to many descendants, even after it had been caught. As a result, the spectators become very confused. Is the boar really alive, or is it a picture? Is it an imitation or is it real? What is real, what is imitation? It seems as if all have entered the period of darkness in which one cannot see clearly. We are surrounded by evil against which we are powerless. It is the time of the boar, when good intentions come to naught.

The maker of the painting grows increasingly apprehensive. His creation has come to life. It lives and overpowers the environment. He realizes that he cannot even rely on himself, that he is carried by the stream of life, that he needs the courage to accept his condition. He has become a boar himself, wallowing in success, born to money and fame. His quiet days are over—he is not his own master any more; he is going with the flow.

Is there a gaur (symbol of Megawati Sukarnoputri's party) that can take on the boar? But the boar has fallen apart into those numerous servants of the old regime. They defend themselves. They remain in their positions. They are as avaricious as ever; they feed on the people. They are not in the mood to surrender. Was there really a new era dawning? Had the time of the Queen arrived? Many doubt whether her time has come. The evidence that we still dwell in the era of the boar is too striking.

The painter is nonplussed. How come his pictures have misfired, came to have unintended consequences? Was it because he was under an evil spell? His life history gives us a clue. When he started out as a painter, he was a man of the people, and his art was done in their service. The people demanded the right to the freedom they had fought for— the right to be free from landlords. He pictured their suffering, and personally joined the demonstrations against imperialism, colonialism, and feudalism. He opposed those who defended art for its own sake.

The change of regime landed him in jail. His family fell apart, and so did his ideals. He could not create any longer. He became an outcast. When he was finally released, he had to earn his living with a sewing machine. And all this because of one man whose power and riches were built on the suffering of the people. How he hated that man! This hatred bred a desire for vengeance. His paintings misfired because they were inspired by resentment. He thus released the boar into this world, where it happily multiplied. Even when he would burn his paintings, the boar of vengeance, greed, and arrogance would still be roaming about. Basically, the boar—or is it boarishness—had taken possession of its maker.

The painter is conscious of this. 'But isn't it so that all people carry a boar within themselves? Name me somebody who is not pretending and hypocritical?' (105). Since he became successful, his style of life became bourgeois. Is he the one who advances the interests of the people? When still in jail, he was privileged, had more to eat and better living conditions than the others. The boar has always been deeply ingrained. Even now he craves for more, is ever after more fame and goods.

He has become like the man he hates. Originally that man came from the common people. But he was driven by inexorable ambition, to the extent of rewriting his past. He seemed to have forgotten his origins, and decided to be base. His wickedness is like that of King Amangkurat Agung who also ruled for more than thirty years. His regime was characterized by cruelty and evil, killing and torture, stealth and abduction, robbery and rape. He set people up against each other; he sowed the seeds of discord and suspicion. Then, imagining the man he hates, the painter pities him. He begins to feel affection for the boar. Is he really that bad? He can smile so beautifully. He is a simple man. If he became evil, it is merely because the force of evil took possession of him, a force that now also pervades the painter himself. It appears to imbue all those in power, all those who possess, not only the successor clown-president, but also the Queen (Megawati Sukarnoputri), the Kang (Amien Rais), and the Gus (Abdurrahman Wahid). Nobody among them embodies the aspirations of the people; none of them dares to knock the earthenware boar to pieces. When the crazy woman finally destroys it, it spills hundreds of pictures of the painter himself. We live in crazy times, in which all sorts of boars prosper; the painter is one of them.

To find a cure for this condition of evil and vindictiveness, he has first to accept it, and then to quest for the Well of the Boar. The water of that well comes from the tears of the boars who lament their fate. That water is a cure against human pain and worry. At that well, he learns to accept himself as he really is. It frees him from his hatred and grudges. He recognizes that life is an endless struggle with the boar within. The merit of that struggle is not in hatred but in the courage to engage the boar. This inspires his last painting, 'Without Condolences 2000,' that cannot misfire because it comes from a calm heart.

This final canvas depicts the rotting carcass of a giant boar on which flies and ravens are feasting. The dead body is situated in a desolate, mountainous landscape, far from the people, and far from the city and the elevated highway that we see in the distance. But the painting is harmless this time. It symbolizes that the worst is over, that people can have hope again, that a new government and a new period are upon them. The painter is happy that no jinx will arise from his latest work. Then, however, strange things happen!

At the opening of the exhibition, a kind of pantomime, 'Not Waiting for Your Applause,' is staged. It is about recent political events, and the desire for reform and democracy. But the leeches, the traitors, manipulators, *agents provocateurs* and 'developers' also feature, even the boar shows up. 'Why?,' the painter asks himself, 'I have honestly left all hatred behind me.' Toward the end, the director of the play brings out Yudhistira—symbol of justice and peace. It is obvious that we have come to the pantomime's end, but nobody applauds. The director and the young boys who fill the stage, all of them with their backs turned to the public, wait. The director feels irritated: 'I performed from the purity of my heart.' Yet, can people be so true to themselves? Hasn't he overlooked something? Then, slowly but steadily the masks—all the masks—drop. On stage, among the audience, all show their boarishness, become boars, naked and honest-to-goodness boars. Shame has been vanquished, and it all turns into an exuberant party. Before 'Without Condolences' was created, the spirit of the boar had already spread. It is the spirit of modern society, of all society.

Message and image

In a few chapters, the author sets the major political occurrences of the past few years in fantasy environments that are clearly recognizable. One chapter describes 'Queen' Megawati's campaign and the miraculous expectations that surrounded it. Yet, even if her gaur attacks the boar, the outcome will be uncertain. Uncertainty breeds fear and loss of hope. Another chapter characterizes the Habibie reign as a sham. The leader is a clown who always reneges promises. Nothing ever really changes. People pin their hopes on the new leadership, on Mbah Megawati who has no ideas, on Kang Amien who calls for jihad, on Gus Dur who is unpredictable. Do they reflect the aspirations of the people? Does the new president connect with the heart of the populace? The author is not at all optimistic.

As he sees it, in the long period of the boar, something very basic has changed. People have learned to cope with greed. They prioritize their own survival, whether they are poor or extremely rich. They are subject to an all-pervading force that drives them on; they are not their own masters any longer. They compulsively forage. The big boar is out of the way, but its mentality prevails. Now people, as individuals, have taken on the qualities of the boar, with abandon.

UMAR KAYAM, *DEVIATIONS* (1999)[10]

Deviations is a sequel to Umar Kayam's *The Priyayi*[11] and has as its subtitle *The Priyayi 2*. These works comprise the history of four generations of the Sastrodarsono family. It begins in the early years of the twentieth century when a man of humble origins has the opportunity to learn and to establish himself as a teacher, a civil servant of the colonial government. He has made the transition from peasant to *priyayi*. These *priyayi*, in all their diversity, constituted a conservative class of people thoroughly loyal to their ruler, and roused by the ideal of service both to the government and to the people they administered. These convictions inspired the life of the (great-)grandfather who epitomizes *priyayi*ness. It is a style of life and a Javanese cultural ideal.

Through the tumultous times of the Japanese occupation, the revolution and early independence, it seems that *priyayi* ways were being lost. The new generation get themselves publicly into trouble, lose honor and face—the worst things to do. They engage in mixed marriages, and even divorce. They get involved in political activities. As a result, when the first volume closes in the 1960s, it is safe to conclude that most characters have diverged from the old ideals and are living lives that are at a considerable remove from colonial times.

Deviations is set in the 1990s and traces the fate and fortunes of the third and fourth generations. The main story line revolves around Eko, whose divergence is most formidable: for him, America has become home; he has even married into a Jewish family. Still, I think it safe to pluralize the title's theme, because the book treats many deviations— quite fundamental ones, in fact. These will be brought into focus as we concentrate on the images of contemporary Indonesian society that the narrative affords.

The first chapter opens a perspective on life under the late New Order, at a time when the regime has lost all of its flexibility. Increasingly suspicious and jealous of its power, it develops a clear case of paranoia. It sees ghosts in broad daylight, against which it defends itself by means of oppression, vengefulness, injustice, and a callous contempt for humanity. This is exemplified by Harimurti, Eko's father. In the 1960s, he was involved with the Left that was outlawed when Suharto came to power. As a result, he and his betrothed became two among the hundreds of thousands of political prisoners. She died when giving birth in jail.

This loss devastates Harimurti. He is grief-stricken. Only long after his release could his parents convince him to marry. They even found him a wife. At that time, his wife-to-be was pushing forty. Their only child was Eko, an extraordinarily gifted boy. Because of this, he was granted a scholarship to finish high school in the States.

After his detention, Harimurti's life takes a new turn. Thanks to the efforts of his uncle, a high-ranking army officer, he is exonerated and finds a job as an editor in a publishing house. Then, after many years, his past catches up with him. The company is threatened with closure if it continues to employ people who are stained, who are 'unclean.' And knowing New Order ways, Harimurti and his wife realize this means that there is no future for their son in Indonesia. Heavy-heartedly, they advise Eko to stay where he is.

Harimurti, his wife, and elder brother Lantip stand for cultural continuity. They live simple lives. They are dedicated to duty, are devoted to each other, intensely loyal, and definitely not avaricious. They are content with playing Javanese classical music and listening to their turtledoves. They embody a way of life that is of the past. When you are outside their yard, you have left Java too.

Their style of living stands in stark contrast to that of some of their cousins. Two of them are very well-off. Maridjan is very rich, and lives in Mexican hacienda-style surroundings, but still prefers to eat Javanese food. Tommi is more than very rich, he is a business tycoon, owner of a conglomerate of enterprises, and wallows in filthy lucre of obscure origin. His surroundings are palatial, and so are the retinue he keeps, his fleet of conspicuous automobiles, and the park-like garden that, despite Jakarta's heat, has weeping willows in it.

Their lifestyles have far diverted from anything commonly Javanese. They are archetypal *nouveaux riches*. Especially Tommi is interesting: spoiled and born to privilege, his empire has ever expanded. He is hardheaded, tenacious, and very authoritarian. He knows what he wants, and gets it, including his gold-digger mistress who, in her turn, gets what she wants.

Tommi does not appreciate his own traits in others, and so it is quite a confrontation, and a family scandal, when Ana, his daughter, reveals that she is pregnant. She had been traveling around with the son of Tommi's Middle-Javanese, Chinese business partner, and had seduced him. Tommi exploded: 'A Chinese, Chinese blood defiling our line!' The way he puts it is insulting to Harimurti as his Eko was going to marry a Jewish girl, also pregnant.

When that came out, Harimurti and his wife were very upset. Eko had written them a very straightforward letter explaining his situation. More upsetting even than the unlikely mixture of an Islamic Javanese and a white, American Jew, was the *fait accompli* they were confronted with. Had he, a Javanese, deviated so much as not to consult his parents and, worse, not even to ask for their blessing? Had parents lost their importance altogether? This particularly hurts his mother's feelings. As far as Tommi is concerned, he washes his hands of Ana, and will not show up at the marriage in Semarang where she is going to live.

The deviations from how life should be lived abound. Yet, interestingly, not all concerned are aware of it. Maridjan is, at least, conscious of the discrepancy between his 'Mexican' entourage and his preference for hearty Javanese fare. Tommi, however, takes his excessive *nouveau riche* life style for granted. The food at his home is catered by the best hotels. The furnishings and decorations hail from the global market. English is generously interspersed in conversations. Even sanctified Javanese traditions are affected by the whims of the parvenu.

The case in point is the Javanese cult of the dead, of revering ancestors. Once every year, the descendants are supposed to make a pilgrimage to the ancestral graves where they commune with parents and grandparents. They may seek their blessing or pray for the well-being of their souls. It is a deeply emotional encounter, the normally rather simple gravesite becoming a kind of storehouse of the merit of the deceased. This power can be accessed or revered by the living progeny.

The first two generations of the Sastrodarsono family are buried at Wanagalih, the small, backward regency town where the grandfather lived his life. There he was accepted as an equal by the regency's doctor, police chief, and other notables. They talked and played cards together. After their demise, they were buried next to each other, as if to continue their conversations and games. Later on, the remains of the parental generation were also interred there, and every year the living faithfully fulfill their obligation of pilgrimage.

At a family gathering, Tommi reveals his grandiose plans to honor the first Sastrodarsono couple and their own parents by converting their graves into a mausoleum complex worthy of a Roman emperor. It is evident that Harimurti and Lantip do not agree. To do so is disturbing a sacred site, an environment in which the ancestors are at peace. But then, once again, they are confronted with a *fait accompli*. Persuaded by Tommi's money, the descendants of Grandfather's friends have already agreed to relocate the graves of their ancestors. To Harimurti this is shocking news. Then again, the construction of the mausoleum has already begun. The marble from Italy has been shipped in; an Italian expert is directing the works. The only remaining question is whether Harimurti will agree to the plan of including the grave of his parents in the monument. Of course he does not give in to that sacrilege.

To get things his way, Tommi uses his ostentatious appearance (London-tailored suits; a Bentley) and his irresistible tea money. With his son Bambang he jokes about the corruptibility of officials, politicians, and judges. They are just greedy little bastards. Everybody and everything can be bought. The power of money is supreme, and the inauguration of the mausoleum becomes an unforgettable extravaganza to which hundreds of guests are flown in and for which all rooms in nearby Madiun have been booked. Even the people of Wanagalih are not forgotten. They are treated to a fun fair and a full shadow play performance. Tommi expects that the mausoleum will become a major tourist attraction and stimulate Wanagalih's economy.

At the inauguration, Bambang bores the guests with a long enumeration of the preparations and the works invested in the conversion of the graves, carefully specifying the billions of rupiahs and the millions of dollars spent. Then his father speaks to express their generation's indebtedness to their grandparents and parents' merit. He also expresses the hope that the gravesite, because of its reconstruction and the many trees and flowers that will be planted, will become an attractive park, devoid of the somber, mysterious atmosphere of common Javanese cemeteries.

Message and image

In order to give insight into life in contemporary Indonesia, and most particularly in its capital Jakarta, the author constructs a striking contrast between idealized Javanese ways and the blatant lifestyles of the new rich. Java is embodied in Harimurti and Lantip. It is the Java Umar Kayam is nostalgic about, the Java of his youth that could still be enjoyed until the flood of 'Development' washed over the island in the 1970s. Development brought money. Where it came from was often unclear, but it changed a formerly rather austere, contented style of life.

The sudden wealth and the choices it afforded posed the problem of what to do with it. There had never been a class of very rich commoners before. The culture of these new rich had to be invented. It became a rat race of ostentation, of aping all sorts of foreign examples, of faking Western lifestyles, of imitating royal wedding rites. The Javanese accoutrements notwithstanding, such rituals are brand new, and their authenticity is literally far-fetched. It is the invention of tradition as just one more ornament of the ways of the *nouveaux riches*.

The author wants to demonstrate that these people have lost their link with the past. If formerly *priyayi* were a privileged class who took pride in cultivating their Javanese-ness, their successful descendants have digressed so far as to have lost the security of tradition. This is the message of the mausoleum. It is the ultimate violation of what the Javanese hold sacred. It is celebrating the victory of money over culture. In Tommi's eyes, the grave of Harimurti's parents has become a stain on the Carrara marble complex. Obviously, Tommi does not know what he is doing any longer. He is driven by wealth.

Are there still people who maintain the old ways and its virtues? According to several authors, maintaining *priyayi* culture with its respect for hierarchy, obedience and conformism is an obstacle to progress.[12] Does this judgment also invalidate the Javanese way of life, with its wisdom of acquiescence and self-restraint, and its fine arts? Of course not, but it seems to be bulldozed over by money, consumer culture, and the disinterest of the new generations. Umar Kayam is nostalgic about many good things disappearing. It is the drone of traffic spoiling the peaceful atmosphere, of pop songs drowning out the sound of the gamelan percussion orchestra, of exhaust fumes suffocating the turtle doves. It is progress and development all around, and the monetary crisis just accentuates the primacy of economy and technology. In that limited domain, essential humanity seems to have gone missing.

COMMENT

The four authors reviewed in this chapter, to whom we may add Lualhati Bautista and Ayu Utami of the previous one, comment on the current condition of society in Southeast Asia. Often they compare the situation with that of bygone days. In Wimon's work, former times are exemplified by Old Man Khong and his uncorrupted villagers. In José's *Viajero*, the benchmark is native culture and identity before these were destroyed by Spanish colonization, before the Filipinos were vanquished and brought into servitude. Similarly, the pristine past provides the background for Sindhunata, who notes a transition from humanity to bestiality. For Umar Kayam, the past consists of idealized Javanese ways from which the current generation is deviating.

Even as the Philippine condition may be rooted in distant history, the current situation in the three societies under consideration seems to be remarkably alike. It is as if people are losing identity, roots, dignity. They are no longer self-possessed but exposed to overwhelming forces of modernity. There seems to be an absence of national leadership and moral guidance. Wimon targets the degeneracy of the Buddhist monks. José points to the self-serving elite who is not interested in much more than exploiting people and country. Sindhunata describes the Suharto regime as violent, arbitrary, injust, callous, cruel, mendacious, and oppressive. Umar Kayam's parvenus are alienated from their past. It is as if amoral power reigns, and that ideals and the desire for moral order cannot mobilize significant force to oppose it. In Javanese parlance, we simply live in 'crazy times' in which everybody—certainly those on their way up—is corruptible by nature. Lies are held for truth, ordinary people are denied their dignity, everybody is beyond shame and has to struggle for survival. The idea of moral order appears to have gone lost; what remains are self-centered individuals, mere boars.

In Wimon's Thai perspective, greed or the desire for power, violence or anger, and gullibility or ignorance are narrowly related. Without referring to this lofty Buddhist wisdom, the other authors appear to agree as to the interrelatedness of these qualities. They seem to be inextricably connected, and characteristic of modern times.

Gullibility is the principle on which *The Lord of the Land* is based. It pairs with the general lack of historical and social awareness noted in José's narratives. Sindhunata warns that ordinary, simple people are especially vulnerable to manipulation, but he is also doubtful that the house of lies, so carefully constructed by the New Order architects, will readily collapse. Umar Kayam dwells on the delusions of the *nouveaux riches*. In the absence of cultural identity or continuity, anything goes— no matter how outrageous. Posturing and hypocrisy have been elevated to a form of art that pervades life; they constitute important instruments to play politics with. After all, what people believe to be true is true and, in these uncertain, lonely times people pin their hopes on irrational beliefs. Others simply seek escape from the harshness of existence, or from their own confusion. These are golden times for soothsayers, amulet vendors, and sectarian cult bosses.

The only things that count are money and power. *Deviations'* Tommi is after ever more of both, and to facilitate this he corrupts, 'buys' everybody on his path. José notes the same mechanism in the Philippines when he writes about how the tentacles of the oligarchy reach through the whole of society, even into the classroom. Morally, the social edifice seems to be an empty shell. People are driven by greed, and greed alone. Of course, to this end they need power—and in the process they become like the insatiable boar. They forage compulsively, and while they still hold themselves to be righteous and rational, they fail to see that they have been overcome by their greed and desire for power. As a result, they become moral runts, using whatever means is available to serve their purposes.

The obvious means is violence, whether born from stone-heartedness or vindictiveness. Ayu Utami's novel is set in the structural savagery of Indonesia. Lualhati Bautista protests Marcos's brutality, but according to José's vision, things did not turn out to be better under Aquino or successive regimes. In Wimon's novel, violence is the ultimate means to get things done. Sindhunata even compares the previous dispensation with King Amangkurat whose murderous reign is remembered as the most ferocious of all. Umar Kayam's book draws its main story line from New Order disrespect for humanity and its oppression of all dissent. As a result, culture, civilization is violated.

Painted by the hands of these contemporary novelists, modern society in Southeast Asia is not a pretty picture. Instead of the orientalist myth of Eastern spirituality, we see extreme materialism. The shameless mix of business and politics results in a rapacious elite incapable of, and uninterested in, providing moral leadership. On the contrary, they corrupt society, rendering both old ways and modern ideals irrelevant. Whereas there is some civic action in Lualhati Bautista's and Ayu Utami's narratives, the other authors make it clear that it does not stand a chance in changing practice as long as greed, gullibility, and violence prevail. For the foreseeable future, the latter will be the driving force of public life in Southeast Asia.

CHAPTER 9

RELIGIOUS REVIVAL

The rapid entry of Southeast Asian societies into a modernizing and globalizing world has left many individuals nonplused as to their moral worth and identity in an anonymous urban environment. To fill the void, the religious option is attractive to many, and reinforces the tendency of judging social life in moral terms.

TOWARDS RELIGIOUS INDIVIDUALISM

On Sunday mornings in Bangkok, people dressed in white are picked up by buses to visit the Dhammakaya temple near Rangsit, to the north of the city. The grounds of this temple look impeccably clean. Its main temple hall is surrounded by park and pond. An artificial waterfall adds to the pleasant surroundings the sound of cascading waters— uncommon in these flat plains where the temple is located. The colorful villagers on the other side of the canal that separates the main entrance to the temple from the settlement, are not welcome. The land they once used to cultivate rice has been taken up by a temple that does not perform rituals for the common man. They cannot even hope to cremate their dead there.

Apparently, the sect takes pride in presenting itself—and they rehearse for it—as a disciplined lot, its propaganda material showing its votaries seated in long straight lines; walking in disciplined fashion; sitting in meditation posture; posing in uniform rows under forest monks' umbrellas. In contemplating the temple hall, one is struck by its extraordinary, elegant, modern, yet stern appearance. It evokes at first exotic images of Japan, of a modern Zen temple perhaps. But the temple is Thai. The male students who are to join for a two-month period of meditation exercises during the hot season of April–May must undergo three days of military drill first. Dhammakaya at once provides its followers with a quick meditation course to discover and develop the dharmatic spiritual body within oneself, and stresses discipline and obsequiousness. It is also, and certainly no less importantly, a sect with very considerable financial resources.

In the Philippines, the Iglesia ni Cristo also demands discipline from its devotees. It builds upon the mandatory tithe its members pay. The latter are also expected to be present at services twice a week, and attendance records are kept. Members absent for any length of time are visited by a deacon who attempts to convince them once again that there is no salvation outside the Iglesia.

Theologically, and also in its militant propagation of the faith, the Iglesia reminds one of the Jehovah's Witnesses. It tries to persuade through the eclectic citation of texts from the Bible. Interestingly, it rejects the divinity of Christ. As such, it does not count itself among the Christian churches proper. Stressing purity, worldly discipline, and exclusivity, it has all the characteristics of a sect for those few who have been 'chosen' among a humanity that is on its way to eternal doom.

Drawing on dissatisfaction within the Catholic Church, this militant sect has made deep inroads into the flock of Rome. It now probably counts among its followers up to eight percent of the urban population, at least on the island of Luzon. The people who feel attracted to this, until now, almost exclusively Filipino denomination, are not the university students among whom the Dhammakaya recruits. Its typical members are literate, mainly urban, lower middle class. Generally speaking, it is a church for the common man; yet, increasingly, people of higher social standing can be found among the congregation.

Although many individual priests feel called upon to serve the poor, the mainstream Catholic Church addresses a slightly higher situated public of professionals, office workers, and urban politicians. Among them, members of Opus Dei constitute an influential yet select circle. Many more in this public are members of the Knights of Columbus, an urban confraternity that unites many of the notables in town; collectively they are often referred to as the bishop's bank because they constitute the main funding agency of episcopal projects. It is from among such circles of people that the *cursillistas*—people willing to go through an intensive three-day confrontation with the faith (*cursillo*)—are drawn. These circles also form the recruitment base for retreats, marriage revival weekends at resort hotels, and other organized Catholic activities.

The vast majority who come to mass, however, are not likely to be hooked into such networks and activities, and are not committed members of the Church. For them, the Catholic Church is a powerhouse, and their devotions, novenas, prayers, vows, pilgrimages, processions, and sacrifices are means of securing immediate and future benefits. They are, therefore, just as likely to put their trust in a favorite saint, an amulet, or to turn to one or the other of the many thriving charismatic movements—among whom El Shaddai and Jesus is Lord currently stand out—that promise the devotees to share in God's power, which results in miracle cures, in finding work, and all kinds of blessings.

The long-time observer of Java is struck by the impressive upsurge of Islam. In the past, certain Islamic parties and groups were politically distrusted, and the faithful fulfillment of the Muslim tenets was unfavorably commented upon by those who pursued a Javanese mysticism-inspired style of life. Now, however, Islam enjoys the favor of the powerful, and the execution of Muslim duties commands greater prestige. The new popularity of living the faith, or at least of giving it space in one's life, appears to be pervasive, even in the principalities of South-Central Java. For the first time ever the ruling sultan of Yogyakarta is a hajji and Sri Paku Alam, the other prince of the realm, begins his speeches with the elaborate Muslim greeting.

Juxtaposed with thriving Friday prayers, Koran study clubs, Ramadan rituals, and other Islamic identity markers, lie the languishing symbols of Java-centered civilization. The sultan's palace is no longer the center of life in Yogya; interest in shadow play performances is waning; the past lies irretrievably hidden in Javanese script; royal ritual goes unnoticed; young people are no longer well-versed in the refinements of language and manners. It seems as if the local great tradition has given in to another, more universal one.

There is more to the appeal of Islam in the Javanese heartland than the decapitation of its high culture and the detraditionalization of life. Islam was formerly associated with backwardness and centered in remote rural boarding schools that provided an educational experience that bore little resemblance to that provided in the urban, secular mainstream schools. These days, these boarding schools also teach the state curriculum, and modern schooling is no longer an exclusive privilege open only to the children of civil servants, professionals, and administrators, collectively known as *priyayi*. Its expansion has given rise to a generation of modern Muslim intellectuals, committed to their faith and to secular careers. Besides, in the later Suharto years, Islam was supported even by the temporal authorities, with the then president setting the example by going on pilgrimage to Mecca.

Of course, there are always connections between politics and religion, whether for purposes of legitimation or enhancing power and influence. In the middle 1980s, the ascetic Buddhist Chamlong Srimuang was able to successfully ride a wave of moral indignation to the Bangkok metropolitan governorship, and then on to national prominence. In Manila, Cardinal Sin has, since long, been throwing his weight around in national affairs. And in Indonesia, most national Muslim organizations had supported Suharto until shortly before his fall. Meanwhile he has been succeeded by two staunchly Muslim presidents and one so-reputed vice-president.

Middle-class frustration with contemporary political and social conditions can be channeled into demands for moral righteousness and political protests. Such appeals for a more ethical way of life can be sufficiently annoying to the establishment; it reacts by granting concessions, and by trying to subvert and co-opt the religious leadership. In order to maintain their moral credibility, it may therefore be wise for such leaders to dissociate themselves from the government whose power corrupts. The leadership of the Iglesia ni Cristo provides a case in point. Adept at political bargaining, it sounds out who will be its favorite candidates in the period running up to election time without committing itself to actual politics, a position which was underlined by the Iglesia's refusal to take up the two seats it was offered on the commission that drafted the new Philippine constitution in 1986. Also the mass-based Nahdlatul Ulama under Abdurrahman Wahid knew how to evade direct state meddling in its affairs by stepping out of the political process in 1982; in this way, and unlike most other Muslim organizations, it could maintain both its independence and political clout.

The appeal of religion to the educated urban middle classes is rarely directly political, Chamlong's The Force of Righteousness party being the exception rather than the rule. As a distinguished member of the Santi Asoke Buddhist reform sect, Chamlong embodied the desire of the urban middle classes for a regular, accountable, and honest government; for the rule of law; and political openness. For a while, these desiderata have made Chamlong a Mr. Clean, an attractive white knight fighting against the privilege, 'corruption,' monopoly and violence that belong to traditional politics.

Chamlong's direct involvement in politics naturally set him on a collision course with established politicians and bureaucrats. Government authorities responded to his challenge by striking out against his home base, the Santi Asoke sect, through declaring the movement's monkhood illegal. At that time, Chamlong, for his part, was intensively involved in the long drawn-out battle against the military usurpation of power which ultimately resulted in the Bangkok massacres of May 1992, the restoration of traditional politics, and the gradual setting of Chamlong's star.

While the political arena seems to be the logical place to contest for power, the support that aspiring middle-class politicians can muster is extremely limited, and largely confined to the metropolitan areas. Besides, most of their potential constituency is not very interested in playing politics and taking responsibility for the affairs of the realm. Many of them decide to practice religion more seriously in order to put their own house in order, a motivation that underscores the activities and practices of most Santi Asoke members as well as the followers of Buddhadasa Bhikkhu.[1] This is also the case with the members of the Iglesia ni Cristo who even vote *en bloc* for the church's preferred candidates. Similarly, devout Catholics, who go to mass every day, participate in nocturnal adoration groups, or are involved in the Legion of Mary may perhaps be influenced by the cardinal's preferences, but are primarily interested in following an ethical way of life and proving their own moral worth through strict adherence to religious injunctions. And so it is for the vast Nahdlatul Ulama membership, the followers of Muhammadiyah's Javanese mainstream,[2] and the many who now attempt to observe more seriously 'orthodox' Islamic practices. These individuals are not necessarily committed to voting for Muslim parties, and are often rather apolitical.

A religious way of life is generally seen as a personal affair. This emphasis on the individual person, in turn, tends to be linked to the conviction that if everybody faithfully fulfills the duties of his denomination while respecting and tolerating the religious practices and commandments of others, society will be in good order. This apolitical conviction that steers clear of critical social analysis while emphasizing trust in a potentially benign universal order is very widespread and characterizes, in a sense, societies in which sociology remains to be invented.

In Southeast Asia, the emergence of vast middle classes in a market-driven, consumeristic environment, is a novel phenomenon. It resulted in equally vast masses of upwardly mobile people who have to operate in a new, businesslike society where their parental moral teachings have seemingly become irrelevant. In the new world they experience, they are eagerly looking for means of creating and shaping identity. To do so, some of them discover religion, or set on a moral way of life, while others indulge in materialism, the goodies of consumer culture, and the excesses their money permits them. They search for lifestyles that befit them. Sometimes they may even choose a religion-tinged lifestyle if that is fashionable, and often it is.

In many respects it seems that religion is not merely the fountainhead of eternal truth but also a child of the times. While for some religion provides a fundamental epistemic framework, for others it appears to be more ornamental. Sometimes, the ornamental and the epistemic may even combine into distinguishable lifestyles. This appears to be the case among the adherents of the Santi Asoke who express their 'simplicity' through vegetarianism, and through donning a blue 'peasant' shirt when congregating at their 'Buddha Land' near Nakhon Pathom. Similarly, the 'true friends,' as they like to call each other, of the Dhammakaya sect wear white and take pride in the curious design of their temple and images. So do the members of the Iglesia ni Cristo whose distinctive architecture marks the town and village landscapes. The charismatics and born-agains within and without denominations who prosper all over the Philippines, on the other hand, have put their particular mark on their conversation, addressing all and sundry with the greeting 'God bless you,' while frequently interspersing their sentences with 'Praise the Lord' and 'Halleluiah,' even when they are not attempting to convert their interlocutor.

In Yogyakarta, 'the' Islamic lifestyle has taken visual shape in the popularity of the headscarf. Muslim girls and younger women apparently exercise considerable pressure upon each other to don the veil that was formerly the almost exclusive trade mark of Muhammadiyah schoolgirls. Interestingly, this headgear that only exposes the face says nothing about the other garments worn by a woman. While some of them modestly cover all that should remain invisible of a female in public, others wear blue jeans, enticing variations of Sumatran dresses, or fashionable shoulder-padded blouses. For the latter, wearing the veil has become a fashion statement of sorts, just as Mecca has become a favorite travel destination, the hajj a sign of being abreast of the times, and 'We are the Muslim' stickers a young man's counterpart to his sister's scarf.

Lifestyle and fashion magazines have discovered a new market in Islamic dress design and compete in propagating the contemporary Muslim look in which orthodoxy vies with graceful presentation. During Ramadan the society pages report who is breaking fast with whom at which luxury hotel, while the movie *Music and Mission* shows the popular preacher Zainuddin M.Z. with music star Rhoma Irama at their natural best, playing themselves, such as they do on the stages of the super revival rallies where they are further supported by Rendra's poetry reading and businessman Setiawan Djody's guitar. Their fulfillment of the hajj together attracted so much publicity that they became religious pop stars overnight.

In the Philippines one also finds that religion provides entertainment that draws happy crowds. Catholicism's colorful carnivals and processions, fiestas and ceremonies have always enjoyed great popularity, with locals as well as with tourists. Such festivities are very much alive, and so it hardly comes as a surprise that the local Church's celebration of the Holy Virgin's 2000th birthday in 1985 became a real party at which huge birthday cakes were carried around to the cheers of 'Happy Birthday, Mama Mary.' While this exuberance is also a characteristic of the many Thai merit-making festivals, Thailand does not know, at present, the type of religious revival rallies that are staged in contemporary Jakarta and all over the Philippines. In the latter country, they often include charismatic faith-healers performing healing miracles to the sounds of music, singing, and clapping.

In brief, religion appears to be alive and well in Southeast Asia where it has even taken on some traits of modern consumer culture. While many take their religious duties seriously and consciously strive to shape their faith in a world of money, materialism, and urban anonymity, others do no more than just attending ceremony and ritual. Yet, whatever the motivation underpinning this interest in religion—whether it is faith, a moral stance, or merely a means to gain public acceptance—it does not seem that religious revival is stimulating the spirit of universalism and the brotherhood of all.

As an exponent of a more basic understanding of social life, religion almost seems to move in a contrary direction, and this is not only so because of its emphasis on personal ethical behavior. The broader ideals that fired the imagination of the founding fathers of the modern states of Southeast Asia—constitutionalism, democracy, education for all, social justice, the rule of law—have gradually vanished from the popular imagination, and have been replaced by the new creed of economic development, with its stress on money, technocracy, and material success. The religious upsurge is partly a reaction to the amoral rule of money and a response to the ethical vacuity of the wider social environment. The ideals of active citizenship and nation-building have given way to the experience of an anonymous scene ruled by political and economic expediency where people strive for survival, caring for themselves and their immediate dependents only. As a result, civil-society ideals, such as responsibility for and active participation in a shared public world, have difficulty in taking root, and may be out-competed by the promise of religious righteousness.

Rulers and elite politicians continue to conceive of social arrangements in a patrimonial way; their position at the top of the pile is legitimized as a natural state of affairs through notions of hierarchy and moral inequality. While this perhaps once led to the obligation of extending protective patronage, the commodification of relationships has since long eroded its practice. The high and mighty now jealously guard their position of privilege against claims of others. To them, individual-centered religious obligations and ethics come in handy. Add to this the replacement of the older notion of nation by the new stress on state and market, and the particularistic reaction to modernity logically follows. People care for themselves, especially their families. Indeed, the old family ideology now justifies any profit-taking in the 'public' world outside.

Family ideology, with its concomitant demands of loyalty, obligation, and respect for age, certainly does not contradict the prevailing understanding of religion. This is especially so because the Southeast Asian concept of sin is located in concrete bonds, most crucially, in parent-child relationships. Not respecting or going against one's parents constitutes the cardinal transgression that will be punished by unavoidable supernatural retribution, and cause feelings of guilt. Beyond the core of the family, however, religion is primarily seen as the means of securing protection, blessing, and good fortune. It is directed toward the future, and not concerned with a sinful past. Although the committed members of Santi Asoke, the followers of Buddhadasa, serious Catholics, and reflective modern Muslims will hold ideas to the contrary, theirs is a small milieu, not representative of the upsurge of religion in general.

Generalizing, it would appear that the very visible vitality of the urban religious scene has everything to do with the rapid emergence of new middle classes in societies that are market-driven, and that have opened up to the wide world while running away from history and 'tradition.' Ruled by political and economic expediency, the resulting environment is morally vacuous, and the politicians' appeal to 'nation,' 'law,' or 'democracy' merely breeds cynicism, and reinforces the moral particularism that befits the new 'individualism' or 'liberalism.' While occasional political protest surfaces, and some social concern is channeled into the activities of civil-society organizations, religion appears to be the most likely candidate to fill the moral vacuum, not only as an implicit or explicit protest against elite decadence, alien ways, and the vagaries of the economy, but especially as personal identity marker, claim to righteousness, and source of protective blessing.

Interestingly, the common religious reasoning that the good order of society depends on individual moral conduct, brings the individual person into focus while drawing attention away from the structural roots of social process and problems. This religious individualism dovetails nicely with a patrimonial perception of the wider society, a distrust of critical social analysis, and ultimately, elite interests. It is hardly surprising, then, that the powerful will support religion and cultivate its leadership, so also compromising its moral stance while undermining its political potential.

CHAPTER 10

CIVIC MALAISE

Here we shall trace the evolution from early nationalism to the current ideas filling urban space. On this trajectory, we can identify a modern phase in which society was envisaged as constructable and individuals as concerned citizens. For the time being, these ideas have withdrawn into the margin in competition with surging individualism and gobal capitalism.

FROM NATIONALISM TO GLOBALITY

Among the many Filipino firsts in Asian history is the nineteenth century arising of modern nationalism. While it is most improbable that this concurred with Spanish intentions, in retrospect it is safe to conclude that the colonial church did all it could to promote its growth. This became clear when the struggle between the Spanish regular clergy and the locally ordained secular priesthood came to a head with the judicial murder and martyrdom of the Philippines-born priests Gomez, Burgos, and Zamora in 1872. This shocking event galvanized the Filipino into being.

The non-ecclesiastical basis of Filipinism lay in the early establishment of modern, European education, initiated by the Jesuits upon their return to the country in 1859. This combined with the presence of a small class of rich, native entrepreneurs desirous to invest in advanced schooling of their offspring. The conjuncture of education and martyrdom proved to be irresistible, and when the first generation of Filipinos went overseas, Spanish intransigence and the former's desire for emancipation, such as formulated in their Reform movement at home and the Propaganda in Spain, directly led to the formulation of a nationalism that did not envisage independence yet, but at least equality of status with the mother country.

Well-known is José Rizal's novel *Noli Me Tangere* (1887) in which friars and church, official arrogance and injustice, corruption and racism, are depicted as the cancer that needs to be cut from the body politic in order to give it a chance to prosper. This very influential book, and its sequel, *El Filibusterismo* (1891),[1] created an atmosphere that sought for more than provincial status and representation in the Cortes. When the popular Katipunan started its uprising in 1896, the Spaniards sealed their fate by martyrizing Rizal on the penultimate day of that year. Whatever the latter's intentions and political vision, he had already grown to become a legend in his own time, inspiring nationalism and, irrespective of his wishes, the fight for independence.

Being born of colonialism, the Philippines was the first Asian nation to rebel against foreign domination, and to fight successfully for its freedom. Doing so required more than an abusive regime; it demanded the unifying idea of nationalism. The depth of this idea was soon demonstrated by the long drawn out resistance against American rule, both on the battlefield, and on stage through many 'seditious' theater productions in Tagalog.

This early Philippine nationalism discovered the Filipinos as a people, and aimed at independence, pure and simple. Concurring with the views of Rizal, Pardo de Tavera, and later Mabini, the elite is there to rule and will shape independence in their best interest; the others are to follow. But also the nonelite Katipunan did not envisage a social revolution; it was the fight against Spain that mattered, not the shape of tomorrow; it was the realization of the mystique of nationhood, of brotherhood; it was nationalism as religion.

Similarly, early Thai nationalism was cultic rather than programmatic. As a royal fabrication, King Rama VI (r. 1910–25) sought to unify his subjects through propagating that the people of his realm shared in the Three Institutions of nation, religion, and king. Under this trinity all belonged together. To substantiate this doctrine, national days and public ceremonies needed to be invented, together with schoolbook history, to serve as the timeless frame in which the nation was to celebrate itself."

When the Dutch finally opened opportunities for their East Indian subjects to pursue advanced education, nationalism was soon to arise. While the word Indonesia was already occasionally used in the 1910s, it became clearly the emblem of people who feel or imagine themselves to belong together when, in 1922, the Indonesian Students' Association was founded in the Netherlands. A few years later, in 1928, the idea was institutionalized at the Second Youth Congress that formulated the famous oath that Indonesia is one country with one people and one language. While such enunciations still had a 'religious' tinge, the intellectual climate had been changing, especially because of the influence of Marxism, utopian socialism, and humanism; society had become constructable; people could be educated; progress and improvement had become a possibility.

This was already apparent in the philosophy of the Taman Siswa school movement of 1922 that combined Javanese educational principles with modern, humanistic ideas. It was also expressed in the Marxism-inspired hopes of the left wing of the Sarekat Islam association. Modern social thought surfaced in Sukarno's essay on the compatibility of Marxism, Islam, and nationalism (1926) as well. During his political trial of 1930, nationalism and critical analysis of the political economy were firmly combined in his defense oration *Indonesia Accuses.*[?]

The Thai king's nationalism notwithstanding, the commoners who, as a consequence of the 1892 administrative reforms, were educated abroad to fill the posts in the new bureaucracy and the modernized army developed their own ideas, and were not precisely charmed by the claims of royal absolutism. When they took power in the revolution of 1932, they not only changed the polity to a constitutional monarchy, but also presented an economic plan that would have radically restructured the country's political economy. That Pridi Banomyong's ideas were never seriously implemented—much like Moh. Hatta's concepts about the cooperative organization of the Indonesian economy—does not lead away from the fact that, from the late 1910s or early 1920s onward, a social engineering approach often combined with nationalism, and that the idea of the democratic citizen caught on, at least in the heads of the founding fathers of the modern states of Thailand, the Philippines, and Indonesia. Juxtaposed and simultaneous with these ideas we find the modern, intellectually attractive Buddhist teachings of Buddhadasa Bhikkhu that emphasize personal improvement and responsibility; society and the individual could be made.

The combination of nationalism and the belief in social constructability is less apparent in the Philippines. In spite of Quezon's battle cry for 'Immediate, complete, and absolute independence,' America's colonial tutelage led to the denial of history, a future orientation, vacuous nationalism, and a political conception of the public world. The Filipinos the Americans co-opted to collaborate with their administration were the pliable descendents of the elite and, once given power, they went all out for the playing of politics per se, divorcing its practice from the democratic demand for good government. Quezon may have been visionary when the country got what he was said to prefer, 'A government run like hell by Filipinos to one run like heaven by the Americans.'

The founding fathers of the Philippine-American Commonwealth (1935) and the Third Republic (1946) cannot be credited with attempts to fill the public world with nation-building or social reconstruction. Elitist by nature, they cared for their own interests and had nothing to gain from popular mobilization. In their mercenary culture of the public sphere, the adaptation to local conditions of the American institutions of government resulted in a travesty of democracy. To keep the people in place, they subscribed to the idea that the good order of society follows from individual moral awareness, such as spelled out in Quezon's *Code of Citizenship and Ethics*.

In the Philippines, nationalism was never combined with the idea of social reconstruction, at least not by the people who held center stage in politics. While labor-union activities surfaced during the early years of the American occupation, and while concern for the oppression of peasants and laborers was already expressed in Lope K. Santos's novel *First Rays and Full Brilliance* in 1906, it was well into the 1920s before Crisanto Evangelista established a workers' party, the forerunner of the Communist Party of the Philippines (1930) that, in 1938, fused with Pedro Abad Santos's Socialist Party. Then as now, however, the ideas they carried remained marginal to the political process.

As idealistic imports from the West, constitutions, democratic aspirations, and programmatic politics carry little weight in a hierarchizing environment that focuses on the person of a patron-leader.

So, not before long, and in an era when fascism was fashionable, the first president of the Commonwealth arrogated so much power that he virtually established himself as the strongman of the polity. In order to perpetuate his position, he even got the constitution amended, all the time seeing himself as the fulfillment of national destiny.

The grant of independence to the Philippines in 1946 had little to do with the war and its aftermath; it was on schedule at a time that the Americans were hailed as liberators. Rather than the culmination of a fight for freedom, it ushered in a period of profound dependence on the United States, culturally, economically, and even politically. Independence, and with it the spirit of nationalism, needed to be reinvented as it were.

At the same time the spirit of nationalism provided the fuel for the fledgeling Republic of Indonesia to drive out the Dutch. Achieving independence, though, brought many cleavages and contradictions in Indonesian society to the fore, and all through his turbulent presidency, Sukarno felt he had to prioritize nation-building, to the practical neglect of the economy. The same was true in the late 1950s and early 1960s, when nationalist fervor ran high again, first because of the campaign to liberate Western New Guinea from the Netherlands, and then to defeat the British imperialist project of creating Malaysia.

In the late 1950s, we witness the attempt to recreate the spirit of nationalism in the Philippines. Then presidential candidate Claro M. Recto reminded his countrymen that continuing dependence on the U.S. was a betrayal of their nationhood, and that the attitude of mendicancy was an insult to independence. Somehow, this message came home, and most concretely resulted in President Garcia's economic Filipino First policy. Later on in the 1960s, it led to the recognition of the colonial nature of the Philippine school curriculum.

In Thailand, nationalism was reinvigorated by Phibun Songkhram's successor, Field Marshal Sarit Thannarat (1957–63), who set the country on the course of stimulated economic development, and propagated the unity of the nation around the king. He, and his political heirs, were not particularly tolerant of democratic, let alone social-utopian interpretations of progress. This drove, for instance, the author Sriburapha into exile in Peking, with the result that he never finished his monumental *Look Forward* (1955/57) that depicts the betrayal of the democratic spirit and ideals of social justice of the revolution of 1932. Khamsingh Srinawk's gifted, social critical short stories were not welcome either, and 'communist' dissidents, such as the brilliant intellectual Jit Phumisak, were liquidated in the cold-war environment that welcomed the Americans to conduct their air raids against Vietnam from Thai territory. Their massive involvement resulted in speeding up economic development, at the same time that the high visibility of the American presence triggered a strong nationalist backlash. Among university students, it stimulated visions of a truly democratic and more egalitaran society.

It is most interesting to note that this volatile mixture of ideas surfaced roughly at the same time among university students in the three countries under discussion. In Indonesia, the agitated atmosphere of the early 1960s led inexorably to the terrifying confrontations of 1965–66 and to the students' campaign to destroy the communist party while forcing the first president from office. Their democratic aspirations and hopes for constructive citizenship were expressed in their newspaper *Harian Kami* and the monthly *Mahasiswa Indonesia* that, in the early years of the Suharto dispensation, were allowed to voice remarkably frank opinions about the state of the realm. Then, as fortunes were built and repression grew, the voices of the students and other critics were gradually pinched off. Their frustration still exploded in the violent, anti-Japanese Malari event of January 1974 that signaled the end of whatever remained of a free press. Their last expression of protest against state authoritarianism was the nation-wide campus demonstrations against the self-appointed 'reelection' of the president. These resulted in the showcase trial of Heri Akhmadi whose published (and banned) defense oration (1979)[3] reminds one of Sukarno's *Indonesia Accuses* forty-nine years earlier.

The persistence of traditional politics, anti-authoritarianism, democratic ideals, and feelings of political irrelevance also fired the imagination and protests of the Philippine studentry who took upon themselves the role of 'conscience of the nation.' The pressing of their demands for democratization culminated in the protracted demonstrations that became known as the First Quarter Storm of 1970. Campus activism came to an end when martial law was declared in

September 1972. What stayed alive, at least at the University of the Philippines (UP), was the desire for genuine independence that was stimulated by Constantino's anti-colonial and anti-elite rewriting of history (1975),[4] and a quest for a cultural nationalism that came to full bloom in the 1980s at UP's Diliman campus. Be that as it may, the results of the nationalist project have, until now, not been very convincing.

For a long time, Field Marshals Thanom Kittikachorn and Prapat Charusathian seemed to be comfortably established while administering Sarit's legacy of rapid economic growth and intimate alliance with the Americans. Yet, their arrogance was irritating, and when the promised constitution was never forthcoming, the pressure of popular discontent exploded in the bloody demonstrations of October 1973 that forced the 'tyrants' into exile. For three years to come, students played a prominent role in politics; progressive ideas circulated, and the works of Sriburapha, Khamsingh Srinawk, Jit Phumisak, and Buddhadasa Bhikkhu were printed and reprinted in unprecedented editions, together with translations of Marx, Lenin, Mao, and other then fashionable gurus. Thai society should be reformed, the practice of Buddhism modernized, the Americans forced out, the peasants emancipated. Students even toured the countryside to educate the rural population in democracy and socialism, trying to make them politically aware while spreading the message that a just society could be built. The counter-revolution of 1976 forced many of the more convinced students 'into the jungle' where they joined the armed communist struggle. Toward the end of the 1970s, most of them resurfaced and were welcomed back into the fold of mainstream society. In the 1980s, progressive, programmatic thinking vanished from the scene. Politically, the campuses became sleepy. The economy boomed.

This was not the case of the Philippines. The excesses of the Marcoses kept indignation alive, and on the far left the National Democratic Front (NDF) and the New People's Army (NPA) were very successful. The Aquino assassination galvanized the urban middle classes into action, too, ultimately resulting in Marcos's flight in February 1986. Interestingly, the NDF/NPA had little to do with the massive demonstrations against the durable dictator, and more with the anger of people thoroughly fed up with their abasement. Although their

People Power 'revolution' was a protest without a program, for a while they became proud Filipinos, titular democrats, and nationalists.

Marcos's demise marks the beginning of the undoing of the Left. In spite of declining levels of living, the massacre of demonstrating peasants, the travesty of Aquino's land reform, environmental degradation, the return of Marcos's cronies and wife, and a hundred other issues that merit protest, the motivational power of the Left is waning, and in the 1990s the 'progressive forces' with their plethora of small socialist parties appear to be in total disarray. At the same time traditional politics have been resurrected, so that the once Proud Filipinos have little left to be proud of and identify with.

The Southeast Asian students of the late 1960s and early 1970s were the third-generation heirs of the pioneers who thought about democracy, social justice, equality, citizenship, and who looked at society and its individuals as capable of amelioration; society could be made a better place. These students were elitists, in the sense that higher education was a privilege still; they were idealists, at a considerable remove from the masses whom they 'discovered' and whose problems they formulated. They went to the countryside to teach.

Simultaneously, though, a new type of society was in the making; urbanization and the changing structure of the economy began to render advanced schooling a necessity; the demand for diplomas steeply increased. Education, as the handmaiden of the credo of development, became a massive enterprise. With this ideational shift, technocracy and economy took precedent over idealism, while societies were opening up to the international world. In the process, the status of being a student changed: students were there to become professionals, not social critics or critical citizens.

These developments were spurred on by martial law in the Philippines and New Order repression and regimentation in Indonesia, but also in Thailand it is hard to believe that, some twenty-five years ago, campuses were buzzing, often blaring, with political energy. Since then, students appear to be motivated by career prospects and the money they need to put their mark on themselves and on society. They seek and shop for lifestyles and the goodies of consumer culture; they watch television and discuss international sports. Meanwhile, the outlandish ideas on democracy, social constructability, and active citizenship fail to develop. At the same time, however, old patterns and values are seemingly reasserting themselves in an environment that is increasingly driven by business and market.

The subconscious return to ideas that existed before society was supposed to be constructable and when it was a moral order still, was already adumbrated by the two neo-Buddhist movements that were founded in Thailand around 1970 and that, at present, enjoy a wide popularity among members of the urban middle classes. These two movements are separated by a far cry from Buddhadasa's rationalism and intellectualism. The first, the Santi Asoke, emphasizes the merit of faithful religious practice, conscious respect for the commandments, and a simple way of life. This movement stands at the beginning of the fad of vegetarianism, a thing unheard of among the Thais in the 1960s. Also its position outside the official Thai Brotherhood of Monks makes the Santi Asoke movement somewhat special.

While the Santi Asoke with its exclusivism and strict lifestyle does not appeal to a vast audience, its counterpart, the Dhammakaya, enjoys wide popularity among university students and other members of the urban middle classes. Although operating within the Thai Brotherhood of Monks, it also strikes one as strange, not because of its emphasis on the benefit of meditation, nor because of its method and speedy progress, but because of its discipline, uniformity, and order.

Like the Iglesia ni Cristo and other sects in the Philippines, or the Islamic upsurge in Indonesia, the new streams in Thai Buddhism focus on individual fulfillment and lack social programs. To them, personal behavior is the well-spring of good society. It is not social reconstruction that matters, but individual morality and discipline. This moralistic approach finds its roots in a hierarchical order where people are aware of and fulfill their place, and where disorder follows from moral decay, from people who are not conscious of duty and who have lost their manners. This way of understanding comes 'naturally,' and tallies with the persistent view that society is, like the ideal family, an integral, moral edifice.

This twin idea of wholeness and wholesomeness precludes distinguishing between things private and things public. What is not personal is of the king, or the state, who, as other private possessors, happen to be superior in the social hierarchy. The public sphere is not of the public—even though it is allowed to cast votes, it is not expected to actively participate in or take responsibility for the commonweal. The public is at the receiving end of political decision-making, and since economic development is the most prominent policy goal, it is business and the state, or money politics, that have become the main players in the political arena. With little in place of a tradition of public control over general affairs, the wider society evolves into an anonymous scene that is animated by the economy with its current ideals of privatization, free-market, technology, career-oriented education, and media control.

What is emerging is a society of consumers, not of citizens. The rapid rise of the urban middle classes has produced novel people in search of a format and a culture. They pattern themselves after the old elite or purchase the international lifestyles that are momentarily fashionable. Their orientation is global; they show a solid preference for what is foreign made; they like to travel abroad; they take little interest in programmatic politics, and if positive, their ideas are businesslike rather than national or ideological.

Their experience of the world outside the home fits with the older image of an area where one does not really belong, where one moves to make a living but carries no responsibility. It is the world of the monarch, patron, corporate manager, or political boss who sees to it that order is imposed. It is a rather violent world because it is about power and thus is driven by competition, prestige, and privilege. Basically it is an amoral environment, subject to the whims of the powerful—and nowadays that most often means corporate business. If charismatic leaders could once still evoke the spirit of nationalism, the transcendence of the (transnational) economy misses this personal touch. United by the market, people have little to identify with and appear to be cynical about and not committed to political affairs. In this situation, the public world does not generate much moral content, and becomes an area of expedient action. In such an environment, the discussion of the rights of citizenship is reduced to empty talk, and the rule of law, a mere illusion.

The image and the reality of this post-national and post-citizenship public world is highly unsatisfactory, although some *nouveaux riches* relish their quest for status and social prominence. This world of make-believe is shared by almost everybody who has some spending money to buy blue jeans, an obscure imitation watch, an earring and a coke, or the paraphernalia of the 'executive look,' including portable telephone, Samsonite luggage, and Gucci frills. Deep down, in one's self-experience, this is little to go by, and other identity-affirming choices need to be made. The ongoing religious revival is a clear indication of the desire of many to adopt a stature and identity independent of the market-driven rat race. Other primordial choices fare well too, the option for one's family and its welfare being the most obvious, at the same time that people are drawn to ethnic and cultural identification in the vague world of the multi-ethnic nation-state. Besides, those who still believe in activism have stopped their politically programmatic agitation, and are now engaged in the more surveyable civil-society associations that fight symptoms rather than basic structures. In brief, the current phase of post-modern contemporaneity seems to foster the moral particularism an older generation of modernists and idealists predicted to be on its way out.

SECTION IV: THE PUBLIC DISCOURSE

CHAPTER 11

THE SOCIAL IMAGINATION

In this chapter, the various bits and pieces of information that have been presented in the previous chapters will be integrated, together with materials concerning the public discourse that I collected in the three predecessor volumes of this study. With the comparative perspective that has guided the selection of the nationally specific topics throughout, we will develop a comprehensive picture. The bibliographic note at the conclusion of this volume will specify the source of the data.

Thus, the data that have been offered on, for instance, Thai ideas on democracy, Filipino thinking about values, and the national debate in Indonesia, will be combined with comparable observations relating to all of the three discourses under discussion. This, in turn, will enable us to propose a concluding sketch of underlying patterns of thinking that, according to my analysis, demonstrates a certain commonality of Southeast Asian conceptualization regarding the public world.

DEMOCRACY

The person

Comparing approaches to democracy and citizenship, it is important to note that these are explained within the constraints of a national doctrine in both Thailand and Indonesia. The Philippines has no such creed. It has a new constitution and values education in school that serve as idealistic guidelines. Interestingly though, while Thailand expects citizens to be loyal subjects of the king, the parts nationals play have been more elaborated in both Indonesia and the Philippines. Indonesia envisages the Pancasila Man, or the Whole Indonesian Human Being. This particular species is entirely embedded in group: it is part of family, community, nation, and state. It blends with its social surroundings; its actions concur with the common welfare; it is the embodiment of harmony.

According to Philippine teachings, the New Filipino has arisen in fulfillment of the progress of the nation. The course of history was full of obstacles to democratic practice; the nation still had to be formed. Now, however, freed from the debilitating clutches of the Marcos dictatorship, a new citizen can emerge who, conscious of rights and duties, actively participates in national and civic affairs. As responsible citizens, new Filipinos are expected to enjoy their autonomy within the bounds of the common welfare.

The fact that Thai teachings do not propose a new type of human being is in line with what these implicitly tell us. To be a Thai Thai, inspired by 'beautiful culture and traditions,' and leading an ethical way of life (which entails the meticulous execution of tasks and duties) is good enough.

Thai and Indonesian teachings warn against the free exercise of rights. Such practice leads to self-centeredness and could well endanger social harmony. Thai instructions emphasize a seemingly Buddhist remedy. Be self-aware! This self-awareness, which is also invoked in Indonesian and Philippine civics texts, is thought to stimulate reason and moral consciousness, tolerance, and sense of belonging to group, and thus acts as a disciplinary measure. This results in respect for customs and law, in ethical and well-mannered behavior. Such self-aware people are not only nice to associate with; they are, like the New Filipino, eminently democratic. They follow the rules, thus creating order, and thus enjoying happiness.

From these considerations, interesting differences appear. The Indonesian citizen is located in the future, and will be the product of the consistent practice of Pancasila democracy that leaves no room for individual dissent. Of course, individuals hold a variety of opinions, but these can be reduced to a common denominator. Then harmony will prevail, the group will carry the day, the nation-state will prosper. The Thais look for the key in the past. Yet, also they assume that individuals are primarily components of an encompassing family or nation, and that their ethical behavior and duty consciousness result in a democratic way of life, in quiet happiness. It is the Filipinos who appeal to active citizenship, which seems to imply a little more than the claims made by all that the government derives its power from people, and that 'the' or these people are involved in political decision taking. Civic activities, open disagreement, and civic liberty are expressly mentioned as ingredients of democratic practice. Nonetheless, like the others, Filipino textbooks also readily assert that duty comes first. The government must be supported by its citizens. People must be loyal to the republic. They should be gainfully employed. They must be responsible. They are members of their family, which is, according to the constitution, 'a basic autonomous institution.' They are encompassed by or under that institution, like they are under God, and under authority that must be respected.

The oscillation in Philippine teachings is present in the Thai and Indonesian materials too. It is bound to come up when discussing the basically confusing ideas of rights and equality. While it was explicitly stated that human rights are vested in individual persons, that they are intrinsic to their being human, and that people in this sense are equal, the elaboration of these ideas did not proceed smoothly. While the Thais appeared to be most serious in attempting to clarify rights, they went awry when explaining the consequences. Finally nothing much happened but a listing of the rights the constitution specifies, followed by a safe retreat to the subject of obligations.

The Filipinos, too, listed rights, without any attempt at explaining these in despite of their legalistic approach to the subject. Somehow, in the school presentation, they de-individualized rights as 'right to welfare,' 'right to education,' and 'right to protection.' The Indonesians were even more exhaustive in specifying the rights people are declared to enjoy—which is quite remarkable in view of the then prevailing dictatorship. Less remarkable, though, was the caveat that people should not insist on exercising rights. That, as was expounded in the Thai curriculum too, could disturb harmony and good neighborliness, and thus lead to punishment. And so all and sundry paired rights with duties as a matter of course, and stressed the latter.

Equality, in Southeast Asia, is perhaps the most difficult of all notions to explain. Often, the very idea of equality is equated with anarchy and loathsome individualism. Looking for the safe side of things, equality has therefore not been properly elucidated in any of the books. It has merely been asserted. People are equal before the law. The Thais illustrated equality by 'a poor and a rich man each has one vote.' And then, of course, all are said to enjoy the same rights.

The collectivity

'The people' are proclaimed to rule the country. Government is of, by, and for them. The government listens to them. They voice their opinion in representative bodies. All teachings agree on these clauses. The Thais and Indonesians then idealize the people as an undifferentiated mass. In Thailand, they become nation, under king and religion. In Indonesia, they become a family inhabiting an integralistic state. In both, they are embedded in state ideology. The state is represented as a father-knows-best, its king or president the head of the national family. The rules of democracy, therefore, become the rules of the family—a hierarchical arrangement in any culture. 'Do as we have always done'—mutual consultation, or respect for parents and king—and we are democratic. Somehow, democracy belongs to being a nation, and being a nation is being a family. The Filipinos are not blessed with a strong sense of nation and openly complain about lack of unity and solidarity. The state is not seen as a father and does not command much confidence or loyalty. But this is to change. The state is evolving towards nationhood. Under the constitution and with the practice of democracy, nation, rule of law, respect for human dignity, freedom, and equality, will come into being.

So, what the Thais say they have, and what the Indonesians are aiming at—the fulfillment of the Pancasila state—the Filipinos hope to realize through implementing constitution and democracy. They are all set on nationhood, on unity, which they connect with an interpretation of 'democracy' in which the dutiful 'citizen' is embedded in the national family. Still more important than constitution and democracy in bringing forth national community is the condition of the family. If this 'foundation of the nation' is in good order, if people are loving and reasonable there, society and democratic practice will be fine. Respect for parents, teachers and God leads to 'peace and happiness,' to 'harmony,' and to 'democracy' as an ethical way of life.

In spite of the highly critical, negative evaluation of the state of the polity Philippine school texts afford, hopes have been pinned on achieving a nation. That nation is a moral construct in which individuals are not self-centered, in which civil servants do not abuse office, in which politicians are not self-serving, and in which all will feel the pride of belonging. This thinking is undiluted moralism, call it idealism, in stark contrast with the evaluation of practice. We noted that this contrast also surfaced in Thai texts. Old ways of doing things are said to obstruct 'the democratic way of life' and cause divisions and upset. Nation must, therefore, be reconstructed. Nobody doubts that it existed—only democratic reasonableness needs to be added. Even the Indonesians recognized that, as yet, not all is well. 'Certain individuals' still are so self-possessed as to act against the Pancasila. Parliament falls short in initiative, and still acts as a rubber stamp for the executive branch. But in the end—and these are shared teleological interpretations of history— a peaceful national collectivity will come into being, thanks to constitution, democracy, ideology, and doctrine.

The moral society

Although school texts primarily in the Philippines, but also in Thailand and even Indonesia, can be read as hinting at certain structural problems—the gap between rich and poor, self-serving civil service, opulent lifestyles—all of them steer clear of sociological analysis. Problems are noted in passing; their historical and economic roots are decidedly left underground.

The prevailing social imagination seems to be inspired by family ideals. Not only that—individuals are seen as integrated parts of family, group, and community. There they have tasks and duties. They functionally depend upon each other. Such an imagination does not allow for conflicts. It allows for moral solutions to differences. The social responsibility it places on the shoulders of individuals is to watch themselves and to toe the line. Otherwise, peaceful social life will be disturbed.

In this world of ideas, the public realm becomes highly ambivalent. Sometimes it appears to be articulated to the private domain, at another moment the two are separated by putting the public world at a firm distance as an area of immoral politics and abuse of power. In the latter case, it is hoped that the public world can be brought under control when 'the people' are democratically represented, when they raise their voice and speak their will. In this they are still thwarted by elitist, privileged power holders; if the latter would be true democrats too, the public welfare would flourish—public and private interests would fuse.

The articulation of the public with the private world appears most clearly in the moral—and thus individual-centered—advice and exhortations aimed at improving social and national life. The Philippines has its Moral Recovery Program and obligatory values education at all levels of schooling. The course on Pancasila and citizenship is the Indonesian equivalent. In Thailand, the doctrine of the Three Institutions pervades the social studies curriculum. Supposedly, private morality can be applied to the public world. Society is not seen as a realm different from community. As a result, 'the people' are thought to deliberate in parliament. They may voice different opinions—all books say so—but will find solutions that serve the 'common interest.'

The community or family approach also plays havoc with the explanation of human rights. Individuals are not seen as autonomous agents, but as parts of encompassing groups. So, while all of the teachings at some place recognize that rights are vested in persons per se, they make it appear that such persons are parts of groups and therefore under their authority. Rights then appear as something granted, and thus invite reciprocal obligations; hence, the pairing of rights and duties as a matter of course, with the emphasis always on the latter.

Democracy?
Seen in a sociological and Western-historical perspective, the public world, or the abstract vastness of society, is an area of contention and strife, of anonymity and businesslike behavior. The experience of it individualizes. It is the area where everybody pursues his own interest. This public world is animated by power play, that is politics, and by the pursuit of wealth, or the economy. Left to themselves, these two 'independent subsystems' are expected to dominate the lifeworld in many of its aspects. Since this is threatening, they need to be brought under control and a democratic government is a possible means to that end. A vigorous civil society of autonomous yet committed citizens, and civil society organizations, are similar means. Such autonomous citizens

are people who insist on their rights. These are an inalienable part of their humanity. Since they are committed, they insist on the rule of law—and are thus willing to contribute their share.

These things have not been explained in the texts we reviewed. As a result, democracy remains vague—an obviously foreign transplant in a hierarchizing and patron-seeking milieu. While in Philippine books civic associations and public opinion have been mentioned, it remains unclear how these would invigorate democracy and civil society. Individualization—also exercising one's rights—are recognized as endangering harmony and peace. It is from the individual that strife originates. He should be taught morals lest he lose self-control and pursue egoistic interests.

The focus on morality and individual behavior keep practical societal matters from view. While representative institutions and the three branches of government have been presented, their practical operation has been sidestepped. 'Politicians are self-seeking'—but explaining practical politics and politicking has been avoided. While it has been made explicit in both the Thai and Philippine texts that the present, traditional political system of politics does not serve the public interest, concrete questions have not been addressed. An old-fashioned mentality, lack of popular education, vote-selling, person-centered politics, cupidity, and the fooling of voters have been mentioned but have not been reduced to causes. As a result, many questions remain. What is corruption? Why is it so widespread? What is the nature of the collusion of business and bureaucratic interests? What is the material basis of all sorts of conflicts? What is patronage? What do 'traditional politics' mean? Such practical things are never discussed, and students are thus left with high-minded ideas about one form or another of a democratic nation without any bridge to practice or to problems.

NATIONAL COMMUNITY

When surveying Filipino views of their imagined community, we noted strong tendencies to assess national existence critically and negatively. The public domain seemed to be in a mess, the government weak and unwilling to or incapable of imposing order. People were said to be short of nationalism and discipline, cutting corners was the rule, and untamed individualism became the guiding principle in public life. In academic literature the country has been characterized as 'an anarchy of families' ever defiant of central authority. The stinging criticism of their own condition is known as 'self-flagellation' or 'Philippines-bashing' among Filipinos themselves. Now, if we look at all this in comparative and historical perspectives, can we then assess whether the bond that ties Filipinos together is really as brittle as it is popularly perceived to be?

In order to understand Filipino grumbling at 'lack of identity' and 'absence of nationalism,' we need to go back to the Spaniards who justified their dominion by bringing the Christian religion to the natives of the territories they conquered. They were highly successful in this endeavor. They established white, Catholic supremacy, which they arrogantly maintained for more than three hundred years. Their colonization was primarily cultural. They imposed their religion and their racist standards. In the process, the Filipinos lost themselves; they lost their soul. They had begun to believe in what they were taught.

When the Filipinos finally achieved their freedom, nationalist fervor was effectively doused by a second wave of racialized cultural domination. The Americans brought modernity, progress, democracy, education in English, and Protestantism. Again, the Filipinos were overwhelmed. They were truly a vanquished people, losing their own civilization by accepting an alien one. Such are the roots of Filipino resentment, not just against the white world but primarily against themselves and their state of being. They developed a love-hate relationship with themselves, and with their colonizers.

Does this confirm the schoolbook messages of lack of identity and nationalism? I do not think so. The contrary is the case. Colonialism established a transcending culture of which Filipinos are very conscious. They are the only Christian nation in Asia. They consider themselves to be the largest English-speaking country in that part of the world. They identify as modern people, almost as cosmopolitans. They take pride in democracy. They still see their relationship with the United States as something special, as a privilege, and take pride in progress, or rather, a future-orientation that leads away from the past. In other words, there is quite some cultural substance and conscious identity among Filipinos.

The problem with the school texts, and with the press for that matter, is that they perpetuate legalistic and political visions of the nation, and fail to take culture seriously. The nation is reduced to rules of citizenship, artificial symbols, tourist spots, anthem singing and flag raising, practical politics and the constitution. In other words, in the approach taken, public disorder, loathsome politics, and constitutional hopes stand out, while the historical and cultural ties that unite Filipinos receive little attention. We can understand this type of presentation when we are aware of the unconscious resentment against the history of Philippine becoming, which is overtly demonstrated by the irritation at authors, such as Nick Joaquin and O. D. Corpuz, who take Filipino rootedness in the Spanish period seriously.

There may be a second error of judgment. The emphasis on state and politics, and thus on an unruly public world, makes identification with it problematic. There is, indeed, little to be proud of. But identification with state and public affairs is very different from identification with nation, with motherland. The latter appears to be quite strong, and if it is, sometimes, still characterized by a self-bashing attitude, it only demonstrates a healthy love-hate relationship, that is, a powerful emotional bond.

When we juxtapose Philippine cultural unity with the Indonesian situation, we see a world of difference as far as national community is concerned. The Indonesian islands, stretching along five thousand kilometers of equator, were effectively brought under Dutch sway only around 1900. Despite their long presence in the archipelago, their cultural influence was, excepting some Christian communities, minimal. They were interested in trade, in earning money. So, by the time the idea of Indonesia dawned upon its intelligentsia, in the 1920s, nothing was in place really in terms of culture and shared history but the fact of the Netherlands' supremacy. As a result, creating unity through creating common culture has always been high in the minds of the Indonesian founding fathers and the strategists of Suharto's New Order regime. Under the latter this resulted in massive indoctrination efforts.

Already under the Dutch, fissures, or tensions that could spread feelings of hatred, were recognized to exist, and the propagation of such differences was a criminal offense. They were specified as differences in ethnicity, religion, race, and among groups or classes. Ethnicity refers to clefts between the four hundred or so distinctive cultural groups, and their dissimilar ways of life, that compose the Indonesian population. The issue of religion is far more complex than the Philippine opposition between Muslims and Christians. Among themselves, Indonesian Muslims are highly divided, along ethnic-cultural, ideological, and political lines, and many are the battles fought among themselves. Besides, there are also Hindus, Buddhists, Protestants, Catholics, and so-called Confucianists in the country. The idea of racial tensions normally refers to original Indonesians versus people of Chinese descent, while inter-group tensions can refer to anything else, although it is class struggle that is commonly meant.

Because all such clefts were made taboo and ignored during the long Suharto period—national unity was proclaimed to prevail—tensions built up. They exploded during the waning years of the regime, most visibly since the politically motivated attack on the headquarters of Megawati Sukarnoputri's Democratic Party on 27 July 1996. Soon, this state-instigated ransacking was followed by anti-Christian, anti-Chinese, anti-employer, anti-authority, and anti-migrant violence. All of this was aggravated when the Asian monetary crisis began to bite. Then sheer poverty and deprivation gave an added dimension to plunder and rioting.

The New Order regime's emphasis on unity, integrity, and stability also led to administrative and economic over-centralization, the dominance of Javanese in government and military, and the exploitation and subordination of the non-Javanese regions. Several provinces, especially Aceh and Papua, developed active movements of armed resistance, and so finally it is the army that holds the country together. These armed forces, however, do not seem to be able to call a halt to the civil war in the Moluccas; its culture of violence appears to have become the norm. In the final analysis, there is little that culturally holds the country together other than a national school system and the successful establishment of the non-controversial Indonesian language.

Compared to Indonesia and the turmoil that plagues it, the Philippines appears as a wonder of integration, and Thailand as a idyll of rest. Still, we should not belittle the rifts that divide society against itself. Both the Philippines and Thailand have their Malay Muslim minorities that are not precisely pleased with Christian or Buddhist assertions of authority. They feel that they are second-rate citizens, suffering from the claims of the center. This centralization of government and administration is a general problem of the provinces that breeds dissatisfaction and disloyalty to the state. In a way it is also expressed by the rather recent cleavage between the big cities and the countryside, with the latter clearly subsidizing urban economic growth and relative prosperity. The latter phenomena are highly visualized by the ever-growing, yawning gap between the rich and poor. In the Philippines this set of problems is enhanced by what some call the great cultural divide between the English-speaking, America-oriented elite, and those who are ill-educated and seemingly left behind by all progress.

Compared to the actual situation in Indonesia and perceived disunity in the Philippines, Thailand appears both practically and ideationally well integrated. This did not come for free, and is the result of Bangkok's persistent endeavor of exorcising the specters of national instability and disunity. Already early in the twentieth century, King Rama VI (1910–25) recognized a relationship between nationalism, and the country's unity and strength. Because of this, he created many modern symbols of the nation, among them the doctrine of the Three Institutions. That doctrine, as we have seen, is a royal creed that aims at establishing a certain bond between the monarch and his Siamese subjects in all their diversity. When, in the subsequent, highly patriotic, 'republican' period the country was renamed as Country of the Thais, non-Thais could easily feel excluded.

While a certain homogeneity seems to prevail in Thailand these days, in the recent past it was much less apparent. Ten percent of the population is of Chinese origin, and direct immigration went on well into the 1950s. A third of Thailand's people live in the Northeast, and refer to themselves as Laotian. In the North, the last signs of recalcitrance against Bangkok's domination appeared shortly before the Second World War. Besides, and this is lasting well into the present, the various 'mountain peoples' living there and in the western border tracts with Myanmar are still far from integrated into the population.

Even so, in one way or another, historical clefts are being overcome in Thailand. Most people of Chinese descent have been assimilated as Thai citizens and feel themselves as such. Regionalism in the Northeast and North seems to have given way to the general, modern complaint about Bangkok's internal colonialism, and the blatant exploitation of the country by its businessmen-politicians. So, while there is still a good deal of discrimination against uplanders and southern Muslims, certain old fissures are less pronounced at the same time that modernity and economic development cause new cleavages that are shared throughout the developing world, such as highly educated versus barely schooled; rich versus poor; having effective political power versus being part of the voting mob; living in the city versus struggling for survival on the land; being cosmopolitan in a globalizing world versus the quest for identity in regionalism, ethnicity, and life's religious foundation.

From all this, it is safe to conclude that national community, as an imagined fact, has been rather successfully developed in Thailand, and has a strong basis in Filipino culture. Philippine self-doubt about it has plausible historical roots, while this situation is exacerbated by the economy-related cleavages just mentioned. These also explain much of the trouble with the southern Muslims and, of course, with the national democratic Left and their long-running fight to establish a just social order. Yet, apart from Islamic secessionism, the Philippines appears as a well-integrated nation-state, at the same time that the survival of the Republic of Indonesia as we know it today must be seriously doubted.

STATE MORAL GUIDANCE

In the 1990s and into the new century, elementary and secondary schools throughout Thailand, the Philippines, and Indonesia are devoting considerable attention to the teaching of values. This emphasis on morals, ethics, and appropriate behavior is nothing new; it is based on the idea that the cradle of knowledge is the study and understanding of ethics, of discovering the unity of the good, the true, and the beautiful. The wise person, the one who is aware, cannot behave in an ignorant, unenlightened, and thus despicable way.[1] Contrarily, it is the absence of wisdom that leads to undesirable action, saliently expressed in the notion that obnoxious behavior equates with falling short in learning. There is therefore no dispute that people's awareness needs developing, and that it can be trained through study and learning— which is an individual, intellectual pursuit.[2] In brief, ethics can be taught and learned; state-guided values education in school makes sense.

In the courses concerned, ethics and rule-following are seen as being at the core of civilization. This idea fuses with the perception of society as a moral construct in which people relate to each other on the basis of obligation and inequality. As a result, knowledge of the ethics of place—and behaving accordingly—is at the heart of social harmony.

Next to this cultural view, we can identify a more pedestrian, sociological reason that lends the teaching of values its urgency, namely, the social organization of the people along the littoral of the South China Sea. This organization is not based on encompassing principles, such as membership of castes and clans with their religious obligations. On the contrary, Thais, Filipinos, and most Indonesians reckon their descent bilaterally, that is, according to the also Western idea of the equal importance of the female and male lines. This effectively limits the depth of descent, and the devotion or piety to unknown clan ancestors or caste deities simply does not make sense. What is emphasized is obligation and devotion to parents and relatives; these are formulated as a principle of reciprocity, namely, as the debt of gratitude—a principle that implies that people know each other concretely. As a result, people are at the center of personal networks of relationships, and further only encompassed by their patron-client ties, ethnic groups, and the state to which they belong.

Because bilaterality is that person-centered, the governments concerned are wary of their citizens whom they try to bind to the center as nationalists and/or as morally obliged subjects. This circumspection is, especially in Thailand and Indonesia, enhanced by the advent of modernity, of progress, of capitalism. After all, urban living, and commercialized life in general, individualize and set people free in anonymous environments where they are beyond the older means of social or state control. Official apprehension is further aggravated by the clash of time-honored perceptions and the modernist ideas of democracy that seemingly stress individualization, emancipation and equality. The latter have always been suspect in a hierarchicizing environment where power concentrates rather than diffuses. Consequently, the notion of the democratic citizen as a responsible, morally autonomous individual is disorderly in itself; it is threatening to social harmony.

For these, sometimes explicit, sometimes subconscious reasons, the Thai state has, from the 1960s onwards, massively propagated the ideology of Nation-Religion-King, in which King, as the quintessential protector of the nation, became an object of worship. He became the superpatron, the superfather of the people as a family. This implies that the people are seen as children in need of guidance from not only King, but also from Religion, which, as a moral mother, assists King in bringing harmony and prosperity to Nation. No wonder that Nation is tied by the bond of the debt of gratitude to King and Religion; it is obliged to demonstrate loyalty and obedient devotion.

This ideology of the Three Institutions is very similar to what is propagated in Indonesia. The founding principles of the republic are, among others, the idea that the state is *integralistic*, that is, it incorporates all and sundry, and is run on the family principle under a fatherly president. In later Pancasila thinking, the principle of belief in God Almighty, or religion, was added as the fountainhead of morality and good citizenship. People, in their turn, are seen as pupils in need of guidance and care.

Thai and Indonesian ideology both privilege the family as the basic building block of the nation and see the nation-state as a family. This implies hierarchical organization under a father-leader, assisted by a moral mother—religion—and a devoted populace. As in the family, all strive for harmony and execute mutually different tasks and obligations that complement each other. This results in the ideas that there are no conflicts of interest and that society is a moral community.

Although the Philippines has less of a national doctrine other than the Constitution of 1987 and its preamble, also there the individual is seen as embedded in families that are constitutionally considered as 'autonomous institutions' that form the foundation of the nation and that 'public policy cherishes and protects.' The recognition of that autonomy may be at the basis of the Philippine 'anarchy of families,' and pre-empts the image of the nation-as-family. This realism, however, is juxtaposed with the national Moral Recovery Program and, more pertinently, with values education in school. So, also here the state takes it upon itself to provide moral guidance, while the emphasis on the family places individuals in a network of hierarchic and obliging relationships that supposedly rein them in.

In comparison, it is clear that the nation stands at the heart of state moral guidance in Thailand and Indonesia. In the Philippines it is the family as such that is stressed, while the nation is recognized as problematic. Yet, the Philippines shares the same deficit as Thailand and Indonesia by not offering an alternative model to the moral doctrine propagated in preparing the students to come to grips with societal conditions. How to live with or in society as an area of opposing interests, contention, and strife is settled as a matter of personal ethics. As a consequence, the historical and sociological imagination of the public remains underdeveloped, which is also clear from the approach taken to social problems and their solution.

PROBLEMS

Open to the West
In spite of ideology or because of realism, we noticed the recognition of sometimes baffling lists of problems in the three countries concerned. In Thailand, it was change itself that was seen as the root cause of problems. Obviously the past was commendable, and the present questionable. According to Indonesian teachings, it is the future that holds promise: then Pancasila society and the Complete Indonesian Man will be realized. This orientation also surfaced in the Philippines where the Constitution of 1987 and the democratic New Filipino augur a just and prosperous society.

Aside from such idealizations, many problems appeared. While the Thais would like to see them as signs of progress—change is progress with problems—they also thought Asians to be wiser, and thus capable of avoiding the problems that arose in the West and its history of industrialization. Yet they worried about their youth. The young go to karaoke bars, are possessed by material values, behave rudely, or un-Thai, and their sense of morals is eroding. Moreover, many people claim their rights but are remiss of duty, thus threatening to upset the order of the nation.

The last problem also stood out in the Indonesian teachings, and like the Thai, they warned against insistence on rights. Duty should prevail. Even so, many people are influenced by improper Western values, such as individualism and materialism. Shouldn't the country protect itself against foreign influences? Well, apart from preventing national development, the current process of globalization would render such efforts impossible. Inner-Indonesian solutions must therefore be developed.

In contrast to the Thai and Indonesian views, the Western idea of individual rights was not seen as problematic in the Philippines. There, the outstanding problem was identified as the very long period of colonization that destroyed the wholesome social fabric of native society. This problem became increasingly acute during the period of American colonization. Its heritage is to be blamed for the popularity of things foreign, often referred to as 'our colonial mentality,' and an inferiority complex vis-à-vis Caucasians, thus giving rise to a culture of slavish imitation. This pernicious admiration pervades the system of education and the media in English, and makes the mastery of that language the prime token of self-esteem. As a result, it is claimed that Philippine schooling is out of joint with the living culture of the Filipino people.

Power

The evolution of political culture is seen as a grave problem that is rooted in hierarchical organization and patronage. Of old, people are said to admire power, irrespective of who holds it. Those who are powerful are potential patrons, and receiving patronage obliges. It activates the glue—the debt of gratitude—that sticks Southeast Asian relationships together. People are not tied together by abstract loyalties to their state or by socio-political ideologies, but feel obliged to patrons and protectors. Because of having a concrete king as a moral superpatron, the Thai state can mobilize considerable nationalism. In the absence of such an exemplary center, the ties to the state are much weaker in both the Philippines and Indonesia where regionalism is much more pronounced.

But then, below the level of the king, things appear to be very similar: people who wield power are admired. In practical Thai politics, the electorate is said to choose unworthy candidates who, because of their resources, can buy the vote. These businessmen-politicians are very influential, and can thus go against the law while still being held as honorable. They are in politics because they want to promote their personal interests in a materialistic, competitive environment. This is money politics *pur sang* that neither serves the national interest nor the common good.

In the Philippines this is known as traditional politics or loathsome politicking. The whole system, including the civil service, is politicized, and thus highly corrupted. We find hardly any popular representation in Congress and Senate. On the contrary, these Houses consist of elite politicians who promote the interests of their clans. They are guided by money and materialism, and have no loyalty to either party or nation. Like in Thailand, parties are mere *ad hoc* groupings of political entrepreneurs whose wheeling and dealing is far from transparent. The only thing democratic about them is that they depend on elections— and thus on the manipulation of the vote—to achieve political prominence.

What the free vote in post-Suharto Indonesia is going to mean is as yet unclear. The problem of power, however, has been squarely recognized. The system, so far, has been driven by patronage, by cronyism, by money. Filthy lucre has become the measure of everything, which exacerbates status competition, and leads to elite exclusivism. They think themselves to be better than the others; they are the new feudal lords, privileged, and thus way above the law. What is important to them, as well as to anybody else, are connections to the right people. It is the system known as corruption, collusion, and cronyism that not only pervades the civil service but society itself.

Concrete problems or attitudes?

While the three countries similarly recognize the foreign assault on wholesome culture and the bedeviling ways of power, the representation of social problems is rather different between Thailand, on the one side, and the Philippines and Indonesia, on the other. This may have to do with the avoidance of all structural analysis in the teachings of the latter two, and a combination of Thai realism and optimism.

In the Thai teachings, change is seen as inevitable development. Urbanization is a fact to live with, and small families and businesslike relationships have to be accepted in its stride. Modern people are informed people; the media flourish, and the government smoothes the transition, also through expanding public services, and promoting pride in Thai culture. Even so, a certain measure of consumerism and materialism is acceptable; they are part of modernity.

There also is a negative side to all this. Urban traffic is jammed; it pollutes the air and affects the nerves. Besides, when it moves it causes many accidents. Industrialization brings pollution and ecological destruction. Migration of ill-educated people leads to poverty, slums, crime, drugs, prostitution, and poor health. The city is simply overrun by poor people. With this, the enumeration of problems stops, and we hear nothing about their structural rootedness.

Identical lists of shifts and problems could of course have been drawn up in the Philippines and Indonesia. What they did in its stead was specifying attitudes that they see as problematical. It was noted that people shy away from social responsibility and seemingly only care for their personal well-being. In this setting, people grow indifferent to the common welfare, and thus tolerate corruption and irregularities. It seems as if they have no moral conviction, at least, not in the public world. There they have no discipline, sense of duty or initiative. They gladly depend on patrons or government, and try to get away with all sorts of dubious behavior.

Again, these supposed attitudes could also be integrated through structural analysis, but that never occurs. As a result, and this goes for all three of them, people are confronted with an avalanche of problems that threatens to overwhelm them. Since the problems lack clear context and contours, the best that can be done is to arm people morally—and thus individually—to resist them.

SOLUTIONS

There is remarkable homogeneity again in the ways proposed to solve the sudden exposure to a market-driven society. All call for the development of social and self-awareness, and of moral consciousness. People are advised to bring their lives in harmony with law, ideology, and ethics. In Thailand, the stress is on seeking knowledge and education, on understanding cause and effect; in the Philippines, on love for God and fellows to develop individual conscience and attitudes; in Indonesia, on self-mastery and willingness to sacrifice for the well-being of the collectivity. In other words, all clamor for moral solutions to societal problems.

These appeals agree with a basic imagining of society as a moral community. In such a society, individuals bear the burden of knowing their place and its inherent duties. This makes, as we discussed, values education eminently compelling, but sidesteps the question of society as an arena of conflicting interests, of different value-orientations, and competition. That we have arrived at such a society is, in many ways, acknowledged, but a critical analysis that relates problems to structural developments and change does not appear to be part of the social imagination.

QUALITY OF EDUCATION

The relative absence of sociological reasoning makes people depend on experiential knowledge. Such knowledge is highly realistic; it even surfaced in Philippine values education. Yet, it is not really necessary to make it explicit in school: the contrast between a moralistic image and life's practice is just too obvious to ignore. Things that are true within the school yard are fiction on the other side of the fence. So, while students may be ignorant of sociological analysis, of causes and consequences, most of them have a good notion of how things are, how money politics proceed, and how to expedite matters. Consequently, school may instill moral indifference and a firm measure of cynicism.

Even so, an incredible amount of time is spent, especially in Thai elementary, on the preparation for tractable subjectship. In the two upper grades, 75 percent of school time is devoted to social studies. Much of this time is sheer waste, because many of the moral and behavioral messages are not only very repetitive, but have already been instilled at home. Besides, nobody is under the illusion that school-taught ethics stick when students stream on to high school. The excessive emphasis on social studies causes a further problem because, upon entering higher grades, the children generally show a deficit of linguistic and arithmetical skills.

The Indonesian and Philippine situations are different, but not better. Whereas in Thailand the diffusion of the national language has been very successful, probably also because the dialects are rather closely related to it, the diversity of tongues is much greater among the overseas neighbors. While the Indonesians have also been successful in spreading the national idiom, it is, so far, the home language of some 15 percent of the population only. Most students, therefore, have to learn the language of instruction as a second language. This does not need to be problematical if the quality of teaching and textbooks were high—but this is not the case. The confused use of language—and thus muddled thinking—is a grave problem up to the highest levels of education.

The Filipinos, too, have been quite effective in throwing up hurdles to the development of clear-thinking minds. School is supposed to spread Tagalog as the national Filipino, which is a second language to approximately 70 percent of the population. To complicate matters, English is strongly promoted—one period a day—through all school years. This is founded on the brilliant policy of bilingualism: the soft subjects are taught in Tagalog, and the sciences, including elementary arithmetic, in English. No wonder that most students have muddled minds. The few who survive this pedagogic violence gather in the top three sections of the four high-school years where English and science receive extra attention (and where the course on values need not be taught). The others are simply left behind to provide resources to the many diploma mills if they can afford a few years of college. They have been deprived of the privilege to learn to think keenly in any language. Be that as it may, there are many people in the Philippines who are at ease with English, while it is rare to find university students in Thailand and Indonesia who are capable of making sense of a text in that language.

In Southeast Asia, the educational establishment has developed explosively over, especially, the last three, four decades. This fast growth has eroded its quality at the same time that no good policy goals have been envisaged or implemented. The teaching methods remain largely old-fashioned and stimulate rote-learning. This is enhanced by the weak preparation of teachers, of whom some 50 percent are underqualified and who only weakly comprehend the subject matter they are teaching.

The fact that a market-driven, urban society is evolving is nowhere reflected in the teaching materials, which is also obvious from the recent introduction of values education. In Thailand, the excessive emphasis on being good dates from the reactionary curriculum reform of 1978. In Indonesia, Pancasila Moral Education was introduced in the same year, while the Philippine program became official in 1989 only. In other words, students are not precisely prepared for creativity, modern living, or mental and moral independence. Academically, they are poorly trained, committing a vast vocabulary of difficult words to memory without having any theoretical insight into how these rarified terms stick together. This is most obvious in Indonesia where we find a vast production of scatterbrained newspaper columns clearly influenced by equally inconsistent indoctrination.

The quality of intellectual life is rather alarming. Of course, the voices that can clearly be heard are those of the best, most often foreign educated intelligentsia, but these cannot be considered to set the tone of the public discourse. Many people simply do not understand the messages they send. In the Philippines under the long Marcos dictatorship and in Indonesia under the New Order culture was effectively destroyed. The students who were trained in those days are sarcastically known as Martial Law or New Order babies, not educated to be critical or socially attentive. Apart from that, they grew up with television rather than with books. The low priority of reading is also reflected in the unavailability of books, the absence of real bookshops, and the very low production of book titles. Both the Philippines and Indonesia produce eleven hundred titles a year only, which makes Thailand, with over six thousand, a book freak's paradise. In that country one also finds genuine book stores where one cannot buy pencils or erasers, and where one's concentration is not tested by loud music.

The quality of schooling is often discussed in the public debate, although comments are most commonly addressed at school fees and accessibility. As a reaction to the distressing state of public education, more expensive private schools have proliferated, centers of excellence have been established, and new levels of academic qualification have been introduced. In Thailand, curriculum reform is a perennial item on the official agenda. In the Philippines, the Ministry of Education planned to append a college preparatory year to the four-year high-school course in 2002. That year would concentrate on forty-eight units of English, Mathematics, and Science, to be followed by a test to see whether students qualified to go on to college or should downgrade their ambitions to vocational training. No wonder that those who exploit diploma mills heaved a sigh of relief when it all blew over. In Indonesia, one-time technology czar Habibie strongly pushed to send as many students as possible abroad, primarily for training in Australia. Altogether, however, it seems that real reform is as elusive as it is needed.

INSTITUTIONAL DEVELOPMENT

In our review of the topics that are brought forward in the Indonesian reform debate, it became clear that high priority was accorded to building strong, stable, and independent institutions of state and civil society. Under the dictatorship, almost all social organizations had been infiltrated by the state, including the political parties, religious associations, and most NGOs. It was only the unbending few who could maintain themselves outside the orbit of an excessively centralizing executive, such as the maverick politician Abdurrahman Wahid, the courageous legal aid institute LBH, the Forum for Democracy, certain groups of ostracized academics, and the gadfly-members of the intelligentsia who had the temerity—and a little space—to express the voices of common sense, justice, and protest all along.

Perhaps it was the regime's promise, around 1990, of striving for a measure of openness that stimulated it developing a severe case of paranoia, most vividly illustrated by its clampdown on the respectable, self-censoring voices of *Tempo, Editor,* and *DeTik* (1994). This, naturally, gave rise to groups of free journalists and alternative magazines, such as *D&R* and *Forum Keadilan*, that consistently questioned New Order conditions. They emphasized the absence of justice, the venality of and executive influence on the judiciary, and the police as a servant of the powers-that-be. Interestingly, these criticisms were allowed to flourish; in its blind arrogance, the New Order obviously considered the subject of justice a trifle, unworthy of attention.

At the same time, severe but subtly worded criticism was regularly voiced in the columns of the English-language *Jakarta Post* (it claims that its readership is 70 percent Indonesian). Its dual targets were the conduct of politics—or rather their absence—in which the president totally dominated the institutions of parliament, and the appalling condition of education. To bring out the rot in the realm, such columns normally exemplified the state of institutions through analyzing cases of individual conduct, such as those of bombastic 'civil' servants, self-righteous 'popular' representatives, and bigoted principals.

The attack on Megawati Sukarnoputri's party headquarters on 27 July 1996 illustrated the severity of the mental delusions the regime was suffering from. It augured the long period of continual unrest that is pervading the country; obviously, the New Order's culture of violence had established itself, had become national. In this climate, it was even tolerated that, in his collection of poetry, *Eyewitness*, Seno Gumira Ajidarma exposed the horrors of East Timor. The military did not consist of heroes; they were butchers.

From this short survey, it is clear that throughout the waning years of the Suharto regime many of the topics that were later—and currently—articulated in the reform agenda were part of the public debate all along. Their focus was clear too: the institutions of state need to be disentangled; army and police must be civilized. When the discussion about reform could fully develop, two further foci were added: for one, the intimate connection between state-political might and economic power must be broken and civil society should urgently develop.

Meanwhile the hopes for—and necessity of—stable institutions sadly contrast with a state of affairs in which the state itself is threatened with disintegration, with civil wars, and a murderous army 'guaranteeing the integrity of the realm.' This unfortunate scenario in a way underscores the eminent reasonableness of the points raised in the reform debate; it also demonstrates the debilitated state of Indonesian institutions and the grave underdevelopment of civil society.

Despite their longer traditions of open debate and discussion, it is of interest to compare the issues brought forward in Indonesia with those raised in the Philippines and Thailand. In recent years, both these countries had to deal with the urgency of reform as well and, at the time concerned, both were convinced of the imperative of institution building. This exigency was expressed in new constitutions.

In the Philippines, the Constitution of 1987 clearly reflects the desire of sweeping away the abuses Marcos permitted himself during his dictatorship. The three branches of government should be firmly separated; corruption and the abuse of power should be eradicated; economic and social justice should prevail. Meanwhile, some fifteen years later, the high hopes the constitution was thought to shape, have vanished. Problems were not swept away but merely landed under the carpet. Institutional development, then as now, retains the same urgency.

Certain constitutional mandates, such as decentralization and empowering local government, have already resulted in a measure of democratization. Democratization can also be perceived in the effects of massive outcries against the threat of presidential manipulations of the constitution, the People Power II street demonstrations that forced President Estrada from office, and the later People Power III demos that protested the perennial cleavage dividing the Philippine polity, namely, the comfortably established elite versus the impoverished masses. The question that remains, though, is whether these signs of democratic health will bring about relevant changes in the practice of government, in the relative positions of elite and masses, and will result in the establishment of viable, mutually independent institutions of state and economy.

It is especially the last point that dominates the discussion in the Philippine print media and that is high in the minds of public intellectuals. Issues other than the cozy relationship between political and economic power, identified in consciousness-raising talk shows, can hardly been brought to life—and such shows have been characteristically short-lived. In their stead, people like to discuss political personalities and their antics. Politics is living people and their show. It is double-dealing and venality, abuse of justice and power, grandstanding and hypocrisy, that obsessively receive the spotlight, blinkering out all other issues save for the most spectacular, such as Abbu Sayyaf raids, eruptions and typhoons, and criminal drama. Still, it can be observed that the political debate has one outstanding structural dimension. It bares the consciousness of the strong ties between political and economic interests that feed into the practice of 'traditional' or money politics, and the awareness that, as long as this lasts, all fundamental change, that is, institutional reform, will be effectively blocked.

For a while, the debates in Thailand were somewhat more varied than in the Philippines. First of all this was the result of the lengthy constitutional crisis of the 1990s that started as a military protest against the first Buffet Cabinet in which businessmen-politicians were too conspicuously sharing the cake. The subsequent National Peace-Keeping Council (NPKC) promised to reorganize the realm, and for a year to come the discussions on a new constitution, the country's fifteenth, demonstrated the deep divisions between the military and their arch-conservative allies, and the voices of democratic hope and reason. After the bloody events of May 1992, the military had lost all legitimacy, and a new process of constitution-writing could begin. The wide-ranging debates this stimulated yielded loads of academic columns, and certain—alas short-lived—talk and phone-in shows in the electronic media. For a while, it felt as if the voices emanating from civil society were setting the agenda.

When things returned to normal, privilege, authoritarianism, godfather politicians, and businesspeople were all back in place, demonstrating that constitutions are no guarantee for the separation of the branches of government, for economic justice, or political decency. The power of money, of vested interests, and the collusion of business and politics is simply overwhelming, which brings—very visibly so in Thailand and the Philippines—clearly identifiable elites to the fore (in a way comparable to the Suharto clique in Indonesia) who have no interest in a state built on strong, independent institutions or in the development of a sturdy civil society. And so it seems that traditional or money politics—the 'dark influences' of godfather-ism as they are called in Thailand—will carry the day into a foreseeable future.

WHITHER THE PUBLIC DISCOURSE?

It is of interest to note that Thai, Filipino, and Indonesian public intellectuals debate more or less the same topics, such as the necessity of democratic institutional development, educational reform, social justice, and the importance of public participation, which equates with the development of civil society. They agree that money politics are at the root of obstructing the realization of their reform agendas. To counter its pernicious influence, they aspire to the rule of law and an open society of modern citizens. In many ways these programmatic wishes clash not only with living reality, but also with the official and popular imaginations of social life. Democracy—and thus inter-human equality—is hard to imagine, and after lengthy elaborations on its merits, Thai school texts concluded that it is Thai culture itself which prevents it from taking root. In the legalistic teachings of the Philippines, democracy exists on paper. In Indonesia, the democratic message is still wrapped in statist paternalism. For all, being democratic is primarily expressed through conducting elections and having a parliament.

In official quarters they worry more about globalization than the intelligentsia does, and this worry enjoys a strong public resonance. Yet all know that the nations are defenseless in face of mondial streams of information, transnational finance, free markets, recessions, tourism, and worldwide fads and fancies. The discrepancy between erosion caused by global flows and the aspired-for conditions formulated by public intellectuals seems enormous. The development of culture simply has not kept up with the transformations Southeast Asian societies are experiencing. Besides, within these societies themselves, overawing and antagonistic cultural and economic differences are developing that provide new dimensions to the preoccupation with national integrity.

Culture, the social imagination, is lagging behind and does not develop in pace with the rapid changes taking place. In school, lack of cultural direction is countered with values education programs that seem to be inspired by an idealized past. This endeavor privileges the family as the model for society which is, naturally, way out of joint with experience and urban modernity. It may, however, promote family-centeredness and justify the practice of patronage. After all, the family is widely recognized as a safe haven in a businesslike world. For many, it is the primary locus of identity, and thus a stimulant of the trend toward primordialism that we also noted in religious revival, and in Indonesia-wide and Muslim regionalism.

These various tendencies surface in the public discourse, and tear it apart. Besides, whether the inputs originate from members of the intelligentsia, popular experience, or official quarters, all run against the actuality of money politics, elite interests, individualization, consumer culture, and the cynicism and pessimism we noted among the public and in the diagnoses of novelists. Consequently, the national discourse is disjointed. On the one side we find some transcending idealism that stands in stark contrast with living experience on the other. Whatever the solutions propagated, all of them run counter to rooted realities, and thus, for the time being at least, public opinion remains a weak player in the political economy. It can only grow in importance when a vital, educated, free, and quantitatively significant civil society emerges.

SUMMARIZING THE SOCIAL IMAGINATION

In the dominant view, society is seen in a concrete fashion, meaning as networks of relationships among known persons who, in hierarchizing manner, are expected to behave according to the ethics of place, and to recognize their debts of gratitude and obligations. No matter how attractive such a view may be, it is based on the ideals that hopefully guide family and small-community life. When this imagery guides life's practice in the wider society, it logically fosters the institution of patronage, and related corruption, collusion, and cronyism.

This is at the root of a blurred vision of the public world. On the one hand, life in the wider society is supposed to proceed according to the ethics of family life. And indeed, so it proceeds to the benefit of a small elite and their client-protégés. All those excluded from the inner circle of privilege then start, on the other hand, to evaluate the public world against familiar-communal norms, and find out that it is an area of immorality, nepotism, and self-serving 'traditional' politics.

This conundrum leads to advising moral measures to remedy the social condition. If all individuals act righteously, society will be in good order. It is obvious, though, that all individuals do not act in this way, and that power corrupts. This, in its turn, results in a firm separation between the private and public realms. The private becomes exemplary, the public loathsome. Consequently, the prevailing view of the public world is cynical rather than constructive.

These days this dominant imagination is challenged by the modern-constructive ideas of certain public intellectuals—including the critical press—who think that social justice is a serious matter, and who clamor for institutional reform. In contrast to the concrete, moralistic view of society, theirs tends to be more abstract and sociological.

CHAPTER 12

TOWARDS CIVIL SOCIETY?

In the introduction we noted that the rise of civil society is an emancipation movement from the influence of state and big business that, in the history of modern Europe, can be traced back to its early urbanization. Then citizens emerged who, in modern terms, could be seen as middle classes. Of course, when these acquired political power next to their economic might, they became aristocratic elites from whom new generations of middle citizens sought emancipation. A cardinal tool for the latter on that road was literacy, education, and thus critical thinking. From this, we may deduce some of the necessary preconditions for the emergence of civil society: an urban setting; middle classes; a desire for emancipation and power-sharing; a developing economy; formal education and information. To these we may add the present, global flows of ideas and culture.

We also noted that, in Southeast Asia, these preconditions have only recently been met; that the history of local civil societies is not one of linear development; that the ideas they carry vary over time. The desire for emancipation from imperial power fired the imagination of the members of early Philippine civil society. In Indonesia and Thailand, nationalism and emancipation combined with modern, optimistic thinking about the constructability of society and individuals. When new generations took over, we see, especially in Thailand and the Philippines, that the legacy of the ideas of the 1920s lived on into the 1960s and 1970s, at the same time that nationalism was becoming less important, and that the desire for emancipation directed itself against the power of the indigenous elite.

Meanwhile we have arrived at a different juncture again. While old ideas of reconstruction are still carried on by the national democratic movement and their New People's Army in the Philippines, most ideational energy has flowed into the calmer waters of the NGO scene. It seems as if these ideas have been overtaken by a new mentality that sets on economic development, or survival, and that is no longer interested in the ideals of the past. This mindset arose in the period of economic change and educational expansion beginning in the 1960s that concurred with the spread of media, consumer culture, rapid urbanization, money politics and cynicism, globalization and decreasing state sovereignty, while giving rise to new middle classes.

We noted that a civil society of sorts has grown in the countries of Southeast Asia. There is an active intelligentsia spreading all kinds of ideas. With nominally free media, there is a measure of public debate. NGOs, or rather civil society organizations, are active in many areas where government does not deliver. Peasant protests and labor unrest add to the clamor for justice. Sometimes students take to the streets. Democracy has spread as the official system of political decision making. Schooling has become available for most. So, at first glance, it seems that many things are in place that can enhance the growth of civil society, and we may expect that society to play its part as an effective counterpart to business and state. How sound is that expectation?

STRONG, HEALTHY CIVIL SOCIETY

Let us make this immediately clear: civil society is political. It is about empowerment of the citizen in relation to state and market. Civil society does not necessarily oppose state and market; it tries to civilize them, to tame the nature of power and money. Furthermore, civil society does this for the sake of the public good. It hopes to promote good governance. It therefore monitors the actions of the state, and participates in public policy making. It may even share in implementing public policy, especially at the grassroots, but may also strive for self-governance. In brief, civil society mobilizes private action for the common welfare.

Concretely, civil society does this through voluntary associations. Ideally, these associations are autonomous, which means that they have their own resources—preferably deriving from their own membership—and that they can only satisfactorily operate in a political climate that respects the freedoms of association and expression. This implies that the members of society must be interested in public affairs, that they think these are worth agitating for, and that they believe that their actions and mobilization can result in, for instance, justice, better education, a more equitable system of taxation, protection of the citizen, less racism, etc. Since there is no end to matters affecting the public in their private and wider social lives, different and specialized associations addressing new issues will arise all the time.

Often, the strength of civil society is thought to be indicated by the number of associations, and the density of their network of mutual relationships. This is not strange, because civic activity is lodged in a mentality of participatory citizenship, which concurs with the aim of civic associations. This presupposes strong democratic inclinations, exemplified by institutional pluralism, tolerance, willingness to cut across social cleavages, and cooperation.

In order to be engaged in such a manner, a good measure of social capital needs to exist, or to be created. In the discourse on civil society, social capital stands for the available quantity of trust, reciprocity, tolerance, inclusion, respect for law and regularity, and other qualities needed to effectively cooperate, exchange views, and act collectively. Hopefully such qualities also exist in the partners in dialogue, such as governments and corporate business.

Because of all the above qualities and conditions, a strong, healthy civil society is built on a good sense of citizenship. As citizens, its members not only take public affairs to heart, but also feel responsible for the good of society as they see it. This means that they have to think about public affairs, that they form their opinion. At the level of the individual, they do so personally, consulting each other and their conscience. This assumes a measure of moral autonomy and a critical, constructive mind. In a society the experience of which naturally produces self-serving individuals, such constructive citizenship is the only guard against lawlessness, political corruption, and the rule of the free market.

When we reflect on all these qualities of a healthy civil society, we see that its arising is related to a certain social imagination. An active civil society aims at the empowerment of the citizen, and at social reconstruction for the sake of the public good. To think this way is an act of abstraction from concrete experience—it is about the 'general other,' rule of law, equality, emancipation, and constructability. It is a sociological way of thinking that analyzes social life critically in the hope of being able to reconstitute it in a more desirable fashion. Society is not just networks among concretely known persons, but a blueprint of a structure that can be made. To me, the prevalence of this modern imagination is one of the conditions necessary for a purposive, effective civil society.

CIVIL SOCIETY IN SOUTHEAST ASIA

It is against the above background that we can evaluate the chances of civil society developing in Southeast Asia. There is no doubt that strong civil societies are necessary in face of the messy circumstances the countries are in. Realistically, there is a great need for civilizing the public world.

Actual practice

Most clefts and cleavages that divide society have economic underpinnings. If Muslims want to break free in the southern Philippines, it is not necessarily because of religion, but because they have been deprived of their land, exploited, and treated as second-rate citizens. This seems to be the fate of all sorts of minorities. They are not just slow in adapting to and integrating with mainstream society. It is the latter throwing up hurdles by neglecting and discriminating against them. Sometimes the settlement of merchants or unfairly advantaged state-sponsored migrants cause tensions with the locals, and may trigger off violence that, at first sight, looks as if Christians and Muslims are at each other's throats. Yet, once set in motion, mere religious differences may begin to live a life of their own, and spark off further violence.

At this point in time, after so many years of 'national development' and the availability of unprecedented means of mercilessly exploiting the human and natural environments, we see formidable societal dislocations. These have brought new rifts to the fore, and lots of frustration. It is that frustration—being left behind, exploited, without justice—that, on the one hand, stimulates violence against others, and that, on the other, bares the main cleavage dividing society against itself, namely the yawning gap between the national elite and the rest. This makes the majority a minority in their own country. They have been colonized once again. They despair, and are prone to resentment.

Resentment is a very volatile ingredient in a region where conflicts are not solved but terminated, and where violence is thus endemic. Whether resulting from interpersonal friction, competing business or political interests, old grudges or oppression, it easily ruptures the surface 'harmony' of smiles and conformity, as everybody knows. People thus avoid confrontation because of its explosive potential, but these days the sources of frustration cannot be easily avoided, even as they are difficult to pinpoint. They are no longer lodged in personal and hierarchical relationships, but in anonymous, systemic arrangements. Nonetheless, these cause resentment and invite violence where mechanisms of conflict resolution have not developed in pace with the transformation of society.

In Thailand, the Philippines, and Indonesia, the state-owning class has grown filthy rich. This elite thrives on money politics, on patronage, on corruption, collusion, and cronyism. They set the law, or rather its implementation, to their own advantage. The political arena serves to negotiate competing intra-elite interests while elections are mere ways to buy political prominence. Consequently, parties just are *ad hoc* groupings of political cum business entrepreneurs. The political process is driven by money and expediency. Those in the opposition are given to begrudge the coalition temporarily in power, which they try to undermine and destroy. No wonder that the practice of politics presents a messy image: it is confrontational, violent, arrogant, opaque, and has little to do with good government or the public welfare.

The elite is not just self-serving. For a long time, the post-colonial elites have been branded as a comprador class, meaning that they are intermediaries between international economic interests and the exploitation of their countries. These days the name of the game is globalization, in which a new, supra-national layer of governance has emerged that not only affects decision making at the national level but that can even dictate what is locally going to happen.

This higher layer of political and economic power—embodied in UN, IMF, World Bank, TNCs, WTO, Internet, international NGOs, etc.—

reduces the authority and sovereignty of states and, paradoxically, strengthens the position of the state-owning class. Because of their being meshed in the international network, the elite is less dependent on local support. Part of their legitimation derives from their global embeddedness, from their cosmopolitanism. Naturally, this strengthens their hand in exploiting the country and its people.

Education too maintains the gap. In the modern world and its global economy, a good command of English and quality education are indispensable to maintain oneself and one's class in positions of economic power. The elite not only can afford to send their offspring to the few expensive schools offering quality education, but they can also top it off with schooling abroad. As a result, they nearly monopolize the mastery and knowledge needed to run the system, and are not very interested in upgrading the level of national public education. They are comfortable with their privilege, or with what the Indonesians call their exclusivism and feudal attitudes.

With so many people excluded from the nice life and deprived of good chances to make it, there is good cause for protest, conflict, and frustration that could, ideally, be mediated through a healthy civil society. Yet, will it? In modern, urban society people would, naturally, like to improve their situation, and the observation that many of the members of the middle classes clamor for participatory democracy, the rule of law, and quality education is correct. Yet, they also are the people on the other side of the great divide and, very often, dependent on the patronage that the elite provides. So, whereas their 'people power' street demonstrations have toppled regimes in the three countries concerned, they cannot change the system.

Despite a considerable number of vociferous activists, the encouraging expansion of NGOs, and people's empowerment movements, most modern urbanites feel they have good reason for their cynicism. For them, the best thing to do is to focus on their personal careers, to earn well, and to have access to the goodies consumer culture offers. If they can send their children for training abroad, the latter may even leap the gap. With these sorts of aspirations, civic debate and public affairs become luxuries. Besides, there are less tiring things to do, such as enjoying internet and virtual reality on screen, exposing oneself to the foolish products of the local culture industry, or the violence of US-made B-movies.

Urbanization and the resulting anonymity throw people back into themselves. For many, this results in social inattentiveness and egocentric choices. Regarding the socio-political system, individuals feel powerless to change it or to solve its problems, so why bother with anything other than survival? The best thing is to solve your own problems, and thus to play the system, to know the shortcuts, and whom to approach to get things done. If people still have scruples, they may gas up on moral righteousness by partaking in trendy religious revival. They may also look for identity through celebrating ethnicity, regional origin, or other peculiarity markers, such as the personal family.

The untidy picture of the social environment seems to be reflected in the material one. There are overwhelming problems everywhere. The fuming gridlock in the streets, the staggering production of garbage, vendors all around, beggars at every intersection, the neglect of pedestrian crossings, no containers to deposit waste—in brief, an appalling deficit of public services in tandem with the eminently corruptible police and bureaucracy; everything seems to be polluted, from mentality to highway. The only things that apparently escape from the decivilization that surrounds most are the estates, condominiums, office towers, hotels, and shopping malls—and their security services—that mark the social divide.

Ideals lost

The image of actual practice is complemented by certain images of the past. The period in which early civil society arose is very different from the present. The intelligentsias of those times were well-educated, and fully conversant with the modern Western discourse. Especially in Thailand and Indonesia, optimistic ideas about social reconstruction and individual emancipation through education flourished. These days, however, such ideas are peripheral, and there are not many who understand them well. They belong to a discourse of the past. The understanding of democracy is not very clear; the idea of basic human rights is hazy. The perception of problems is moralistic rather than constructive. Society is not linearly progressing to a bright tomorrow, and the monetary crisis, ecological destruction, and the very experience of urban congestion have driven out the modern spirit of optimism. Because of this we can say that ideals have been lost, that yesteryear's brave new world has not been realized—and probably never will be.

This history of loss of civil ideals is also reflected in the teaching materials used in school. This is most explicitly so in the Philippines where the period of the American occupation is invariably depicted as a golden age of modernity and enlightenment that contrasts with both Spanish obscurantism and the treason to the ideals of nationhood that sets in as soon as the Filipinos begin taking care of their own affairs. Whether values education can reverse the degeneration is a moot point, but the ugly picture of society was realistically revealed in the same course.

In Thailand or Indonesia self-flagellation is not a national habit, although cynicism is as prevalent as it is in the Philippines. Even in the doctrinaire course on state ideology, the Indonesians have to admit that all is not well (yet), and meanwhile such a plethora of problems has come to the fore that the public debate does not even consider yesterday's 'national world view.' Thai texts too are very critical of current conditions, especially as they evolve in the urban setting. The Thais have been said to be unable to grasp the idea of democracy, let alone to practice it, and one may question whether the late-feudal doctrine of the Three Institutions can do much to remedy this situation. Apart from squarely recognizing these problems, the future-as-hoped-for seems to vanish because of the self-indulgence and materialism of the young, the generation to come.

The loss of ideals is probably best mirrored in fiction. Especially Thailand has a long tradition of commenting on social life in novels and short stories that can be read as critical diagnoses of the times. Both Sriburapha and Seni Sawwaphong were heirs to the ideas of the 1920s, and their major works, published in the 1940s and 1950s, breathe a confident mood. Of course, the nature of highly stratified Thai society is oppressive to most, but education will emancipate people from the semi-feudal conditions they experience, and the practice of democracy will even enlighten the spirit of the ruling class.

In the 1970s, prolific writer Boonchoke Chiamwiriya burst unto the literary scene with *The Revolutionary District Officer*. This best-selling novel was immediately popular, apparently fitting in with the spirit of the age. It is a largely autobiographical account of a D.O. who does weird things. He refuses to be corrupted, and sincerely takes the problems and welfare of the district's population to heart. Consequently, he is a misfit in what he calls the mafia of the Ministry of Interior. In order to maintain his self-respect and freedom of action, he resigns from the service in disgust (and becomes an author). His other works send the same message: individuals can maintain their righteousness in a thoroughly corrupt world. If society can't be better, the person can always be improved. In viewing society, the optimism of the earlier generation has disappeared, but the possibility of individual moral growth may still be hoped for.

In the 1990s, as we have seen, the idea of righteousness appears to have lost all relevance. In Wimon Sainimnuan's view, it is useless, and will be eliminated. Violence has become the rule. In spite of professed hopes for redemption, Sionil José's diagnoses were no more cheerful. Javanese authors pronounced that the reign of greed has taken possession of all and sundry, and that whatever wholesomeness still exists will be invalidated as soon as one crosses the threshold that separates home from the public world. Apparently, in the wider society no place for idealism and moral goodness has been left.

Individual-centeredness

Whether these most recent writings truly reflect society's moral condition is a moot point. What is relevant here is that in modern, urban society people have to fight their own battles, whether for more comfort or sheer survival. The experience of anonymous society individualizes and, in the teachings on values, the resulting 'individualism' was seen as a serious social problem. In this section, we shall explore the deeper roots of this individual-centeredness, and dismiss the orientalizing myth of collectivism, at least for Southeast Asia.

We noted in passing that the prevalence of bilateral descent results, very much like in Western societies, in temporally shallow networks of relatives who rarely know ancestors beyond their grandparents. On the other hand, these networks can be very widely cast. Since people do not group in clans or castes, the household becomes the real locus of private life. While such households can be very complex and multigenerational, the ideal is to establish one's own nuclear household, independent of others. To be able to do so is a major boost to self-respect. The nuclear family is, therefore, privileged over other forms of co-existence; it is primarily composed of a couple of parents and their children. Together these people hopefully enjoy a good measure of solidarity and sympathy with each other, helping each other through life.

At the death of parents, inheritance is—normally—equally divided among the siblings and—economically, at least—everybody goes their own way. In other words, the brothers and sisters do not constitute a corporate group. They own their prime loyalty to their own nuclear families. This is not to say that they will not extend some help to needy relatives, or that they will not share certain burdens, but such assistance is essentially voluntary. If there is a measure of unity, then it is ritually expressed when siblings congregate around their parents to celebrate New Year or Christmas, or when they take care of parental graves.

There is no denying that extended family networks—say, aunts and uncles, cousins, nieces, and nephews—often assume a certain importance. Within these, people belong loosely together, on a voluntary basis, and it is private individuals, not groups, that animate these webs of relatedness. In other words, the activation of family networks depends on individual persons who cultivate their own specific bonds with certain preferred relatives—each and everybody in a group of siblings may thus see extended family relationships in his or her own way: such bonds are individual-centered, and cemented through the debt of gratitude that links specific individuals to each other, also beyond relations of kin.

Sometimes administrative legerdemain treated whole villages as collectivities in which people were always willing to cooperate. Especially in Indonesia, such presuppositions led to enforced development and production quota, but such compulsion does not give rise to spontaneous acceptance or collectivism. If others still point to cooperative labor in wet-rice farming, they should realize that such is an economic necessity to cope with peaks in labor demand, and that it is organized in a calculated, reciprocal manner.

Often, a group-orientation is deduced from the persistent stress on smooth interpersonal relationships. Of course, politeness and respect, consideration and sympathy certainly contribute to good working relationships, such as labor exchange. Very often, however, harmony within certain groups is exploitative, and equates with enforced conformity. This may serve the boss's purposes: harmony is agreeing with expectations and obeying commands.

The ideal of harmony is also promoted by status considerations. For the acknowledgement of status respect, a person depends on others. They can make and break his 'face.' People are, therefore, aware of the opinion of others, and fear to be shamed. Socially, it often seems as if their conscience is consciousness of others, and it is sheer stupidity to become the butt of ridicule. It is thus wise to avoid giving offense, to refuse rocking the boat, and to be circumspect of others.

Because of this, the pressure for harmony and conformity leads to a certain individualization. It isolates people from each other, because when others know too much they may be dangerous. They may also be dangerous when they feel hurt because of loss of face, and grudges seem to never die. Because of this vulnerability at the hands of others, people cultivate indirectness and circumlocution, dissemble intentions, and keep others at arm's length. The best thing to do is to be able to take care of one's own affairs, not to be too dependent on others, and not to involve oneself where one has no business. To be able to live according to this self-centered ethic is an ideal in a situation where most people cannot escape from the compulsions of patronage and the necessity of conforming, or at least of shutting up.

The dialectic between harmony and individual-centeredness goes further still. With many, the pressure for conformity leads to the desire to break free, or to steal the show. Such 'individualism' is often mirrored by obstinacy, indifference, and withdrawal, but also by, especially male, irresponsibility, generosity, and womanizing. So, however smooth interpersonal relations appear to be, and however harmonious a community represents itself, these are not indications that people want to cooperate, nor signs of 'collectivism.' Beneath the surface of all-is-well, we will often find strong tendencies to individual-centeredness that root in bilaterality, in the very idea that harmony equates with conformity, and that are now being reinforced by the experience of urban society.

CIVIL SOCIETY?

Actual experience, loss of ideals, and individual-centeredness pose daunting challenges to whatever exists as civil society and its future development. The voices most frequently heard belong to members of a very small intelligentsia, and often their opinions are academic rather than practical. To a large extent this holds true for the debates within and among civil society organizations, such as NGOs, even as many of their activist members have learnt and are learning to deal with obdurate realities at the grassroots, and with obstinate opinion among those who represent the power of the state. Regularly, civil society organizations are blackmailed as representatives of foreign interests because many of them depend financially on sources abroad. Others are simply subverted by the authorities. Even so, we should admire their tenacity in the teeth of intimidating odds, and sometimes they have something to show for their efforts. Not everything goes the way of Father Wis's projects. This is, for instance, visible in a certain measure of success of organized Thai peasant activism, a high level of political consciousness among Philippine labor and peasants, and protestations against unjust justice in Indonesia.

We should realize that civil society organizations have to operate among vast, ill-educated masses of people, and that also the deficient training of many members of the new middle classes is a barrier to understanding what civic action is all about. There simply is a comprehension gap between intelligentsia and the general public whose opinion can easily be manipulated by political and market interests. Often people feel more comfortable with religious and sectarian messages that stress morality and personal righteousness. Other particularistic messages, such as identification with region and ethnic group, or preoccupation with survival or lifestyle, are much closer to the heart than programmatic appeals emanating from civil society organizations.

As we have seen, school education hardly prepares the social imagination to reaching for a better tomorrow for all, and the money-political climate of violence and cynicism are not very conducive to evoking the spirit of participation. School continues with its moralistic indoctrination, which, in a way, separates the public from the private world, the unruly from the moral. When measured against private norms, the outer world is messy indeed, a market place at best. But school does not prepare to act responsibly in the public realm; at least, it does not prepare for morally autonomous citizenship and locates conscience more in group than in individuals.

In the hope of making people more critical of what goes on in the wider society, a few talk and phone-in shows have been presented in both Thailand and the Philippines. These presentations have had great difficulty in maintaining themselves, sometimes because of direct political intervention, but even more so because many members of the public found them repetitious and boring. This, of course, did not boost viewer ratings, which, in a highly commercialized environment normally finish them off. The public in Indonesia is not familiar with the airing of critical views on television. The best they get is sheer endless information on Islam. It may naturally be expected that also there at some time talk shows will stimulate critical debate, but, for the time being, Indonesia lacks the educated, broad social basis on which to graft the national discourse. In other words, its public intellectuals and their debates are further removed from the population at large than in Thailand and the Philippines.

Among the criteria for a healthy civil society, we noted the importance of associations, and their networks, that attempt to remedy one social condition or other. In the highly personalistic sphere of Southeast Asia, we frequently see that serving the association's purpose is secondary to loyalty, or disloyalty, to its leading figure. It is not ideals per se that keep people together, but rather the sense of belonging and acting together as a group of intimates around a dominant father figure. As a result, differences of opinion and the arising of alternative leaders may break up associations; these simply seem to multiply without gaining in clout. Person-focus and individual-centeredness combine in making Southeast Asian societies highly factious, which is reflected in politics, civil society, and other organizations, and in the tendency to admire, and crave for, strong leadership.

Next to the politically relevant groups, we find that many civil society organizations are remarkably parochial in outlook and activities. With these I do not mean Parent-Teacher Associations that attempt to, locally, improve the quality of formal education, but all those so or similarly named committees that merely organize celebrations, beauty contests, or collections for prestige projects (and that were chided by Lualhati Bautista's Lea because of it). Prestige often seems to be the main motivation of Rotarian and other civic-club projects. They merely advertise the members' names, and associate to stimulate the sense of mutual self-importance. So, while the art of association must be cultivated, it does not always lead to active citizenship in the wider sense of having an impact on public projects and policy.

One of the hallmarks of vitality of civil society is the interest of the young in public concerns. With 50 percent of the population under the age of twenty, youth offers a vast recruitment base, but are they interested? We have seen that school does not present critical analyses of the public world, and that it is deficient in preparing the social imagination. Besides, the moral approach it takes breeds cynicism and indifference. Indeed, sometimes students' protests occur—flashes to vent frustration and to protest against the system—but these actions are not sustained. If they are, in NGO activism, they are often carried by college dropouts, that is the people upon whom Mangunwijaya pinned his hopes, versus those who are brainwashed into the system.

It is not only formal education that blunts the mind. Society seems to operate in a cultural wasteland filled with the goodies of modern consumerism, cheap entertainment, violent movies, sports, and the drudgery of urban living. There is, therefore, little to stimulate the spirit, which results in the relative absence of creative culture and critical reflection. This cultural vacuum, in which people consume culture rather than produce it, is more serious than it appears at first glance. An active civil society thrives because of ideas, and thus a good measure of originality. This creativity is throttled by the mass culture of imitative consumption that leads away from authenticity and that sterilizes the mind; it reduces social concerns to soaps, silly shows, sports, and other products of the culture industry. In this way, the recruitment base of civil society, and enthusiasm for its projects, remains severely restricted. As a result, activism and ginger groups remain small, in membership and influence.

The above considerations on the possibility of the development of a healthy civil society are somewhat pessimistic because they result from contrasting with ideal, theoretical civil society, without taking into account the practical achievements we can witness in Southeast Asia. For instance, the quality of the public debate has improved, most clearly in Thailand in the 1990s, and most recently in Indonesia because of the arising of a free critical press. Such newspapers and magazines have a longer history in the Philippines, where their overwhelming preoccupation with politics blurs the sight on societal developments. Besides, the press there indulges in a cynicism that precludes a more visionary approach to issues. Comparatively, the discussions in Thailand cut deepest, while in Indonesia a tradition of investigative journalism and critical analysis is developing. A crucial point, and this is a general problem, is that the imagination of the readers needs to be broadened so that they can appreciate criticism and diversity of opinion. Anyway, the influence of public opinion and protest on public policy making has grown dramatically since the early 1980s in the Philippines, and in the 1990s in Thailand and Indonesia.

This influence has been visualized in amazing happenings. First we saw the People Power-style disposing of intolerable leaders (Indonesia 1965–6, 1998; Thailand 1973, 1992; the Philippines 1986, 2001). These days, this is topped by presidents being forced to render account of their deeds before parliament (Abdurrahman Wahid) or court (Suharto, Estrada, even Thaksin Shinawatra was under threat). Although both types of moves against the power of the executive were not motivated by programmatic politics, they set limits to what leaders can and cannot do, and clearly show that public opinion is carrying weight in the political arena.

The development of press and public opinion indicates that there are quite a few people who have survived school indoctrination; they are perfectly capable of understanding the world in non-moralistic or non-state–ideological terms. The contemporary problem is that their thinking has not been translated into programmatic politics. So far, elections focus on political personalities, while political parties tend to be conservative and self-serving. In the press, these money-driven party machines and the machinations of individual politicos are being identified, and such analyses have proven to have mobilizing power.

Another hope-giving element is the advancing of women on the social stage. They are not rushing, but steadily penetrating the professions— one half of college graduates are women—the civil service and, more slowly, political positions. This emancipatory movement will contribute to civilize debates by challenging male dominance and macho opinion, and will certainly contribute to democratization and a better understanding of human rights.

A most encouraging sign is the establishment of civic activism in the form of civil society organizations, or NGOs, that attempt to organize peasants to protest their deprivation (especially in Thailand), that strive for the implementation of land reform (especially in the Philippines), that mobilize public opinion to demand democratic transparency and the recognition of human rights (all three), or that quietly operate in order to empower peasants and the urban poor (all three). In bringing organization and education to the most downtrodden, the organizations concerned also strengthen the recruitment basis of civil society.

Still, civil society activists need to be courageous people, because landowners, port authorities, industrial polluters, 'developers,' and illegal loggers often unleash rather uncivil means when they see their interests infringed upon; besides, the latter know themselves to be backed by not-so-venerable judges and the might of the state. Even so, the various types of civil activism have proven themselves to be ineradicable, and so keep informing the public on desirable alternatives to make their countries a better place.

The most lively scene of association is the religious field. The burgeoning of sectarianism, especially among the literate, urban public, but reaching high up into the middle classes, is, first of all, a sign of longing for a measure of regularity in public affairs that finds its expression in the quest for personal righteousness. Most often its focus is inner-directed; it concerns the individual in an unruly world. Yet, such sectarian associations have, at the level of their leaderships, great political—and thus public policy—potential. In Thailand, the Santi Asoke sect developed a political branch, the Force of Righteousness, that maintained itself for ten years on center stage, while the Dhammakaya sect was for a time the center of political controversy on a daily basis. In the Philippines, the establishment is keen to cultivate good ties with the Iglesia ni Cristo and the vast, charismatic El Shaddai movement. The vitality of Islam in all its guises is most readily apparent in Indonesia where the secular leader of its biggest, Javanese-tradition-oriented Nahdlatul Ulama association made it to the presidency. Besides, Abdurrahman Wahid expects that very Nahdlatul Ulama organization to operate as a vehicle for the emancipation of its vast rural membership. It should act at the grassroots as a gigantic NGO.

Because of these observations, it is not so clear how to estimate the position of religious sects among civil society organizations. On the one hand we see an emphasis on moralism that articulates well with family values and an idealized past. Yet many sects also promote the emancipation of their members in relation to the wider society and politics. These days, the latter two often appear as emptied of morality, culture, and civilization. This image stimulates personal, particularistic choices, but also the desire to redeem whatever seems to have been lost.

At this juncture, it is difficult to predict how much strength civil society is going to generate. At the same time that we can identify many impediments to its growth, it is also clear that there is considerable practical progress. In Southeast Asia, civil society will not develop according to precooked historical or theoretical scenarios. So much is certain, however: for the time being civil society is developing in the teeth of opposition from the cozy alliance of state and business interests. Its progress is observable, and perhaps even accelerating. Even so, its evolution to becoming the pulsating heart of a democratic society will be a long-term project.

NOTES

CHAPTER 1: THE THAI DEMOCRATIC WAY OF LIFE

1. Bureau of School Affairs, *Handbook to Promote the Democratic Way of Life* (Bangkok: Department of Education, 1992). In Thai.

Program to Support Democratic Activities of the Office of the Committee on National Elementary Education, *Handbook for Organizing Study and Teaching Activities that Promote Democracy in Elementary Schools*, vol. 2 (Bangkok: Department of Education, 1988). In Thai.

2. Educational Technique Bureau, Department of Education, *Studybook Preparing for the Experience of Life*, 5 (Bangkok: Book Development Center of the Educational Technique Bureau of the Department of Education, 1987). In Thai.

Educational Technique Bureau, Department of Education, *Book 6. Section: Our Country and Its Neighbours* (Bangkok: Sales Organization of the Khurusapha, 1991). In Thai.

Educational Technique Bureau, Department of Education, *Book 6. Section: People and Environment* (Bangkok: Sales Organization of the Khurusapha, 1992). In Thai.

3. Educational Technique Department, Ministry of Education, *Social Studies Textbook: Our Country*, vols. 102, 204, and 306 (Bangkok: Khurusapha, 1992). In Thai.

Sukhum Nualsakul and Dr. Preecha Suwannathat, *Social Studies 402* (Bangkok: Watthana Panich, 1991). In Thai.

Dr. Thaemsuk Numanont et al., *Social Studies*, vol. 605 (Bangkok: Watthana Panich, 1993). In Thai.

CHAPTER 2: PHILIPPINE IMAGE OF THE NATION

1. Department of Education, Culture and Sports, *The Philippines through the Ages* (Quezon City: Instructional Materials Corporation, 1987; reprinted 1995). In Filipino.

2. Department of Education, Culture and Sports, *Social Studies I: The Establishment of the Filipino Nation* (Quezon City: Instructional Materials Corporation, 1989). In Filipino.

CHAPTER 3: CIVICS *À LA* INDONESIA

1. The course's materials have been excerpted and paraphrased from Department of Education and Culture, *Pancasila and Civics Education (Junior High School 3; Senior High School 1, 2, 3)* (Jakarta: Balai Pustaka, 1996). In Indonesian.

2. The mention of the Kedung Ombo case is blatant effrontery. The population was, in good New Order fashion, intimidated, cheated, shortchanged, and denied access to an impartial court. Protesting about the unfair compensation could even lead to imprisonment. In those days (1980s), courts decided according to the 'law of the ruler' rather than the 'rule of law.'

CHAPTER 4: CHANGE AND PROBLEMS IN THAILAND

1. Educational Technique Bureau, Ministry of Education, *Social Studies Textbook Our Country 101* and *102* (Bangkok: Khurusapha, 1992). In Thai.

2. Sukhum Nualsakul, Dr. Preecha Suwannathat, *Social Studies 401* and *402* (Bangkok: Watthana Panich, 1991). In Thai.

Duean Khamdee, Nuek Thongmeephet, *Social Studies 606* (Bangkok: Watthana Panich, 1993). In Thai.

CHAPTER 5: CHANGING FILIPINO VALUES

1. *Building a People. Building a Nation. A Moral Recovery Program.* A report submitted by Senator Leticia Ramos Shahani to the Committee on Education, Arts and Culture and the Committee on Social Justice, Welfare and Development. May 8, 1988 (Quezon City: Instructional Materials Corporation, 1988).

2. Punsalan, Dr. Twila G. et al., *Values Education IV* (Quezon City: Instructional Materials Development Center, Department of Education, Culture and Sports, 1995). In Filipino.

3. It is this idea of valuable behavior issuing from individual moral personalities that seems to explain the responsibility of the child for its family. While it is avowed that personality is influenced by the home environment, the school, the church, the media, and the whole of society, it is stated that the person must also individually shape his/her own personality (51).

CHAPTER 6: INDONESIA: THE CALL FOR REFORM

1. The foregoing survey of the main topics animating the public debate is based on interviews, newspaper opinion pages, and the following pertinent literature:

Buchori, Mochtar, *Culture and Politics in Indonesia: Personal Reflections* (Jakarta: Center for Strategic and International Studies, 1996).

Budiman, Arief, et al., eds, *Reformasi: Crisis and Change in Indonesia* (Clayton: Monash Asia Institute, 1999).

Lindsey, Timothy, ed., *Indonesia: Law and Society* (Sydney: The Federation Press, 1999).

Manning, Chris and Peter van Diemen, eds., *Indonesia in Transition: Social Aspects of Reformasi and Crisis* (Singapore: Institute of Southeast Asian Studies, 2000).

Parera, Frans M. and T. Jakob Koekerits, eds., *Mengenang Romo Mangun; Surat Bagimu Negeri* (Jakarta: Kompas, 1999).

Sindhunata, ed., *Mengenang Y.B. Mangunwijaya; Pergulatan Intelektual dalam Era Kegelisahan* (Yogyakarta: Kanisius, 1999).

CHAPTER 7: THINKING WOMEN'S EMANCIPATION

1. Ayu Utami, *Saman* (Jakarta: Kepustakaan Populer Gramedia, 1998).

2. Bautista, Lualhati, *Bata, buta... pa'no ka ginawa?* (Mandaluyong: Cacho Publishing House, 1999 (c. 1983)).

3. 'Salvaging' - being arrested, detained, tortured and killed by Marcos's 'security forces.'

4. There is no legal divorce in the Philippines.

5. The development of a self-aware, autonomous personality is, according to Philippine psychologists, very uncommon. For a discussion of their positions, see Niels Mulder, *Inside Philippine Society*, chapter 2.

6. This is a reference to the famous San Miguel beer slogan of the 1980s, *isa pa nga*, 'one more!'

7. Suchinda Khantayalongkot, *Muean rabam doknun* (Nonthaburi: Bannangsue, 1993).

8. The man addresses her as *tyay* (as *che*, but unaspirated), which means 'elder sister,' and is used for a slightly older woman of Chinese descent. This leaves the woman with the opportunity to address the chauffeur with the equally familiar and polite Thai equivalent *phi*, also meaning older sibling. Playing this endearing trick is only possible because of the Chinese-Thai differential and suggests that the two characters are approximately of the same age.

CHAPTER 8: SOCIETY DIAGNOSED

1. Wimon Sainimnuan, *Chao Phaendin*, 2 vols. (Bangkok: Ton-or Grammy Graphic, 1996).

2. Mulder, Niels, *Inside Thai Society: Religion. Everyday Life. Change* (Chiang Mai: Silkworm Books, 2000), p. 25.

3. Wimon Sainimnuan, Khonsongchao and Khokphranang. (Bangkok: Ton-or Ltd., 1988 and 1990). For discussion, see Niels Mulder, *Thai Images: The Culture of the Public World* (Chiang Mai: Silkworm Books, 1997), pp. 264–76.

4. José, Francesco Sionil, *Viajero: A Filipino Novel* (Manila: Solidaridad Publishing House, 1993). 2nd ed. 1998.

5. In *Sin: A Novel* (Manila: Solidaridad Publishing House, 1994), José chides the originally Spanish part of the elite for their immorality, indifference to the country of their birth, and disdain of anything native. For discussion, see Niels Mulder, *Filipino Images: Culture of the Public World* (Quezon City: New Day, 2000), pp. 166–8.

6. José, Francesco Sionil, 'Cadena de Amor,' in Francesco Sionil José, *Three Filipino Women*, pp. 1–72 (New York: Random House, 1992).

7. Sindhunata, *Tak Enteni Keplokmu; Tanpa Bunga dan Telegram Duka* (Jakarta: Gramedia Pustaka Utama, 2000).

8. Nietzsche, Friedrich, *Beyond Good and Evil*, 1885. This quote serves as the book's motto (p. 16).

9. Sindhunata, *Semar Mencari Raga*. Yogyakarta: Kanisius/Basis, 1996. For discussion, see Niels Mulder, *Indonesian Images: The Culture of the Public World* (Yogyakarta: Kanisius, 2000), pp. 201–6.

10. Umar Kayam, *Jalan Menikung; Para Priyayi 2* (Jakarta: Pustaka Utama Grafiti, 1999).

11. Umar Kayam, *Para Priyayi; Sebuah Novel* (Jakarta: Pustaka Utama Grafiti, 1992).

12. For instance, Arswendo Atmowiloto, *Canting; Sebuah Roman Keluarga* (Jakarta: Gramedia, 1986), and YB Mangunwijaya, *Burung-burung Rantau* (Jakarta: Gramedia, 1996). For discussion, see Niels Mulder, *Indonesian Images* (Yogyakarta: Kanisius, 2000), pp. 185–201.

CHAPTER 9: RELIGIOUS REVIVAL

1. The Buddhist reform propagated by Buddhadasa Bhikkhu has roots in intellectual, modernist exegesis; it is highly critical of 'magic' and 'superstitions.' The movement was founded in 1932. In line with changing times, Santi Asoke emphasizes moral purity, respect for the Buddhist precepts, and a sober way of life. Thammakai is more esoteric, stressing meditation, merit, and discipline. The last two both emerged in the early 1970s.

2. The stronghold of the Nahdlatul Ulama, probably the biggest Muslim

association in the world, is the countryside of East Java. Because of its emphasis on the authority of the ulema, the movement has a reputation for conservatism. Inspired by Abdurrahman Wahid, the association is rapidly adapting to the modern world. It was founded in the 1920s. Earlier, in 1912, the modernist Muhammadiyah was established; it allows for a good measure of individual moral autonomy, and engages in social welfare activities. Currently a new, sterner wing among its membership—represented by National Assembly chairman Amien Rais—seems more dogmatically inclined, and strives to enhance the influence of Islam in politics and social life in general.

CHAPTER 10: CIVIC MALAISE

1. Both novels were written in Spanish but have been translated many times over. Personally I like the early rendering by Charles E. Derbyshire as *The Social Cancer (1911)* and *The Reign of Greed* (1913) respectively.

2. Soekarno, *Nationalism, Islam and Marxism* (Ithaca: Cornell University Southeast Asia Program, CMIP, 1970 (from 1926)).

Soekarno, *Indonesia Accuses! Soekarno's Defence Oration in the Political Trial of 1930*, ed. Roger K. Paget (Kuala Lumpur: Oxford University Press, 1975).

3. Heri Akhmadi, *Breaking the Chains of Oppression of the Indonesian People: Defense Statement at his Trial on Charges of Insulting the Head of State* (Ithaca: Cornell University Southeast Asia Program, CMIP, 1981).

4. Constantino, Renato, *The Philippines: A Past Revisited* (Quezon City: Tala Publishing, 1975).

CHAPTER 11: THE SOCIAL IMAGINATION

1. Note that the opposition is between informed/wise versus ignorant action, not good versus bad, nor righteous versus sinful. The idea of 'sin' is a recent—and ill-understood—introduction to Southeast Asia.

2. Note that this conception of ethics emphasizes knowledge/rationality/wisdom as the basis for moral decision making. Christian-Western thinking stresses feeling (love and conscience).

BIBLIOGRAPHIC NOTE

Since the purpose of eight of the chapters of this book is to open up sources of local image making, I let these texts speak for themselves. In this way, there was no need for much referencing. Yet, some readers may want to delve deeper, have access to comparative data as promised in chapter 11, or just look for introductory materials to the subjects and nations treated. They may consult the three country specific predecessors of my *Images* series, of which this book is the concluding volume. This series charts the culture of the public world, and stands in a complementary relationship to the four *Inside* publications that consider the private world.

Most introductory studies to Southeast Asia are country specific, although Steinberg and his colleagues endeavor to integrate regional data in the first and last sections of their historical *In Search of Southeast Asia*. Naturally, the region's diversity poses interesting challenges to all those who attempt to understand what is and will be going on. Nowhere is this more evident than in the spate of updated editions appearing on Indonesia. Since the projections they afford tend to be belied by facts in the shortest of periods, I refrain from directing the reader to post-Suharto and post–monetary crisis literature. Solid introductions to the country and its vicissitudes are Ricklef's *History* and Schwarz's *Nation in Waiting*. Pasuk and Baker authored the outstanding and lively *Thailand: Economy and Politics* that comprises many more aspects of life than the title reveals. Their subsequent book, *Thailand's Crisis*, complements this study. For the Philippines, Steinberg's *A Singular and a Plural Place* remains the standard text. A most useful, annotated bibliography of the region has been edited by Halib and Huxley.

Approaches to Southeast Asian studies that attempt to rise above at least part of the region's diverseness are few and far between. Most authors seemingly concentrate on single areas, nations, and populations, while virtually all collections on specific topics, such as kinship, 'male' and 'female,' family, politics, or market cultures, bring together disparate materials without much attempt at serious comparison and integration. There are a few historians, though, who try to transcend diversity, and who argue for a measure of unity that lends the region its peculiarity. They do this through pursuing specific themes in certain periods. Outstanding among them are scholars like O. W. Wolters and Anthony Reid. In the anthropology of gender, Atkinson and Errington could integrate various data through their felicitous concept of inner Indonesia (as opposed to areas where things are different) that I, in *Inside Southeast Asia*, expanded to the littoral of the South China Sea in my quest for similarities among Thai, Filipino, and Javanese ways. In *The Spectre of Comparisons*, Anderson offers country-specific essays on aspects of the culture of the three nations under discussion that are loosely integrated in his conception of nationalism. Patterns of regionally characteristic thought are also explored by Vatikiotis in his *Political Change in Southeast Asia*.

Although we touched on gender and sexual emancipation, we did not enter into the gender debates. For the region as a whole, Sen and Stivens' *Gender and Power* is of interest, while Sears, Van Esterik, and Roces provide useful interpretations of and references to the ideas animating the women's movements in the three countries.

Political culture and the practical ways in which politics proceed figure prominently in McCoy's *Anarchy of Families* and Sidel's *Bossism*. Together with Phongpaichit and Piriyarangsan's *Corruption and Democracy* they reveal the commonplaceness of violence in Southeast Asia, for which we only need to follow the news in the case of Indonesia. Media and politics in the region tend to be closely related, and whatever distortions these media produce, they are an influential mirror of the public world. In order to get some idea of especially the press, McCargo's challenging work on Thailand is most revealing. Sen and Hill focus on Indonesia, while the Philippine Center for Investigative Journalism charts recent developments in Indonesia and the Philippines.

With much of this book directed to the possibility of a civil society, it may be advisable to sharpen one's thoughts on the subject. Here, I have stuck to the activist stance as elaborated, for instance, in the

CIVICUS and Burbridge compilations. For a more theoretical discussion of the concept, I recommend Seligman's *The Idea of Civil Society* and Hefner's *Democratic Civility*. Next to the current themes of discussion among members of civil society, it may still be useful to situate their origin in the decolonization debates that enlivened early and contemporary civil society. These discussions are the subject of Christie's *Ideology and Revolution*.

There are many alternatives to civil activism, such as religious renewal and revival. Relevant to this subject is *Sojourn* 8/1 of February 1993, edited by Hans-Dieter Evers. Focusing more narrowly on Islam, Hefner and Horvatich's volume may be useful. Apart from the religious option, there are also more mundane attractions that fire the imagination of members of the new middle classes, such as those exposed in Chua's *Consumption in Asia* and Robison and Goodman's *The New Rich in Asia*. For statistics, see the United Nations' yearly *Human Development Report*.

REFERENCES

Althusser, Louis. 1971. *Lenin and Philosophy, and Other Essays.* New York, London: Monthly Review Press. pp. 121–73.

Anderson, Benedict. 1998. *The Spectre of Comparisons; Nationalism, Southeast Asia and the World.* London, New York: Verso.

Atkinson, Jane M. and Shelly Errington, eds. 1990. *Power and Difference. Gender in Island Southeast Asia.* Stanford, Cal.: Stanford University Press.

Breckenridge, Carol E., ed. 1995. *Consuming Modernity. Public Culture in a South Asian World.* Minneapolis, London: University of Minnesota Press.

Burbridge, John ed. 1997. *Beyond Prince and Merchant. Citizen Participation and the Rise of Civil Society.* New York: Pact Publications.

Christie, Clive J. 2001. *Ideology and Revolution in Southeast Asia 1900–1980. Political Ideas of the Anti-colonial Era.* Richmond, Sur.: Curzon Press.

Chua, Beng-Huat, ed. 2000. *Consumption in Asia. Lifestyle and Identities.* London, New York: Routledge.

CIVICUS. 1999. *Civil Society at the Millennium.* West Hartford, Conn.: Kumarian Press, Inc.

Corpuz, O. D., 1989. *The Roots of the Filipino Nation,* 2 vols, Quezon City: Aklahi Foundation, Inc.

Evers, Hans-Dieter, ed. 1993. "Religious Revivalism in Southeast Asia." *Sojourn 8/1* (February), Special focus issue.

Geertz, Clifford. 1980. *Negara: The Theater State in Nineteenth-century Bali.* Princeton: Princeton University Press.

Habermas, Jürgen. 1989 (1962). *The Structural Transformation of the Public Sphere. An Inquiry into a Category of Bourgeois Society.* Cambridge, Mass.: MIT Press.

———. 1987 (1984). *The Theory of Communicative Action.* 2 vols. Boston: Beacon Press.

Halib, Mohammed and Tim Huxley, eds. 1996. *An Introduction to Southeast Asian Studies.* London, New York: Tauris Academic Studies.

Hefner, Robert W. and Patricia Horvatich. 1997. *Islam in an Era of Nation-States: Politics and Religious Renewal in Muslim Southeast Asia.* Honolulu: University of Hawaii Press.

245

Hefner, Robert W., ed. 1998. *Democratic Civility. The History and Cross-cultural Possibility of a Modern Political Ideal.* New Brunswick, London: Transaction Publishers.

Horkheimer, Max and Theodor W. Adorno. 1944. *Dialectic of Enlightenment.* New York: Social Studies Association.

Joaquin, Nick. 1988. *Culture and History. Occasional Notes on the Process of Philippine Becoming.* Metro Manila: Solar Publishing Corp.

Mannheim, Karl. 1940 (1935). *Man and Society in an Age of Reconstruction: Studies in Modern Social Structure.* London: Routledge and Kegan Paul, 1940.

McCargo, Duncan. 2000. *Politics and the Press in Thailand: Media Machinations.* London, New York: Routledge.

McCoy, Alfred W., ed. 1993. *An Anarchy of Families: State and Family in the Philippines.* Madison, Wis.: University of Wisconsin Center for Southeast Asian Studies.

Mulder, Niels. 1996. *Inside Indonesian Society. Cultural Change in Java.* Amsterdam: The Pepin Press.

———. 1997a. *Thai Images. The Culture of the Public World.* Chiang Mai: Silkworm Books.

———. 1997b. *Inside Philippine Society. Interpretations of Everyday Life.* Quezon City: New Day Publishers.

———. 1998. *Mysticism in Java. Ideology in Indonesia.* Amsterdam: The Pepin Press.

———. 2000a. *Filipino Images. Culture of the Public World.* Quezon City: New Day Publishers.

———. 2000b. *Indonesian Images. The Culture of the Public World.* Yogyakarta: Kanisius.

———. 2000c. *Inside Thai Society. Religion. Everyday Life. Change.* Chiang Mai: Silkworm Books.

———. 2000d. *Inside Southeast Asia. Religion. Everyday Life. Cultural Change.* Chiang Mai: Silkworm Books.

Philippine Center for Investigative Journalism, ed. 1999. *News in Distress: The Southeast Asian Media in a Time of Crisis.* Quezon City: PCIJ.

Phongpaichit, Pasuk and Chris Baker. 1995. *Thailand. Economy and Politics.* New York: Oxford University Press.

———. 2000. *Thailand's Crisis.* Singapore: Institute of Southeast Asian Studies.

Phongpaichit, Pasuk and Sungsidh Piriyarangsan. 1997. *Corruption and Democracy in Thailand.* Chiang Mai: Silkworm Books.

Reid, Anthony. 1988. *Southeast Asia in the Age of Commerce, 1450–1680: The Lands below the Winds.* New Haven, Conn.: Yale University Press.

———. 1993. *Southeast Asia in the Age of Commerce, 1450–1680: Expansion and Crisis.* New Haven, Conn.: Yale University Press.

Ricklefs, Merle C. 1991. *A History of Modern Indonesia, c. 1300 to the Present.* London: The Macmillan Press. 2nd ed.

Robison, Richard and David Goodman, eds. 1996. *The New Rich in Asia. Mobile Phones, McDonald's and Middle Class Revolution.* London, New York: Routledge.

Roces, Mina. 1998. *Women, Power, and Kinship Politics: Female Power in Post-War Philippines*. Westport, Conn., London: Praeger.

Schwarz, Adam. 2000. *A Nation in Waiting: Indonesia's Search for Stability*. Boulder, Col.: Westview Press. 2nd ed.

Sears, Laurie J. 1996. *Fantasizing the Feminine in Indonesia*. Durham, London: Duke University Press.

Seligman, Adam. 1992. *The Idea of Civil Society*. New York: The Free Press.

Sen, Krishna and David T. Hill. 2000. *Media, Culture and Politics in Indonesia*. South Melbourne, Vic.: Oxford University Press.

Sen, Krishna and Maila Stivens, eds. 1998. *Gender and Power in Affluent Asia*. London: Routledge.

Sidel, John T. 1999. *Capital, Coercion, and Crime. Bossism in the Philippines*. Stanford, Cal.: Stanford University Press.

Steinberg, David J. 2000. *The Philippines: A Singular and a Plural Place*. Boulder, Col.: Westview Press. 4th ed.

———, ed. 1987. *In Search of Southeast Asia. A Modern History*. Honolulu: University of Hawaii Press.

United Nations Development Programme. *Human Development Report (year)*. New York, Oxford: Oxford University Press. Yearly.

Van Esterik, Penny. 2000. *Materializing Thailand*. Oxford, New York: Berg.

Vatikiotis, Michael R. J. 1996. *Political Change in Southeast Asia. Trimming the Banyan Tree*. London, New York: Routledge.

Wolters, Oliver W. 1982. *History, Culture, and Religion in Southeast Asian Perspectives*. Singapore: Institute of Southeast Asian Studies.

INDEX

New Filipino 190
New Order 48, 85, 87, 92, 93, 107, 149,
152, 157, 163, 197, 209, 210, 236
babies 87, 95
New People's Army (NPA) 8, 181
NGO 218, 222, 228, 230, 232
nouveaux riches 158, 160
nuclear family 226

O
Oetama. *See* Jakob Oetama

P
Pancasila 41, 87
Pancasila democracy 45, 50
Pardo de Tavera 176
participatory citizenship 219
particularism 173
patronage 204, 214, 215
Pedro Abad Santos 178
People Power 212, 231
person 189
Phibun Songkhram, Marshal 7, 179
Philippine society 127, 138, 207
Philippines 5, 6, 7, 8, 9, 29, 71, 139, 166,
170, 171, 172, 175, 176, 178, 179,
181, 182, 183, 189, 196, 199, 200,
202, 204, 205, 209, 211, 213, 224,
229, 231. *See also* Filipinos
Philippines-bashing 72, 83
political culture 90, 97, 204, 242
politicians 25, 38, 39, 130, 144, 200, 213
politics and religion 168
power 27, 128, 135, 136, 137, 146, 147,
149, 150, 184, 193, 204
Prapat Charusathian 181
press 4, 57, 91, 143, 147, 180, 197, 231,
242
Pridi Banomyong 8, 177
priyayi 7, 156, 161
problems 13, 25, 37, 52, 57, 203
production book 209
professionals 4, 7
public culture 4
public discourse 189, 213, 214
public intellectuals 12, 88, 91
public morality 8
public opinion 5, 215, 231

public world 2, 5, 184, 189, 193
Pudjomartono. *See* Susanto Pudjomartono

Q
quality education 222
quality of education 94, 207
Quezon 178

R
Rais. *See* Amien Rais
Rama VI, King 176, 199
Ramos, President 73
Recto, Claro M. 179
reform 74, 85, 86, 151, 213
regionalism 204
religion 11, 13, 42, 99, 170, 172, 173,
202, 220
religion-tinged lifestyle 170
religious entrepreneur 129
religious revival 165, 172, 185, 243
religious sect 166, 233
Rendra 171
resentment 221
Rhoma Irama 171
rights 24, 42, 190, 191, 194, 204
Rizal, José 127, 176

S
Santi Asoke 169, 170, 183, 232, 238
Santos, Lope K. 178
SARA 92
Sarit Thannarat, Marshal 179
school texts 29
Seni Sawwaphong 224
Seno Gumira Ajidarma 211
Setiawan Djody 171
Sin, Cardinal 168
sin 173, 239
Sindhunata 128, 148, 161, 163
Sino-Thai 120
social capital 219
social engineering 177
social hierarchy 184
social imagination 5, 12, 214, 215, 219,
203
social studies 23, 28, 69
social-critical novels 127
society 23, 53, 194, 203